The New York Times

SUNDAYS STRAIGHT UP

Published in the United States by St. Martin's Griffin,
an imprint of St. Martin's Publishing Group

THE NEW YORK TIMES SUNDAYS STRAIGHT UP.
Copyright © 2023 by The New York Times Company. All rights reserved.
Printed in the United States of America. For information, address
St. Martin's Publishing Group, 120 Broadway, New York, NY 10271.

www.stmartins.com

All of the puzzles that appear in this work were originally published
in *The New York Times* from August 2, 2015, to December 27, 2015; June 4, 2017, to
May 27, 2018; February 3, 2019, to March 31, 2019; or January 5, 2020, to April 25, 2020.
Copyright © 2015, 2017, 2018, 2019, 2020 by The New York Times Company.
All rights reserved. Reprinted by permission.

ISBN 978-1-250-89606-3

Our books may be purchased in bulk for promotional, educational, or business use.
Please contact your local bookseller or the Macmillan Corporate and Premium
Sales Department at 1-800-221-7945, extension 5442, or by email at
MacmillanSpecialMarkets@macmillan.com.

First Edition: 2023

10   9   8   7   6   5   4   3   2   1

The New York Times

SUNDAYS STRAIGHT UP
100 Sunday Crossword Puzzles

Edited by Will Shortz

ST. MARTIN'S GRIFFIN
NEW YORK

1 STRESSED OUT

ACROSS

1 Stuffs with bacon, say
6 Convention handouts
10 Second of the 10 biblical plagues
15 Mission-driven org.
19 Underway
20 Congress person
21 Ancient neighbor of Lydia
22 Intl. group founded in 1960 with five members
23 "We can't hear you in the back, Johannes!"?
26 Winter leaf covering
27 "Oops, my bad!"
28 Fixtures at most airport lounges nowadays
29 Boston ___ (former Sam Adams offering)
30 Place to fill up in Canada
31 Not just -er
32 Canal trouble
35 Triage sites, briefly
36 Brown in a Food Network kitchen
37 Not leave alone
38 Put on a production of a classic Sondheim musical?
41 Subjects of "birds and bees" talks
44 Knowledgeable about
45 Pirate's chant
46 Scottish cap
47 What composers do when they add the finishing touches?
50 Lets out
52 Put away, as a sword
53 "What's the ___?"
54 Place to park at the bar
55 Police, informally
56 Comedian Andre with a self-named Adult Swim show
59 Russian assembly
61 Super-duper
65 Western Hemisphere grp.
66 What workers at the sticker factory do?
70 ___ Royal Highness
71 Words before "Remember" and "Forget" in song titles
73 Shooter of arrows
74 Code part
75 Brown in the kitchen
76 Scarfs (down)
79 Do some pogoing
81 French France
83 Jackson nicknamed the "Queen of Gospel"
86 Shorten words like "forecastle" and "boatswain"?
89 Equal
90 Stretching muscle
92 Certain yearling
93 What a private detective might photograph
94 Ignore what you have in reserve while taking inventory?
97 Morn's counterpart
98 Assignment that might have a page limit
99 #MeToo ___
100 Underground places with bats
102 Anti-bullying spot, for short
105 Toiling away
106 Computing pioneer Lovelace
107 Side dish with kalua pig
108 Betrays a sibling, say
110 Statistician's worry
111 Encouragement at an N.B.A. mixer?
115 Irish novelist O'Brien
116 Pull
117 Lake near London
118 Country ruled only by kings named Tupou since 1845
119 Obstacle to overcome
120 Loses sleep (over)
121 Hinge (on)
122 Made a choice

DOWN

1 Mental slip-up
2 Hairstyles for Pam Grier and Angela Davis
3 Take a break from flying, say
4 Martial arts center
5 Audiophile's purchase
6 Nymph pursuer
7 Drag wear
8 Soccer phenom Freddy
9 Be nominated
10 Some scuba gear
11 Overcharge ridiculously
12 In the world
13 Samoa salesperson
14 Worth heeding
15 Utterly useless
16 Nonbeliever, now
17 Not always available
18 Nascar and FIFA, e.g.
24 Ibex's perch
25 Brinks
33 Google Play buys
34 Big snapper, informally
35 Book of Mormon book
36 Ready for romance
37 Trim, in a way
39 Spectacle
40 "I totally forgot!"
41 End result
42 Take up again, as a case
43 Like foods said to be good for hangovers and bad for skin complexion
44 In ___ (not yet delivered)
48 Singer who was in 2018's "Mamma Mia! Here We Go Again"
49 Has as a mount
51 Right-angled joint
54 "Quién ___?" (Spanish "Who knows?")
57 Fateful day in 44 B.C.
58 No purebred
60 Cosmo, e.g.
62 What's the big idea?
63 Dimensions
64 Something you don't want to be under
66 Noodle, for example
67 Colleague
68 Put on the books
69 Giving up time
72 Carrier until 2001
75 Rudder's place
77 Place
78 Dispersed, as a search party

by Will Nediger

80 Retro Chrysler
82 Corroborates
83 Did some gambling
84 Former Haitian leader Jean-Bertrand
85 Defenders in the Battle of Trenton
86 ___ Nostra
87 Film director Nicolas
88 Tangent introducer
91 Funny
95 Watched a kitty
96 Target of an air freshener
97 Series finale abbr.
101 Baseball's Chase
102 Confederate in an audience
103 Ridged fabric
104 Syrian strongman
106 Doesn't just sit
107 Writers might click them
109 Sporty roof feature
112 Solemn statement
113 Poetic "before"
114 Feel bad

2   STATE OF CONFUSION

ACROSS

1 Some Japanese cars
7 Judean king, in Matthew
12 Medical insurance grp.
15 Freedom of the ___
19 Like a short play
20 Brick material
21 Sushi fish that's never served raw
22 School with its own ZIP code—90095
23 Voice box? [Wolverine State]
26 33-Across's sound
27 "Dang!"
28 Like a soufflé
29 ___ Kea
30 2014 film with the tagline "One dream can change the world"
31 Losers
33 Safari sighting [Golden State]
35 Captain of science fiction
36 Spleen
38 Wiggle room
39 Rehearsed
42 Device that keeps fish alive
44 Pay a brief visit
48 Stashed for later [Blue Hen State]
53 Whom a warrant officer might report to, informally
54 "___ Lang Syne"
55 Letters on an ambulance
56 Times before the present?
58 Revealer of the Wizard
59 Following, as a detective might
63 Gave up the ghost
66 It's condensed
67 Editorialist's skill [Mountain State]
72 Banned pollutant, for short
74 West Coast birthplace of John Steinbeck
75 Like some candles
78 "No way, José!"
80 Fairy tale prince, perhaps
81 "There it is!"
84 Big Island city
85 Events for socialites
87 Knight's accouterments [Ocean State]
92 Brother or sister
95 School
96 ___ Schwarz (toy company)
97 Like some wallpaper patterns
100 In which a single raised pinkie is an "i": Abbr.
101 Wilbur's partner in an old sitcom
103 Sushi bar offering [Centennial State]
107 Cockney and others
111 Pilots' flights just after training is finished
112 Face-planted
113 Detach slowly (from)
114 Hit playfully on the nose, slangily
115 Rights-defending org.
116 Has been around the block [Evergreen State]
119 What locks are made of
120 Hawaiian word that's also a common Chinese surname
121 Layers
122 Ready for publication, say
123 "Like that'll ever happen"
124 Lead-in to Brown or Robinson in #1 song titles
125 Sport on a range
126 Not for ___ (sign)

DOWN

1 Disney heroine of 2016
2 Invalidate
3 Cocktail garnishes
4 ___ City, Yukon Territory
5 Nail
6 Bit of party decoration
7 Puts up
8 Pushing the envelope
9 Letters after CD
10 Most of the 2010s
11 Insomniac's order
12 Tush
13 Poses a danger to
14 Cry with an accent
15 Emphatic rejection
16 Food inspectors test for it
17 Thrifty competitor
18 Sticky roll
24 Snub
25 Let fly
30 One leaving a trail
32 What scared horses do
34 "That's so sweet!"
36 Article
37 40 make up a furlong
39 Exam for the college-bound
40 ___ fortis (another name for nitric acid)
41 Noted export from Holland
43 Something North Carolina's Alcohol Law Enforcement regulates, aptly
45 Charlie Brown catchphrase
46 Ask the obvious question, so to speak
47 "Ouch!"
49 Indolent
50 "___ here!"
51 Maintain
52 Reading on the dashboard of the DeLorean in "Back to the Future"
57 Improv offering
60 Fed. agency that helped take down Al Capone
61 Secretive org.
62 Wide gap
63 Walgreens rival
64 Symbol for viscosity, in chemistry
65 Short swim
68 What phonies put on
69 Word before cap or shoe
70 Shakespearean schemer
71 Classic pop brand
72 Flat-faced dogs
73 Kind of tea
76 "___ Minnow Pea," 2001 novel with an alphabetically punny title
77 Dummy
79 Setting for some pickup basketball
81 Uses sigma notation, in calculus
82 Tow
83 Nelson Mandela's org.
86 George Eliot's "___ Marner"

by Evan Mahnken and David Steinberg

88 It's no bull
89 Musician Marley, son of Bob
90 Outlander
91 Command to a dog
93 Go-ahead
94 Many a dad joke
98 Stella ___ (imported beer)
99 Big name in theaters
102 Flotsam and jetsam
103 Japan's largest brewer
104 English class quiz subject, informally
105 Skateboard jump
106 Imitates Daffy Duck, in a way
107 Many a founding father, religiously
108 Terra ___
109 Dry (off)
110 Fine china
113 "This is fun!"
116 Airline with a crown in its logo
117 1–1, for one
118 Something that might accompany a dedication

3 BIOTECHNOLOGY

ACROSS

1 Homeowner's action, for short
5 Things blockers block
8 1979 film inspired by Janis Joplin's life
15 Indistinct shape
19 Receptionist on "The Office"
20 Be bothered by
22 Island nation west of Fiji
23 Possible consequence of default, in brief
24 Wildflower with spiky, purplish blooms
25 Secure
26 Ruling family of Edward I
27 Finished
28 Adam's ___ (water)
29 Hole in one's head
31 Humpty Dumpty, e.g.
32 "Dallas" family name
33 The Anne of "Anne of the Thousand Days"
35 Feverish
36 Put back on
38 Insinuating
39 -
40 James who won an Emmy two years in a row for the same role on different shows
42 -
45 Ignorant person, in slang
47 Security system array
49 Total
51 Angered by
53 Ancient monuments
54 Gaston ___, "The Phantom of the Opera" novelist
55 Latte choice, informally
58 The "she" in the lyric "She would merengue and do the cha-cha"
59 W.W. I French biplane
60 Capital of Albania
61 Like much of Iowa
63 1980 Olympic hockey champs
66 Up
68 Shark fighters
70 "Believe ___ not!"
71 Biological manipulation suggested four times by this puzzle
74 First African-American Davis Cup player
75 Beethoven's birthplace
76 Comprehension
77 Tender spot?
78 Like the sun god Inti
79 Some liturgical vestments
81 ___ de Triomphe
83 It's down in the dumps
86 First National Leaguer to hit 500 home runs
87 Fall color providers
88 Some instant coffees
90 Cheyenne Mountain org.
92 Stays out of
93 Closes in a thin membrane
95 Disappointing response to an application
98 Remarkable ability of a starfish
99 Use a rototiller on, say
101 Lack of variation
103 "ER" actress Laura
105 Turn out
106 Service with more than 1.5 billion users
107 Home of the Latino Walk of Fame, informally
108 Composer of the "London" symphonies
111 Big e-cigarette brand
113 Anti-athlete's foot brand
115 Good for leaving handprints in
116 State without reservations
117 -
119 Provider of child support?
120 -
121 Polynesian carving
122 Dreamer
123 Half in advance?
124 Unique individual
125 Starting point
126 Broadway's "___ Todd"
127 "Hamilton" Tony nominee Phillipa ___
128 Loch ___, site of Urquhart Castle

DOWN

1 Goes through physical therapy
2 Anon
3 Beethoven's only opera
4 As a rule
5 City that ancient Greeks called Philadelphia
6 Christian with a big house
7 Winter vehicle
8 Mike and Carol Brady, e.g.
9 Berry receiving much attention in the 2000s
10 Bambi's aunt
11 Bit of ancient script
12 Ingredient in some health food supplements
13 Not occurring naturally
14 Romanian-born writer once in the French Academy
15 Cook on the outside
16 Tribe of Moses and Aaron
17 Available to the public
18 Wimbledon champ, 1976–80
21 First takes
29 Gag item floating in Halloween punch
30 Brother on "Frasier"
32 Breadwinner
34 Ancient Dead Sea land
37 Woozy
39 -
40 Rooms with views
41 Forecast
42 -
43 Phrase of agreement
44 Subject for Kinsey
46 Olden Tokyo
48 Flower part
50 Roman emperor before Hadrian
52 "Nyah, nyah!," e.g.
55 Nursery sight
56 Insurance for the crash-prone
57 Big story
60 Start of a countdown
62 Composer Schoenberg
64 Repair material
65 Skeptically
67 Apostle called "the Zealot"
69 Launched
71 Didn't know but said something anyway
72 Midlength records, for short
73 Full of spirit
78 From Shiraz or Tabriz
80 Country star Womack
82 Greenbacks

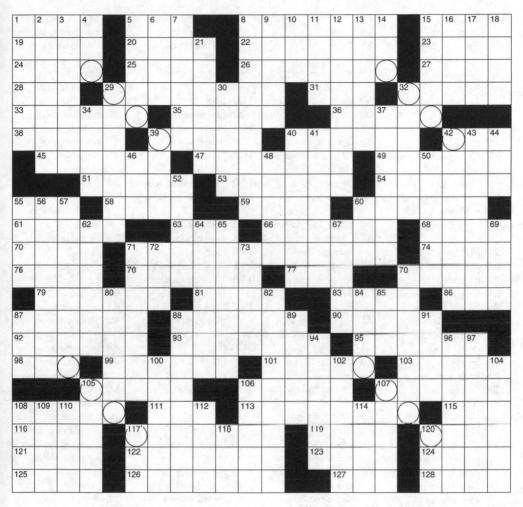

by Victor Barocas

FOOD ENGINEERING

Note: When this puzzle is finished, change one letter in the last word in the answer to each asterisked clue to name a food. The replacement letters, in order, will spell an appropriate phrase.

ACROSS

1 It got some "Xtra" flavor in 2001
7 San Antonio pro
11 Atkins diet no-no
15 What's called a cashpoint by Brits
18 Wage ___
19 Add to the team
20 ___ squash
22 One-named singer with the 2014 hit "Chandelier"
23 *Looks that can be difficult to pull off
25 *"It's 2 a.m. already?!"
27 Half up-front?
28 Tikka masala go-with
29 Gravitate (toward)
31 Singer Morissette
32 Actress de Armas of "Knives Out"
34 "How was ___ know?"
35 Place for speakers
37 Trig function
38 *Data visuals similar to histograms
41 *Swimming hazards in the ocean
44 Crossword-loving detective on "Brooklyn Nine-Nine"
45 ___ Dhabi
46 Celebrations of lives, for short
48 Dance arrangements, familiarly
49 One making frequent pitching changes?
51 Back of the neck
52 It's spoken in Aberdeen

53 "Who ___ knows?"
54 Elderly
55 "I call dibs!"
56 [I'm mad!]
59 Honor for a play
60 Place in the earth
62 South African currency
63 Operatic showpiece
64 *"Man, that was cheap!"
66 *Holder of the single-game W.N.B.A. scoring record (53 points)
68 Something to do before a deal
69 Super, in slang
70 Lisa who "ate no basil," in a palindrome
71 Missiles and such
72 Animal in a "Sound of Music" song
73 Big Super Bowl purchase
74 Easy as falling off ___
75 Nickname for a really thin guy
76 What Mercury and Venus lack
77 Religious observance that's also a past-tense verb
78 "That ship has sailed"
81 Small-time
83 Cause of red-eye
84 Ate
85 Regret
86 *Diner choice
88 *Something visually arresting
91 Chief
92 Coin with 12 stars on one side
93 Ancient greeting

94 El Misisipi, e.g.
95 Source of some South American wool
98 Get groceries, say
100 Sole
102 Film excerpt
105 *Duplicate, in word processing
107 *Disappear suddenly
110 Long-handled tool
111 One with a track record
112 Spore producer
113 Keys of some songs
114 Loan fig.
115 Political worker
116 "A fickle food," per Emily Dickinson
117 Superlatively pleasant

DOWN

1 Children's playroom, often
2 Zen garden accessory
3 Running argument?
4 Frame in a box score
5 Hebrew for "son"
6 ___ Mawr College
7 Sword's place
8 Almost a score of Mozart compositions
9 Receptacle for ancient Greek votes
10 11-Down and such
11 Small siestas
12 Low-pH
13 Follower of CD
14 La ___ Tar Pits
15 Donkeyish
16 Have a connection with
17 Hordes

21 Org. behind 14 of the 15 most-watched TV broadcasts in U.S. history
24 Capital of the Indian state of Rajasthan
26 They help with printing and pointing
30 Made line changes
33 Body of water greatly shrunk by 1960s Soviet irrigation
36 To the point
38 Howl
39 Opposite of the Latin "odi"
40 Busy as ___
41 Less green, say
42 Title woman in a #1 Beach Boys hit
43 Learn by ___
47 Score of zero, in slang
50 Ins
52 Pollution portmanteau
56 People who would object to this clue because of it's punctuation
57 Fixes
58 Issa of "Insecure"
59 "How disastrous!"
60 "No way!"
61 Nonnegotiable things
62 Sound a warning
63 Spanish month that anagrams to a zodiac sign
64 Bit of gum
65 ___-faire
66 Birds on Minnesota state quarters
67 Bad smell
70 "Ugh!"

by Erik Agard

73 -elect
74 Alarmingly
75 Daytime TV fare
76 Back-to-school time
78 "Well, that's that!"
79 Follower of 76-Down: Abbr.
80 Suffix with election
81 Skater's leap
82 Candy discard
83 Not to go
86 Ballroom dance from Cuba
87 Sent packing
89 Actress De Carlo of "The Munsters"
90 Out-eat?
96 E.M.T.'s procedure
97 Tiny battery
99 Smoke
101 Welsh form of "John"
103 Goddess pictured with a solar disk above her
104 Excellent, in dated slang
106 Grade school subj.
108 Shade of green
109 Muslim-American icon

ACROSS

1 Part of L.G.B.T., for short
6 Like wine, but not grape juice
10 Chances
14 Hogwarts headmaster Dumbledore
19 "The Jungle Book" bear
20 Part of a theater?
21 Do for a few months?
22 "Lovergirl" singer Marie
23 *"Soak Up the Sun" singer, 2002
25 *Fictional protagonist who attends elementary school in Maycomb County
27 Smooth over
28 Onetime "Come hungry. Leave happy" sloganeer
29 Tolkien trilogy, for short
30 Hawk
31 Pick up from school
33 Nat ___ (documentary channel, for short)
35 Gentle attention-getter
36 Divert
38 *Actress in "Alien" and "Avatar"
42 Farthest orbital point from the moon
44 ___ smear
45 Patois
48 Grace's partner on Netflix
49 Symbolic item
51 Avoids attention for now
53 Ingredient in bananas Foster
54 Cease
55 Completely lost
56 Speck in la mer
57 Ivanovic who won the 2008 French Open
58 Lend a hand when one shouldn't
60 "Cool your jets!"
62 Directs
64 Really, really hope
65 Aqib ___, five-time Pro Bowl cornerback
67 #carpediem
69 Kitchen timer sound
70 Labors
71 Iowa college city that isn't Iowa City
73 Corrida combatants
75 One of the Spice Girls
76 Swedish vodka brand
79 Tease relentlessly
80 Hamilton and Burr, e.g.
83 "Nice job, dude!"
84 Poker-faced
85 You might gain knowledge through this
86 Direction from Tampa to Orlando, for short
87 "Don't include me in this!"
89 Dipsomaniacs
91 Bronze
92 Costco competitor, informally
94 Italian wine region
95 Bottom of Britain?
96 Some square dance participants
97 Bill passers, briefly
99 Some woolen blankets
103 Peter or Paul (but not Mary)
105 Ballerina's balancing aid
107 Exhibition mounter
109 Anne with the Pulitzer-winning novel "Breathing Lessons"
112 *First African-American U.S. poet laureate
114 Uraeus, in ancient Egypt
115 2017 film nominated for Best Picture . . . or a hint to the answers to the eight starred clues
117 Northern race
118 President whose veep was Dick
119 Lone female Argonaut
120 "Copacabana" hitmaker, 1978
121 ___ St. James, first female Indianapolis 500 Rookie of the Year
122 Comes to light

DOWN

1 Amt. of cooking oil
2 Bobby in the Motorsports Hall of Fame of America
3 Advil alternative
4 "Because I felt like it"
5 Makeup of some meat substitutes
6 Prefix with conservative
7 Ignore orders
8 Romeo or Juliet
9 Mountain ___
10 Covert ___
11 Render harmless, so to speak
12 Wasn't stiff
13 N.S.F.W. stuff
14 Antismuggling grp.
15 Idle periods
16 Elaine on "Seinfeld"
17 Cry from the defeated
18 Jokester Mort
24 Trattoria dish
26 Labors
32 Rainer Maria ___, writer of "Letters to a Young Poet"
34 Baked, in a way
35 Herman Melville's first book
37 Fracas
39 "Eventually . . ."
40 Vittles
41 Sick
42 Island whose name rhymes with a popular thing to do there
43 *Portrayer of Fallon Carrington Colby on "Dynasty"
46 *"The Silence of the Lambs" protagonist
47 Like the Vietnamese language
48 Kegger locale
49 *Singer with the most American Music Awards of all time (40)
50 *Janet Leigh played her in "Psycho"
52 How, with "the"
59 Asian island divided between two countries
61 One on a bender, perhaps
63 Young ___
64 Arroz accompanier, often
66 In the hold
68 Keynote, say
69 R2-D2 or C-3PO
70 Overflows (with)
72 "For example . . . ?"
74 Bigheadedness
75 Weapon with a lock, stock and barrel
76 Passing judgments?
77 ___ fide
78 M.M.A. stats, for short

by Brian Herrick and Christopher Adams

80 Mob bosses
81 Money in the Mideast
82 1040 figures, for short
88 Gawked
90 "The Little Mermaid" villain
93 Certain clouds
96 Stonewall Inn, e.g.
98 Make it to the podium
100 App with an envelope icon
101 Kind of voice or dog
102 Wood that's good for matchmaking
104 Word with house or high
105 Hat part
106 Hit musical with music by Elton John
107 Swear
108 ___ in three (chess challenge)
110 The Father of Art Deco
111 Nutrition figs.
113 Guadalajara gold
116 Horse's female parent

ACROSS

1 With 115-Across, 🦍🐢🏙️
5 Energy-efficient Navajo structure
10 "Take this bit of advice . . ."
16 🐵🏢🎁
19 On the briny
20 Grecian hub
21 Gorge
22 Corporate honcho
23 💍🐱🗡️
26 👁️❤️🏢
27 Gawked
28 Looked over before knocking over
29 Arrive for duty
31 Illinois city or its college
34 Closes
35 80-Down android
36 Close by
37 Have because of
38 🚢🐞🏦
41 Regarding
42 🖼️💰🗂️
45 Unruly head of hair
47 What a future attorney must now take by tablet, for short
48 ___ on a log (healthy snack)
49 Wapitis
50 Not spicy, so to speak
51 QB Manning
52 Outbacks taken back, e.g.
53 Mentally erratic
55 🐘🐨🥤⛲
56 Get the bugs out of
58 Cinque × due
59 Places atop
60 🚀🐻🏂
64 Removal from power
67 Slow, in music
68 Bug-eyed primates
72 🚌🦟🍎
73 Runaway #1
74 Not called for
76 Cartoon character once voiced by Hank Azaria
77 Rhyme for rude and crude, appropriately
78 Kerfuffle
79 Rendezvous
80 Yacht spot
81 Gender-neutral pronoun
82 🍄👜🦌
86 Word with recorder or measure
87 🔪🌷🏬
90 Titular host of TV's "Game of Games"
91 Parent of a newborn, typically
92 Sled supinely
93 Water spirit
94 Like the Magi
96 Unavoidable process
99 Goose
100 ___ climbing, new medal event at the 2020 Olympics
101 👤🎹🌍
102 🍪♀️😮
108 "The Loco-Motion" singer Little ___
109 Need for curdling milk into cheese
110 Knack
111 Buffalo's county
112 🧸📀💪
113 Shows signs of hunger
114 Object of a Kickstarter campaign
115 See 1-Across

DOWN

1 Kit ___ bar
2 Ending with brack or Black
3 Originally
4 Wonder Woman portrayer
5 ___ Productions (media company)
6 Poet Nash
7 "Well done"
8 Pet sound
9 First capital of Mississippi
10 "Sergeant ___ of the Yukon" (old radio and TV series)
11 Some steak orders
12 "Metamorphoses" poet
13 Sardine holder
14 Unappreciative sorts
15 Former Spanish coin
16 Quick comeback?
17 Impolite look
18 Snow construction
24 Like Cheerios
25 ___ couture
30 🔫🐛🐇
31 Hunted à la Ahab
32 Pain in the rear
33 Necessitate
34 Airline to Geneva
35 Penny-ante
37 Chancellor von Bismarck
38 Superseder of a silent
39 Prayer leaders
40 Fast-food option
42 Who famously declared "The die is cast"
43 Indelibly, say
44 Actor Stacy
46 Lowly worker
50 Rwanda minority
52 Like notebook paper and monarchies
53 Manhattan avenue known for its Museum Mile
54 Mother of Apollo and Artemis
55 Major mower manufacturer
57 Chose
58 Puts on
59 Features of teapots
61 New York city where Mark Twain was married and buried
62 Lachrymose
63 John on the Mayflower
64 Capital on a fjord
65 Tip over
66 Underground channel
69 Ingredient in an Italian sandwich
70 Reaction shot?
71 Race with gates
73 Old and worn
74 Looked over slides at home, say
75 German refusal
78 Customs target
80 Space program
83 Charles Schulz strip

by Brian Kulman

84 They block for the QB, informally
85 Postseason game
88 🐱 🕊 🦋
89 Cruise line that owned the Lusitania
91 Seaweed used to wrap sushi
93 Brexit politician Farage
94 Garden pest
95 People of action
96 Aid in illegal activity
97 Bestow
98 "Zoinks!"
99 Onetime iPod model
100 Laurel of Laurel and Hardy
103 Brian in the Rock and Roll Hall of Fame
104 Ailment with a "season"
105 El Dorado gold
106 Take first
107 Below zero: Abbr.

7   NUMBER THEORY

ACROSS

1 "Consarn it!"
5 Kind of case in grammar
11 Shed some pounds
17 Edited, in a way
19 Sister channel of HBO
20 What the answer at 26-Across is written in
21 Low-level, as a class
22 Question that might be asked when hurrying into a meeting
23 Duty for a property owner
24 Relative of marmalade
26 FIFTEEN
28 Oval Office V.I.P.
29 Transition point
30 Period preceding a school break
34 What the answer at 45-Across is written in
36 "Yes, captain"
40 Gaping opening
41 Willem of "John Wick"
42 Toward the stern
43 Howe'er
44 Chicago mayor Lightfoot
45 ELEVEN
46 Whom Harry Potter frees from serving Draco Malfoy's family
50 Spicy, crunchy snack tidbit
53 "Ars Amatoria" writer
54 Area the Chinese call Xizang
55 "Make sense?"
56 Hell
58 Square up with
59 & 60 Take control after a coup
61 SIXTEEN
62 "Just ___ boy, born and raised in South Detroit" (lyric from "Don't Stop Believin'")
63 Specks
64 Sleep: Prefix
65 Not quite right
66 Full of tension
67 "Hallelujah, praise the Lord!"
71 Because
75 TWO
76 Cozy spots to stop
77 Miss in the future, maybe
78 Buzz source
79 Cocktail specification
81 Fictional creature made from slime
82 Restaurant handouts for calorie counters
84 What the answer at 61-Across is written in
86 Final authority
88 Rainbows, e.g.
89 Flour filter
90 & 92 Alternative title for this puzzle
98 On-the-go sort
101 It's SW of Erie, Pa.
103 See 106-Across
104 What the answer at 75-Across is written in
105 Life lessons?
106 With 103-Across, character in Episodes I through IX of "Star Wars"
107 Millennial, informally
108 Things passed between the legs?
109 "Butt out!"

DOWN

1 Title host of radio's first major quiz show
2 Contact lens care brand
3 Broadway opening
4 Declare for the draft, say
5 Items that, ironically, contain nickel
6 "Slumdog Millionaire" co-star ___ Kapoor
7 Be a snitch
8 Wishy-washy R.S.V.P.
9 Plant holder?
10 Funeral ceremony
11 Go across
12 Soldier on horseback
13 Word before card or fund
14 Sloan School of Management sch.
15 Team ___
16 Major Southwest hub, for short
18 In store
19 Like some New Orleans cooking
20 Sloppy
25 Letter in the classical spelling of "Athena"
27 "Here's something that'll help"
29 Some battery ends
31 Amorphous creatures
32 Dreaded musician of the 1960s–'70s
33 Brisk
34 Luxurious affair
35 Symbols of failure
36 1974 Eurovision winner that went on to international stardom
37 "Wahoo!"
38 Immature stage of a salamander
39 Letters of credit?
41 Drops on the ground?
42 "Not on ___!"
44 Where Wagner was born and Bach died
46 Scatterbrained
47 Man's name that sounds like two consecutive letters of the alphabet
48 At any time
49 Oktoberfest vessels
51 Some unfair hiring managers
52 "Go ahead," in Shakespeare
56 Openly controversial opinions
57 Knock out
58 Invoice directive
59 Like most medical journal articles
60 High hairstyle
61 Club ___
62 Egypt's "king of the gods"
63 Excellent conductors
64 N.Y.C. neighborhood near NoLIta
65 "Ciao"
66 Put in jeopardy
67 Muscle cars of the '60s
68 Lyrical, as poetry
69 Facetious response to a verbal jab
70 "E.T." actress Wallace
72 "Ugh, stop talking already!"
73 Sack

by Sam Ezersky

74 Sun ___, "The Art of War" philosopher
79 Where most of America's gold is mined
80 Like the presidency of John Adams
82 Joint
83 Longtime Eagles QB Donovan
84 Suspect
85 Bible study: Abbr.
87 With a wink
89 Kisses, in Cambridge
91 Brown
92 Bring (out) for display
93 Candy wrapped in a tube
94 "I'll come to you ___": Macbeth
95 Eensy-weensy
96 New pedometer reading
97 Beginner, in modern lingo
98 Mammoth
99 Western tribe
100 ___ Salvador
102 What will happily sell its Soul?

ACROSS

1 Feeling of hopelessness
8 Julius Erving, to fans
11 Calendar abbr. that's also a French number
15 "Your choice—him ___"
19 Early online encyclopedia
20 "___-hoo!"
21 The Powerpuff Girls, e.g.
22 Fantasy author Gaiman
23 Going MY way?
24 What's up?
25 Wagner opus
27 "Stop rolling sevens!"?
30 Southeast Asian ethnic group
31 Princess in a galaxy far, far away
32 Lady bird
33 Org. in charge of Tokyo 2020
34 Suffix with expert
36 "Oy ___!"
37 Bay window
39 Home of Mount Rushmore: Abbr.
40 Bobby of the Black Panthers
42 Spew out
45 Build rapport like a presidential candidate?
50 "Livin' la ___ Loca"
51 Celery unit
52 "Hmm, that's odd!"
53 Dance craze of the early 2010s
54 Right on
56 Spot for a laundromat?
58 Color akin to cyan
60 Anger
61 Word with pop or crop
63 Subject of gossip
65 Dance class garments
67 Matter of survival
70 Hate getting ready to move?
74 ___-di-dah
75 Children's book made into a 2012 3-D animated film
77 Singer Bareilles
78 Grunts
80 Tempo
81 Ran
83 Fancy rides
86 Cy Young Award winner Hernandez
90 Requite
92 Board pick
94 Kind of scholarship
96 Dunce cap, basically
97 Makes friends while working retail?
100 Accepts responsibility for
101 "More or less"
102 Model and TV host Banks
103 Billionaire Carl
105 Trickster
107 Understood
108 Today, to José
109 Train schedule abbr.
110 Dutch cheese town
113 This may be at the end of one's rope
115 Event planner's post-banquet task?
120 Winter athlete, not a summer one
122 Turnabout
123 Where first tracks are found
124 Wrinkled fruit
125 "To Live and Die ___"
126 Wichita-to-Omaha dir.
127 Christie's event
128 Start of a Guinness record
129 Rough talk?
130 Our sun
131 Cheer on

DOWN

1 Pullers of Artemis' chariot
2 Georgia of "The Mary Tyler Moore Show"
3 Extent
4 Antiterrorism law
5 Unpaid debt
6 "Indeed"
7 Bad records to have
8 Company that makes products that suck
9 Streaming media device
10 Thrill-seeker's action
11 Utterly failed
12 Prince in "The Little Mermaid"
13 Like medium-rare steak
14 Dress (up)
15 Ending with pseud- or syn-
16 Young woman to call when your data gets deleted?
17 Pooh creator
18 Formal lament
26 Miser, colloquially
28 Berate
29 Reluctant (to)
35 Baby plant
38 Letters before ".gov"
39 Island neighbor of Guadeloupe
41 ___ Ingalls Wilder, author of "Little House on the Prairie"
42 Second person?
43 Be sociable
44 State in both the Mountain and Pacific time zones: Abbr.
46 Locke who was called "The Father of the Harlem Renaissance"
47 Brexit exiter
48 Actress Swinton
49 "Ooh, that's bad!"
55 Runner in Pamplona
57 One side of Mount Everest
59 What many Latin plurals end in
62 "Bull's-eye!"
64 Relative of a xylophone
66 End-of-the-week expression
67 For face value
68 Whitney Houston hit "___ Nothing"
69 Places to swim during school?
71 ___ soda
72 Suits
73 Brief glimpse of a star
76 Slow, musically
79 Runner-up
82 Car with faulty brakes, e.g.
84 Study of birds: Abbr.

by Sophia and David Maymudes

85 Star of "Your Show of Shows" of 1950s TV
87 Way down
88 Travel stop
89 Deletes, with "out"
91 Canyons
93 "The joke's ___!"
95 Screening org.
98 Subject of the 2006 documentary "When the Levees Broke"
99 Rehearsals
104 Move in the direction of
105 "Overall . . ."
106 Home planet of Ming the Merciless
109 Gird (oneself)
111 "Half ___ is better . . ."
112 ___ Park, home of Facebook
114 "M*A*S*H" actress Loretta
116 Wrigglers
117 Spanish youngster
118 Neophyte: Var.
119 Visionary
121 Cassis cocktail

ACROSS

1 Magical healer
7 Maintain
11 Overseas landmark located in Elizabeth Tower
17 "Fa-a-ancy!"
18 Classic Mell Lazarus comic strip
19 Soaring performer
20 GAZACHO
22 Young antagonist in Super Mario games
23 Counterpart of the Roman Aurora
24 Jargon
25 John, to Lennon
26 Mythical archer
27 Suffix with Jumbo
29 SMEILL
34 Poet who wrote "For God's sake hold your tongue, and let me love"
35 Chocolaty Post cereal
36 Org. for which Pelé once played
37 Something many an A-list celebrity has
38 Area with a half-dome
42 Noted Chinese-American fashion designer
44 Mystical ball
47 ENTURIES
51 Payment to a freelancer for unpublished work
53 ___ fixe
54 Informal "Ugh!"
55 Little thing to pick
56 Some p.m. times
57 China flaw
59 Familiar inits. in math

60 Original airer of "The Office"
61 Lapis lazuli shade
62 TECHNIQUEO
66 DEFINITEL
68 Romeo and Juliet, e.g.
69 Adam's ___
70 Air traffic watchdog, for short
71 Literary protagonist named after a king of Israel
72 Violinist Leopold
73 "That's show ___!"
74 Film character introduced in 1977, who died in a 2015 sequel
76 ___ Major
80 French compliment
82 INSTBANT
84 Ability that's hard to explain
85 Handsewn toy
87 Derive (from)
88 Woman in Progressive ads
89 Book reviewers, for short
91 1910s flying star
94 James Garfield's middle name
96 ENVIRONMENAL
101 Yuletide
102 Part of binoculars
103 Fireside chat prez
104 "The United States is not, and never will be, at war with ___": Obama
106 Home of the Sun Devils, familiarly
107 Subj. of Article I, Section 3 of the Constitution
110 RUMYSELF

114 Digitally IDs by location
115 Rock standard?
116 Big name in skin care
117 Features of some dresses and shoes
118 Subtracting
119 Stifled

DOWN

1 Help line?
2 "With any luck!"
3 Uncompromising
4 House of Burgundy?
5 Keyboard key
6 Cabernet county
7 Land between Albania and Serbia
8 Histrionic sort
9 Bird Down Under
10 ___ smear
11 Play's final act?
12 Computer addresses, for short
13 Fraternity and sorority members
14 Carnival or circus, so to speak
15 Delight in
16 Language from which "reindeer" comes
18 Christmas gift bearers
19 Annoyance for Santa
21 Rowing machine, in fitness lingo
22 ___ nova
25 Sierra ___
28 Peachy-keen
30 Like some hair and embarrassed friends
31 Sweetums
32 First Nations people

33 Get perfect
34 ___ counter
39 Tiny amount
40 Something that's not easy to blow
41 ___ sauce (sushi bar condiment)
43 Alpine lodging
45 Happening again?
46 Burdened
48 Millennials
49 Veil over a Muslim woman's face
50 ___-doke
52 No go-getter
55 Org. to which Jordan once belonged
58 "___ complicated"
60 Grendel, e.g.
61 "I knew it was you!"
62 Take to the soapbox
63 Store sign info
64 Curse remover
65 Diana Ross musical, with "The"
66 "Life of Pi" author Martel
67 Reply of faux innocence
70 Have no success with
73 Speak with swagger
74 Spiral
75 Words of wonder
77 Like some web pages and memories
78 Will Ferrell and Tina Fey
79 Chemist's study
81 Muffin choice
82 Leafy shelter
83 U.S. ally in the Gulf War

by Sam Trabucco

86 Nickname of the Miami Heat's all-time leader in points, games, assists and steals
90 Old Spanish bread
92 "Hear ye! Hear ye!" announcers
93 Obstacle-free courses
95 Waterside lodging with a portmanteau name
96 Drinking sounds
97 Put back to level one, say
98 Young salamanders
99 Congeal
100 Cross shape
105 *big kiss*
108 Quick time out
109 Chief legal officers: Abbr.
110 Target of an athlete's M.R.I.
111 Charlotte of "The Facts of Life"
112 "___ changed"
113 Stretch of history

ACROSS

1 Boasts
6 Longtime anthropomorphic aardvark on PBS
12 Australia's national women's basketball team
17 Sounds "everywhere," in a children's song
18 Gloomy
19 Soup server
20 Add insult to injury
22 "Whenever I want you, all I have to do" is this, in an Everly Brothers hit
23 Farming prefix
24 "Gracias a ___"
25 Jam producer
27 Jack Frost's bite
29 Bits of terre in la mer
30 Churns
32 Author Harper
33 He loved Lucy
34 Dry
35 Tea type
36 "A Life for the ___" (Mikhail Glinka opera)
38 1940s vice president who went on to become president
39 "In Praise of Folly" writer
41 How to take glib promises
44 Dog/dog separator
45 Subject of many a negotiation
46 Days ___
47 Jeanne d'Arc, e.g.: Abbr.
48 Enlivens
52 Big feller?
53 Fails to be

54 City on the Brazos River
55 Propeller blades?
57 ___ Crunch
59 Gobs
64 Item often numbered from 3 to 9
65 Boardwalk buy
68 Gush
69 Time magazine's Person of the Century runner-up, 1999
71 Strain
72 ___ Westover, author of the 2018 best-selling memoir "Educated"
73 Big name in theaters
74 Till compartment
76 "Silent Spring" subject, for short
78 Nothingburger
80 Descartes's conclusion
83 Energy
84 Least interesting
86 It gets the ball rolling
87 2002 Winter Olympics locale
90 Looks through
94 Abdominal pain producer
95 Way of securing payment
96 Fizzy drinks
98 Knitting stitch
99 "Holy ___!"
100 Word after bargain or overhead
101 Emulated a kitten
102 ___ expense (free)
103 Org. with the slogan "Every child. One voice"

104 Brand with the slogan "The Art of Childhood"
107 What flies usually become
109 Get cold feet, with "out"
110 It's held by a winner
112 You, according to Jesus in Matthew 5:13
115 Follow
116 Reflexive pronoun
117 Fishes
118 Moved like Jagr?
119 Shaded growths
120 Lil Nas X and Billie Eilish, to teens

DOWN

1 Orlando ___, two-time Gold Glove Award winner
2 Almost won
3 Martial artist's belt
4 Appurtenance for a T.S.A. agent
5 Many Dorothy Parker pieces
6 Big 12 college town
7 Column crosser
8 Brings (out)
9 Time of day
10 Sch. with 50+ alums who went on to become astronauts
11 Warning sign
12 Blast from the past
13 Setting for a classic Georges Seurat painting, en français
14 Fruity quaff
15 South American cowboys
16 Like Havarti or Muenster
17 Reveille player

20 Jack up
21 Repeated part of a pop song
26 Kind of wheel
28 Peak
31 Heroine of Bizet's "The Pearl Fishers"
33 Cozy spot
35 Shows how it's done
36 Climate change, notably
37 State
38 Refried bean
40 Astronaut Jemison of the space shuttle Endeavour
42 Reduction in what one owes
43 Headaches
45 Nursery rhyme couple
48 Gulp
49 Prefix with medic or military
50 Princess Diana, for one
51 Negotiator with G.M.
53 Suckling
56 Disco ___ ("The Simpsons" character)
58 Memorized
60 Exasperate
61 Fabric with sheen
62 Actress ___ Rachel Wood
63 Potential source of a political scandal
66 Evasive maneuver
67 Opposite of "to"
70 Behave like a helicopter parent
75 Attendant of Desdemona in "Othello"
77 Lightly roast

by Laura Taylor Kinnel

79 Continental abbr.
80 Clustered
81 Meted out
82 Best Actress Oscar winner between Streep and Field
84 Agent of change
85 Attention seekers
88 Critical
89 Fictional exemplar of Christmas spirit
90 Stir-fried noodle dish
91 Sews up
92 Senator Joni and Dadaist Max
93 What water in a bucket might do
97 Source of the line "Man does not live by bread alone": Abbr.
100 Boxer, for example
101 Handcuffs
104 This, for one
105 "___ be in England"
106 Not so much
108 Post
111 "Tut-tut"
113 Argentina's leading daily sports newspaper
114 Super ending

READY, SET . . . GETS LOW!

ACROSS

1 Palindromic band with the palindromic song title "SOS"
5 Place for an oxygen tent, for short
8 A whole bunch
13 High-level H.S. math class
19 Exploit
20 Dandy
21 Like many barrels
22 "Yay!"
23 Cheer for beer on campus?
26 Milan-based fashion brand
27 Skate effortlessly
28 Put down in print
29 Part of a strip
31 West of Chicago
32 Discerning judgment
33 Author Calvino
35 Played the fall guy?
37 Half-___ (rhyming order)
38 Hoot at an out-of-focus nature photograph?
43 Chicago university
46 Small three-legged table
47 Two-time Best Actor, 1954 and 1972
48 "___ Old Cowhand" (Bing Crosby hit)
49 Put away
52 "If you ask me," briefly
53 Something populists revile
54 Antsy feeling when one is out of cellphone range?

59 Sport ___
60 One of the dames in 2018's "Tea With the Dames"
61 Like the lion slain by Hercules
62 Cans
66 "Tilted Arc" sculptor Richard
68 Jackie on the Hollywood Walk of Fame
70 Places to sleep
71 Spanish omelet ingredient
72 Isaac's firstborn
73 Fought
75 Bête ___
77 Counterpart of frost
78 Where a demanding dockworker gets supplies?
82 Snack item with a salient anagram?
85 Word that's its own synonym in reverse
86 Symbol of danger or anger
87 Boot
88 Discriminating against elders
89 They've got talent
92 "Ditto!"
94 Landing in Rotterdam?
98 Curry or Rice
99 Snack items with their name on the top and bottom
100 Result of union negotiations, often
101 Lotion bottle abbr.
104 Native seal hunter
107 Part of a college application, informally
108 Unfeeling
110 Roaster or toaster
112 It's not legal

114 Piano that plays only a certain three notes?
117 Slips
118 "Fingers crossed!"
119 Wrath
120 A long time ago
121 Willie Mays phrase
122 A little tight
123 Pseudoscientific subj.
124 Charon's river

DOWN

1 "Waste not, want not," e.g.
2 It has a button in the middle
3 Show to be untrue
4 Reason that some students struggle in school, for short
5 "___ were you . . ."
6 Joint effort, slangily
7 Requiring difficult pedaling, say
8 Exclusive
9 Phone
10 Pseudonymously
11 Manny's last name on "Modern Family"
12 Slip through
13 "Of course!"
14 Bill padding
15 Time out?
16 Stuffed and deep-fried rice balls, in Italian cuisine
17 Name tag holders
18 Political system with a paramount leader
24 Vocal quintet?
25 More or less
30 Work well together

34 Translation of the French "vivre" or German "leben"
35 Rested
36 World capital settled by Vikings circa the ninth century
38 Scourge
39 Apt rhyme for "constrain"
40 Martin Sheen's real first name
41 Name of seven Danish kings
42 "Le ___," Matisse work that hung upside down at the Museum of Modern Art for 47 days
43 Neglect
44 Acts dramatically
45 Bakery/cafe chain
50 Like a bowl
51 Cheat, informally
53 Refusing to answer directly
55 Suggested intake level, for short
56 Glass fragment
57 Correct
58 "Two Sisters" or "Two Young Girls at the Piano"
63 Struck
64 Exceedingly
65 Site of a 1976 South African uprising
67 Quaintly countrified
69 Virtual animals in an early 2000s fad
71 "___ Got the Whole World in His Hands"
73 Attended
74 Alternative to a snake
76 They catch waves

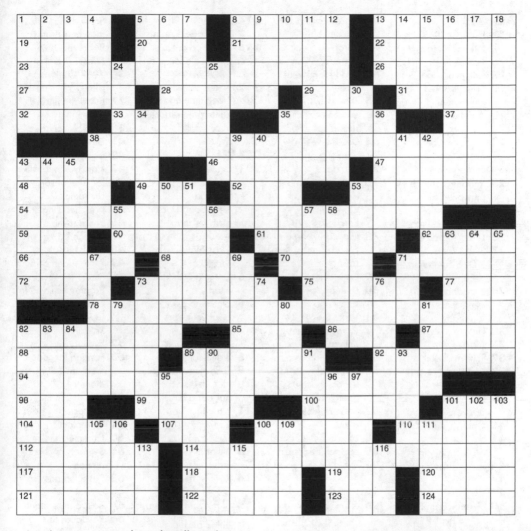

by Nancy Stark and Will Nediger

79 Nickname on "The Addams Family"
80 Shakespeare's "You, too?"
81 Bugs Bunny, e.g.
82 Sob stories
83 Christina of pop
84 "Here, move over"
89 Not much at all
90 Trattoria dumplings
91 New England fish
93 Dork
95 "Catch-22" pilot
96 Cloth that may get a lot of tears
97 Handy types
101 Meager
102 Walker ___, 1962 National Book Award winner
103 Shipping option
105 Sundance state
106 Place for un béret
108 Concessions
109 It beats a deuce
111 Stock sounds
113 Bit of sun
115 Short flight
116 Informal affirmative

BRING YOUR "A" GAME

ACROSS

1 Half of a 1960s folk-rock group
6 Action
12 Car thief's tool
19 Govt.-backed investment
20 Another name for the cornflower
22 Vacuum tube with five active components
23 What the church's music director wanted to do?
25 Stick in a church
26 Difficult problem
27 "I'm With ___" (2016 campaign slogan)
28 Broadband overseer, for short
30 Up
31 Nasty words
32 Truism about unwanted sound?
35 Dull
39 Indian term of address
40 Call ___ early night
41 Sch. on the Mississippi River
44 Robustness
45 Pounds
47 Chatter
50 Greatly dismay one of the Beatles?
55 Picture cards
56 Carousel figure
57 Staple in Creole cooking
58 West Indies city that's home to Lynden Pindling International Airport
61 Classic Halloween costume
62 Affirmed under oath
63 Literary character whose house is uprooted by a tornado
64 Shade similar to claret
65 Times when your archenemy shows up?
68 Decorative throw
71 Quaint giggle
72 In a daze
76 Native of Hrvatska, e.g.
77 One of the Ramones
78 Dipped in egg and bread crumbs, then fried
79 Consider
80 Unimpressive brain size
81 What the antigovernment activist does?
83 Acct. holdings
84 Setting of a 1903 Victor Herbert operetta
87 Spanish letter with a tilde
88 Little kid
89 ___ doble (dance)
91 What's not a good fit?
92 Halloween haul
96 "Aye" or "Oui"?
100 Anne of fashion
103 Pertaining to the lowest possible level
104 Rep.'s opponent
105 One of the N.H.L.'s original six teams: Abbr.
107 Scholarly
109 Facing a judge
111 Geronimo, when his beard was just coming in?
114 Former Indianapolis arena
115 Didn't go out
116 America's foe in an 1898 war
117 Noted satellite of 1962
118 Some green sauces
119 Very small

DOWN

1 Some book fair organizers, for short
2 "The Good Doctor" airer
3 Arouse
4 Class Notes subjects
5 Get into with little effort
6 One who asks "Got your ears on?"
7 Rio hello
8 Significantly
9 Take from the top?
10 Nut seen on the back of a dime
11 ___ chi ch'uan (martial art)
12 Liven (up)
13 Billionaire Blavatnik
14 Recites, as a spell
15 Sight from Catania, in brief
16 Frontman whom People magazine once named "sexiest rock star"
17 "Methinks . . ."
18 Matches
21 Co. that might hire influencers
24 Radiation units
29 TV show with the theme song "Won't Get Fooled Again"
33 Sch. whose mascot is Brutus Buckeye
34 Suffers (from)
36 1887 Chekhov play
37 Spots at the card table
38 "___ bit confused"
41 Director von Trier
42 Gush
43 Hairstyle that calls for a lot of spray
45 Do some prescheduling
46 Ending with "umich."
48 Black birds
49 Actor Noah of "ER"
51 Prophet believed to be buried in the Cave of the Patriarchs
52 Eye luridly
53 Foreign language seen on U.S. money
54 In mint condition
56 Avatar
59 Park place?
60 Extremely dry
61 Symbols of change, in math
63 Protected on a boat
64 Bathroom sealant
66 Ravaged, as mosquitoes might
67 Spoke aloud
68 Rock band whose lead guitarist notably dresses in a schoolboy uniform
69 Actor Armisen
70 Flies into a violent rage
73 Sci-fi bounty hunter Boba ___
74 Golfer Aoki

by Brendan Emmett Quigley

75 Reach out with one's hands?
77 Susan of "L.A. Law"
78 Abolitionist Horace
80 Spot for cannonballs
82 Part of a Victorian social schedule
84 Who wrote "This is the way the world ends / Not with a bang but a whimper"
85 Enticing smells
86 In mint condition
90 Some honors
92 Polishing aids
93 Flatpack retailer
94 Go by
95 Mexican wrap
96 Cancel early
97 Former secretary of state Cyrus
98 Psychotherapist Alfred
99 Diminish
101 Like Machu Picchu
102 Some fruit-flavored sodas
106 ___-free
107 Caustic cleaners
108 Not allow
110 Residency org.
112 Trivial content
113 Benefits plan, maybe

13   KEEP THE CHANGE

ACROSS

1 Company often cited in business studies about disruptive innovation
6 Barbecue applications
10 Center of an ear
13 Authorized
18 Superman, for one
19 Bit of Q.E.D.
20 Brian who created the Windows 95 start-up sound
21 Time machine option
22 Binary, as some questions
23 Settled on
25 "Here's the thing . . ."
26 Make heads or tails of a situation . . . or an alternative title for this puzzle
29 Like a pigsty
31 What an aglet is for a shoelace
32 Some pain relievers
35 Sharer's word
36 ___ parm
39 Give a talking-to
41 Bit of letter-shaped hardware
42 Food catcher
43 Got misty-eyed, with "up"
45 Tricksy maneuver
48 Bearded beast
49 Satellite signal receiver
51 Orange County's ___ Beach
54 Whistle-blower in 2013 news
57 Donkey Kong and others
59 Dresses' upper sections
61 Cherry, for one
63 College town in Iowa
65 Units in linguistics
67 Selfish sort
68 Home to the Alhambra
70 Confused
72 The invaders in Space Invaders, in brief
73 Things held up to the ear
77 Nobel and Pulitzer winner Morrison
78 Part of a mission
80 Unfavorable
82 Some coolers
84 Surgeon's tool
86 Slowpokes
88 "30 for 30" network
90 Lab noise?
91 Lazy ___
93 Relied on no one else
95 [That knocked the wind out of me!]
97 Free offering from a cafe
99 Certain colors in printing
102 Beyoncé's role in 2019's "The Lion King"
103 Having as a hobby
104 No-goodnik
107 ___-Tiki
108 One fighting against Thanos
110 Kind of visual puzzle . . . or what to do with each line in this puzzle's two shaded areas
115 Location in the Beach Boys' "Kokomo"
117 Dog days of winter?
118 House-elf in the Harry Potter books
121 Any one of the Magi, to Jesus
122 Cousin of Inc.
123 Mount ___, much-hiked peak in Yosemite
124 Not hide one's feelings
125 Applesauce brand
126 Drano component
127 Site for handmade goods
128 Introduction

DOWN

1 Kick start?
2 World Cup cry
3 2007 Shia LaBeouf thriller or a 2008 #1 hit by Rihanna
4 Hero of a Virgil epic
5 Bit of raised land
6 Someone with all the desired qualities
7 Craving
8 "Eww, gross!"
9 "Leave it be"
10 ___ the Entertainer (actor and comedian)
11 In addition to
12 [Out of nowhere!]
13 Nintendo character with a green cap
14 Summer complaint
15 State-of-the-art
16 Fuming state
17 X
21 Word before phone or book
24 Little salamanders
27 Word in the corner of a TV news broadcast
28 Paris's Musée ___ (art museum)
29 No-goodnik
30 Pounds
33 Brooks & ___ (country duo)
34 Man's nickname found in consecutive letters of the alphabet
37 Like about half of the OPEC countries
38 Danish tourist attraction since 1968
40 Tone down
43 Society at large
44 ___ ranch
46 Promoter of gender equality, for short
47 Like some tennis shots and most push-ups
50 No-frills
52 Strike out
53 Expert
55 Humdingers
56 The circled letters in the first shaded area
58 Title for many a W.H. aspirant
60 Substance discharged
62 The circled letters in the second shaded area
64 Ink container
66 Went unused
68 Manage to heave the ball before time expires
69 Dispense (with)
71 Hopeless from the start, slangily
74 Job seekers' needs, in brief
75 Egg maker
76 Long stretches
79 The Golden Flashes of the Mid-American Conf.
81 Jazz's Fitzgerald

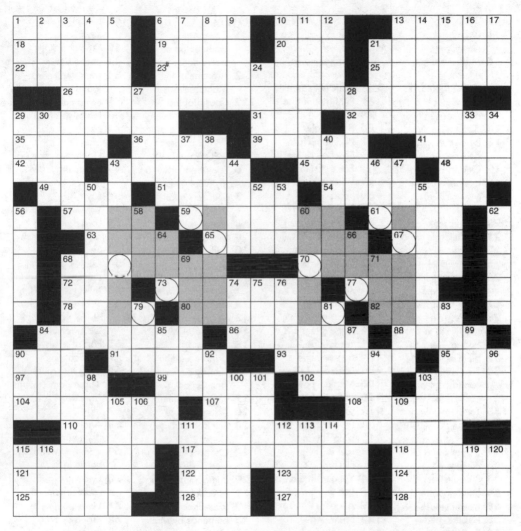

by Ricky Cruz

83 Cartoon character who works at the Krusty Krab
84 Vim and vigor
85 Article of apparel that's an anagram of other articles of apparel
87 Length of time between noons
89 Point out
90 Cries of disappointment
92 With full disclosure
94 Roof part
96 Supporting
98 Somewhat
100 "That didn't work!"
101 Foul mood
103 Earnings
105 Sights in the Jerusalem skyline
106 One of six in Subaru's logo
109 Over
111 Bit of raised land
112 Direction in a film script
113 ___ bro
114 Long stretches
115 Comic book onomatopoeia
116 Big whoop
119 A/C spec
120 Even so

DOUBLE TALK

ACROSS

1 Orchestra heavyweights
6 Mushroom in ramen
11 When tripled, a comment of annoyance
14 "Oh my!"
18 It has a very big bed
19 One of a pair of explorers on the Missouri state quarter
20 Spring feature
21 Golden rule word
22 Run-on sentence?
25 ___-by date
26 Common female middle name
27 Wax theatrical
28 Sharply dressed, shoewise?
30 Boring events
32 Bit of conniving
34 Five-letter world capital that locals spell as two words
35 Tempe neighbor
36 Passing comment?
38 Riding the waves
41 Something a bib catches
43 Busy Bee, for short
44 Single quote?
50 Doesn't touch
55 Head to bed
56 Surreal finale?
57 Big name in student grants
59 Order to attack
60 ___ Paradise, "On the Road" protagonist
61 Weapon associated with the film quote "Here's Johnny!"
63 Sack cloth
65 Hats, slangily
66 Just saying?

72 ___ Roddenberry, first TV writer on the Hollywood Walk of Fame
73 Ancient Greek poet sometimes called the "Tenth Muse"
74 Smear
75 Preschooler
77 Nickname for Baseball Hall-of-Famer Ernie Banks
79 When tripled, "etc."
80 Educational TV spot, for short
83 Square dance move
85 Fireplace item
87 Stock phrase?
90 Not commercial: Abbr.
92 Briskly
93 Bring in
94 Self expression?
101 Trade jabs
104 Sports venue
105 "Outta luck!"
106 Magical powder
110 Prepped for surgery
112 Children's song refrain
113 Uma Thurman's role in "Pulp Fiction"
114 Yonder, in dialect
115 Old saw?
119 Anger
120 Spew anger
121 ___ Mitchell, creator of the Tony-winning musical "Hadestown"
122 Handle
123 "What are the ___?"
124 Deli sandwich, hold the vowels
125 Like stereotypical Seattle weather
126 Symbol of the National Audubon Society

DOWN

1 Coverings on ancient Roman statuary
2 Women's basketball powerhouse, for short
3 Gas-relieving brand
4 "What a relief!"
5 "4-Down-choo!"
6 Poe poem about a mythical quest
7 Scurriers near streams
8 Minor cut, say
9 Makeup holder
10 Suffix with Black or brack
11 "Can't deal with that right now!"
12 Lacking focus
13 Unbridled joy
14 Composer Mahler
15 Low tie
16 Canonized fifth-century pope called "the Great"
17 "Stop right there!"
20 Adorable one
23 ___ Research Center
24 Org. tracking workplace accidents
29 English setting for a series of Impressionist paintings by Monet
31 Neighbor of an Emirati
32 Young weaned pig
33 Monk's digs
36 Word with tippy or twinkle
37 "2001: A Space Odyssey" computer
38 Puts on . . . or things put on
39 Ugly ones sometimes come out in December

40 Nosh at noon, say
42 Diamond stat
45 Second-most common Vietnamese surname
46 Home of Wichita Falls
47 Magnum ___
48 Game ball material
49 The scat got her tongue, you might say
51 Where bills pile up
52 Lower extremity affliction
53 Secret target
54 Capt.'s assistant, maybe
58 Milk: Fr.
62 Where the meaning of life was sold in 2000 for $3.26
63 Part of a job application
64 European museum whose name means "meadow"
67 Sign on again
68 Another name for the moonfish
69 Common wedding hairstyle
70 Undergo rapprochement
71 Stern's opposite
72 "Today" rival, for short
76 "Old ___ Road," longest-running #1 single in Billboard history (19 weeks)
78 You might open one at a pub
80 Kind of book or ad
81 Didn't just float
82 Home of 72-Down
84 Mortimer ___, dummy of old radio and TV

by Jim Peredo

86 Newcomer, informally
88 Org. in charge of the 23-Down
89 Not worry
91 Country whose most widely spoken language is Wolof
94 Democratic politician Julián
95 Flower for a corsage
96 First name in the 1970s White House
97 Gets used (to)
98 Gopher, e.g.
99 Fighter pilot's wear
100 [head slap]
102 Masochist's pleasure
103 Generate, as suspicion
106 Peaceful protest
107 Brown shade
108 Evening hour in Spain
109 Cartomancer's deck
111 Pointed remark
112 Actor Morales
116 Rattle
117 "___ voce poco fa" (Rossini aria)
118 One of the March sisters

BARISTA TRAINING DAY

ACROSS

1 Book that's out of this world?
6 Illuminating point
12 Gilda Radner character on "S.N.L."
20 Took the plunge
21 Ladies' men
22 April 22
23 Gray with a tinge of brown
24 Things got off to a bad start when one trainee tripped and . . .
26 ___ on the side of
27 Father on "The Marvelous Mrs. Maisel"
29 Doctor Zhivago, in "Doctor Zhivago"
30 Flock
31 Part of a Parisian address
32 Roofed patio
35 1099-___ (I.R.S. form)
37 Company with a Gigafactory
40 The carton leaked milk everywhere when another trainee accidentally . . .
45 ___ sci, college major related to psych
46 Kitchen bulb
47 Put back in place, as measures
50 Overly sentimental
53 The drip coffee tasted grainy because they . . .
57 Company whose Nasdaq symbol is its name
58 Having colors in blotches
61 Steinbrenner who took over the Yankees in 2010
62 Moves like Jagger
63 Box score stat
64 It follows more or less
65 Draft choice
67 Nonkosher meat
68 In fact, every cup they served was . . .
75 Writer Rand
76 "This is the worst!"
77 Flier for a magic show
78 Internet address, in brief
79 Lifesavers
82 Headed up
83 "Oh, so that's how it's going to be"
84 Comfort
85 To make matters worse, the espresso machine . . .
88 Some TVs and cameras
89 Fully
90 Home to many Berbers
94 "Surely you don't mean me!?"
95 They worried about their jobs ___ these mistakes were . . .
102 Snitches
105 Attendee
106 Stereotypical dogs
107 Weak ___ (unconvincing argument)
108 "Give it ___!"
111 Polite title
113 Either weekend day, symbolically
114 Sound from a fan
115 Sure enough, when the boss showed up, everyone . . .
120 Speak grandly
122 Bit of contingency planning
123 Pal of Pooh
124 Soap Box Derby entrant
125 Reporter's vantage point
126 Adult
127 Critics' awards

DOWN

1 Makes fit
2 Get misty
3 Source of bay leaves
4 Offering in the Google Play store
5 Like ninjas
6 Premier League rival of Tottenham Hotspur
7 Really stand out
8 Onetime label for Radiohead
9 Depend
10 Spreadsheet part
11 Log-in need
12 Make things interesting, so to speak
13 Sounds of satisfaction
14 Be in the works
15 When you might run away from home
16 Info on an invitation
17 Player of Ben Wyatt on "Parks and Recreation"
18 Unnaturally pale
19 Shakespearean affirmatives
25 Trade gossip
28 ___ Men ("Who Let the Dogs Out" group)
33 Purely
34 "You win this hand"
36 Valentine's Day purchase
38 Takes an "L"
39 Constant stress or heavy drinking
41 Popular children's book series with hidden objects
42 ___ glance
43 Grazing spots
44 N.Y.C. shopping mecca
48 Optical illusion
49 Showy feather
50 Drudge
51 So-called "enclosed" rhyme scheme
52 It beats nothing
54 Absurd pretense
55 Justice nominated by Obama
56 Your highness?: Abbr.
58 Series of missed calls
59 "Do you know who ___?"
60 Singer born Eithne Ní Bhraonáin
64 Team-building activity?
65 "The Wiz" director Sidney
66 N.L. Central team
69 ___ Islands, archipelago between Iceland and Norway
70 They give a hoot
71 Kind of deer
72 Explorer Ponce de León
73 Nail polish brand
74 Trees that line the National Mall
79 Asian city with a monument to John McCain
80 Finish 0–0, say
81 Matin's opposite
83 "See you later"
84 Crass, classless sort
85 Custom auto accessories
86 Excessively promote
87 Pro-___
88 They usually make the cut
91 French chess piece
92 Got takeout, say

by Joel Fagliano

93 Ones concerned with cash flow, for short
96 Man, in Italian
97 More nifty
98 Part of a cash register
99 Destination in the "Odyssey"
100 Render ineffective
101 Many Twitch streamers
103 D and), in texts
104 Ships
109 Sharp pain
110 Escapee from Miss Gulch's bicycle basket
112 Moore whom Sports Illustrated called the "greatest winner in the history of women's basketball"
115 Org.
116 Dinghy thingy
117 Spell the wrong way?
118 Small fry
119 Lead-in to long
121 Snitch

OF COURSE!

ACROSS

1 Big inits. in news
4 Place to visit in a suit
10 Sign of winter's end
16 Purchase that often costs 99¢
19 Something picked at with a pickax
20 Comic Jones formerly of "S.N.L."
21 Fleet
22 Low-___
23 Duffer's approach shots that barely go anywhere?
25 Like kids, but not mom or dad?
26 Gaza grp.
27 Bad position for a server
28 Pick up
30 CD follower
31 Flair
32 Post-Mao Chinese leader
33 Duffer's putt that just misses?
37 Goes on a tweetstorm
39 ___ Reader
40 Tiny insects in a swarm
41 Founder of WikiLeaks
44 Common skirt feature
45 Preparatory time
46 Nickname for a duffer who can't hit straight?
49 "___ on!"
51 Yapped like a dog
55 Make (out)
56 Pauses
57 King Midas' downfall
59 Sport
60 Showing signs of neglect
62 Orphan girl in Byron's "Don Juan"

64 Lodgers
66 Result of spectators heckling a duffer?
71 Rope holding down a bowsprit
73 Course that's free of obstacles?
74 It was "a no-go" in Billy Joel's "We Didn't Start the Fire"
77 "Such is life!"
78 Foaming at the mouth
81 Certain insurance coverage
84 Line on a map: Abbr.
85 Protection
87 Rapper Lil ___ X
88 Duffer's problems with an angled club?
90 Scale starter, per "The Sound of Music"
92 Attach to the end of
94 On the button
95 "I'm listening"
98 Physician Jonas
99 Actress Davis
100 Duffer's reasons to choose a wood?
104 Turntable rates, in brief
108 Letter-shaped fastener
109 ___ order
110 Wolf (down)
111 Button on a DVD player
112 Cool, in an uncool way
113 Something consumed with a cracker?
115 Like the duffer in this puzzle?
118 Palindrome in poetry
119 Box up

120 Cause of fatigue
121 VW predecessors?
122 New York city on Long Island Sound
123 Like the "Mona Lisa" in 1911
124 Civics and Accords
125 School of thought

DOWN

1 Wanderer
2 ___ March, annual June celebration
3 Intel producer
4 Scads
5 Part of the upper bod
6 "Or so"
7 V.I.P. rosters
8 More yellow, but not yet brown, say
9 Like a question for which "maybe" is not an option
10 Capital of French Polynesia
11 Off the internet, to internet users
12 Blue toon in a white dress
13 Chocolate substitute
14 Japanese soybean appetizer
15 Nickname that can be either masculine or feminine
16 Standard outlet connection
17 Grand dwelling
18 Carelessly drops
24 Ankle-biter
29 Move stealthily
31 Weapon sought by Voldemort
33 Woman with a well-known internet "list"
34 Cardiologist's tool
35 Like some personalities

36 Go full ___ (throw a world-class hissy fit)
38 Certain employee at ESPN or JPMorgan Chase
41 Vanquishers of kings?
42 Drink in a little cup
43 Piece of training equipment in boxing
44 Put forth, as a theory
47 Dance that men often do shirtless
48 Europe-based grp. with no European members
50 Org. that employs radio telescopes
52 Principle of harmonious design
53 Absorb, as a loss
54 Ones practicing: Abbr.
57 ___ Purchase, 1853 land deal with Mexico
58 Actor Patel
61 Thorn in a dictator's side
63 Grassy field
65 Kind of rating
67 Road crew's supply
68 House speaker before Pelosi
69 Went green, perhaps?
70 Called up
71 Call to a shepherd
72 Stadium cry
75 Milk sources
76 Disintegrate, in a way, as cells in the body
79 S O S in Gotham City
80 Biblical figure with a tomb in the Cave of the Patriarchs

by Jack Mowat and Jeff Chen

82 Simple shelter
83 Spanish winds
86 Convinced
88 No longer sleeping
89 "Marriage Story" co-star, to fans
91 Simple and ingenious

93 Sparkle
95 Have trouble deciding
96 Headstrong
97 Spot coverage?
99 Like a wunderkind
101 Edie of "The Sopranos"

102 Spoilers, of a sort
103 Witch
105 "Catch That ___ Spirit" (old ad slogan)
106 Exams for some bio majors
107 Pull some strings?

111 Guesses by GPSs
113 Director Craven
114 Play with
116 Thurman of "Pulp Fiction"
117 Word with rolling or bowling

ACROSS

1 1969 hit for Neil Diamond
6 Big dipper?
9 Event at a convention center
13 Southern bread
17 Risk maker
19 What a plastic bag might come with, nowadays
20 Comics mutant
21 Specks of dust
22 Ad label in red and white
24 What Santa does before Christmas
26 They do dos
27 Tempe sch.
28 Invites out for
29 [Let it stand]
30 Pop singer Ora
31 Heats
33 Bête noire
34 Italian pal
35 Burning
40 Some of the American heartland
44 Belief in Buddhism and Hinduism
45 Certain make-your-own-entree station
47 With 86-Across, fixation problem suggested by this puzzle's theme
48 One hanging around the yard
50 Statement that may precede "Wish me luck!"
51 Per ___
52 Arc on a musical score
53 Go back (on)
55 British ending
56 Conventional
59 Deal with
60 Suffix with block
61 China's Zhou ___

62 Hound
64 Some bolt holders
67 Arroz ___ cubana (Cuban-style rice)
70 Demerit
72 Once-ubiquitous electronics outlets
77 A hot one can burn you
78 Stars in western movies, e.g.
80 "That's my foot!!!"
81 Son of George and Jane Jetson
82 Verbal concession
84 Start to pay attention
86 See 47-Across
87 Sea that Jesus is said to have walked on
88 Beloved members of the family
89 Having a fix
90 South American barbecue
91 Rather eccentric
94 D.C. types
95 It fits a big frame, for short
97 1990s Nickelodeon show about a preteen boy
98 Former Saudi king
102 Peninsula with seven countries
106 Hosp. area
107 What torcedores can skillfully do
109 Hierarchical systems, so to speak
111 It may spit venom
112 News items often written in advance
113 Beget
114 Nasdaq, e.g.: Abbr.
115 Things that can bounce
116 Bone connected to the wrist

117 Founding member of the U.N. Security Council, for short
118 Humanities dept.
119 Like the entire 290-page Georges Perec novel "A Void," curiously enough

DOWN

1 Bygone kings
2 Attended
3 Nail polish brand
4 Who said "No good movie is too long. No bad movie is short enough"
5 Dos más uno
6 Worth mentioning
7 Subsidiary of CVS Health
8 Races in place
9 Ken Griffey Jr. or Ichiro Suzuki
10 Short winter days?
11 Alan who directed "All the President's Men"
12 Any nonzero number raised to the power of zero
13 Florida county named for a president
14 Los Angeles's ___ College of Art and Design
15 Where talk is cheep?
16 This: Sp.
18 Way to run someone out of town, idiomatically
21 Heavy defeat
23 QB-protecting group, for short
25 Cousin of cream cheese

31 Not outstanding
32 Aware
33 German city on the Weser
34 Try to see if anyone is home, maybe
36 Adversary
37 Island famous for its nightlife
38 Was livid
39 Slowly disappear
40 Orgs. running drives for school supplies
41 Little piggy
42 Sullivan who taught Helen Keller
43 Temper
44 Enlist again
46 Early king of Athens, in Greek myth
48 Magical rides
49 No longer working: Abbr.
52 Sedate state
54 State
57 Gerontologist's study
58 The driving force behind this puzzle?
63 Cheerfulness: Var.
65 Nonbinary pronoun
66 A dip, or a series of steps
67 Spanish girlfriend
68 Things once tossed in the Trevi Fountain
69 It stops at Union and Penn Stations
71 Understand
73 Agnus ___ (prayers)
74 Banned aid?
75 Lead-in to Aid
76 "Auld Lang ___"

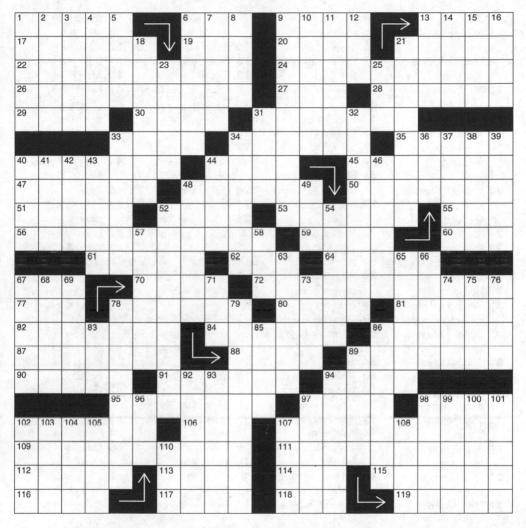

by Royce Ferguson

78 Gambler's alternative to Las Vegas, NV, or Atlantic City, NJ
79 One with special I.T. privileges
83 Throwing away
85 Pond critter
86 Latin version of the Bible
89 Doesn't give a hoot, colloquially
92 Applebee's competitor
93 Kitchen gadgets
94 System of government
96 ___ dog
97 Loading areas
98 Championship
99 Texas A&M athlete
100 Lugs
101 Add oil and vinegar to, say
102 Bit of chemistry
103 Legal cover?
104 Plugging away
105 Testing stage
107 Ratchet (up)
108 Command to a dog
110 Buckeyes' sch.

18 VOWEL PLAY

ACROSS

1 Start of the third qtr.
4 Treatment centers?
8 Sycophant's quality
13 Mr. Dithers's wife in "Blondie"
17 ___-ball pens
18 Ristorante dessert
20 Construction site vehicle
21 Top
22 Richard Simmons diet regimen / London tabloid
24 Records
25 One may have a height restriction
26 Gauge
27 Carpe ___
29 What a red pepper on a menu may signal / Made clear
31 Caninelike animal more closely related to a cat than a dog
32 Three-engine planes
34 Babies grow into them
35 O. J. Simpson trial judge
37 "Goosebumps" author
38 So-called "cradle of civilization"
40 Curse
43 Preceder of free throws / Juice container?
46 Pretended to be
50 Inventor Howe
51 Discombobulated
52 Slimming surgeries, in brief
54 ___ Ste. Marie, Mich.
55 Strategic position
57 Like the data in big data
59 Warriors' org.
60 Really bothered
62 Used, as a chair
65 Chow mein relative
67 Self-reflective question
69 Fooler / Summer Olympics standout
72 Sound signal booster
73 Kind of medicine
75 Lady friend, in Livorno
76 SoCal-based sneaker brand
78 Zeno of ___
79 Colonial Indian title
81 When big bands thrived
84 Bridges of old film
86 "Shush!"
88 Writer Shaw
91 Scheduled to arrive
92 Hypothesized
94 Harry Potter's ex-girlfriend / Register sound
96 National Spelling Bee airer
97 Some prized Prado pieces
99 One of the Kennedys
100 Disappointing
102 Sin subject?
104 Lessens the distance between, in a race
106 Straight or curly hair, e.g.
110 "He's so lame!" / Deer variety
112 Golden apple goddess
114 App developer's milestone
115 Prefix with port
116 Photographer's light
118 Thin neckwear / Assam or Earl Grey
120 Complete
121 Lightly touched
122 Afghan, e.g.
123 Cursive capital that looks like a flipped "&"
124 Mustang feature
125 Mount
126 Little sibling, often
127 Major race sponsor

DOWN

1 Jerusalem's onetime kingdom
2 Nervous
3 Act the middleman
4 Visits for a time
5 Yappy lap dogs, informally
6 Plane calculation
7 Unadventurous
8 Word after "&" in many a company name
9 Minister's home
10 Makes into a movie, say
11 Trusts
12 Richie's mom on "Happy Days"
13 Flare-ups in the hood?
14 OxyContin or Demerol
15 Fixes the décor of completely
16 Canceled
19 Sort of
20 Thin layers
23 Moscow landmark
28 Writer Jong
30 "Hoo boy!"
33 Solidify
36 18, say
37 Is litigious
39 Baby in a basket
40 Actor Patel
41 Resembling
42 Cookies filled with green creme / Flattish sea creatures
44 Best at a hot dog contest
45 Cap
47 Risky / Denim attire
48 See 49-Down
49 With 48-Down, philatelist's collection
53 ___ gland (melatonin producer)
56 Five things in "La Bohème"
58 Pulled a fast one on
61 Part of a wedding that drags
62 Comp ___ (college major, informally)
63 Dog show initials
64 Grp. with wands
66 Often-oval floor décor
67 Puppy
68 "Are you listening?!"
70 Stressed at the end, in a way
71 ___ to go
74 Crime-fighting mom of 1980s TV
77 Jets and others
80 Tried something
82 Lambaste
83 Massachusetts' Cape ___
85 Scan, in a way
87 Storyteller's transition
88 Olympian blood

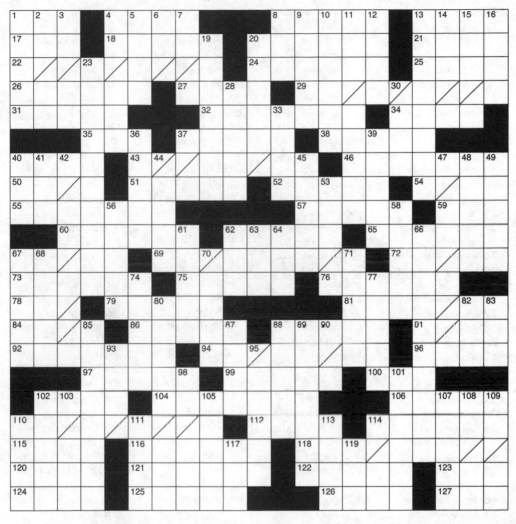

by David Steinberg

19 SUPREME INTELLIGENCE

ACROSS

1 Mike who was the 2017 N.B.A. Coach of the Year
8 Presidential advisory grp.
11 Covers
18 Worked on some screenwriting?
19 Major work
21 Like the French directors Eric Rohmer and Jean-Luc Godard
22 Poseur
23 Kid's creation out of pillows
24 Kind of elephant
25 Last monarch of the House of Stuart
26 Destructive sort
29 Photographer Adams
30 Lines in geometry
31 Android's counterpart
32 ___ Xtra (soda)
34 Scoundrel
36 Worked from home?
39 Cease communication
41 Bug-studying org.
42 Steinbeck novella set in La Paz
46 Topic for Sun Tzu
47 Has as a tenant
49 Shakespearean king
50 Retired chat service
51 Military term of address
52 Perry of fashion
53 "I knew that would happen!"
58 "Twelfth Night" twin
62 Thin pancake
63 Spa treatment
64 Flowery

66 ___ Nation (record label for Jay-Z and J. Cole)
67 Illegal interference . . . or what can be found in this puzzle's 1st, 3rd, 7th, 15th, 19th and 21st rows?
71 Stewbum
72 Noted brand of guitars
73 Use an ice pack on
74 What a conductor might conduct
75 Online admin
77 Where a big bowl is found
79 Indication to bow slowly, say
80 Creator of the "Planet Money" podcast
82 Like a boiled lobster
83 Buoy
85 Poe ode
89 Nicknamed
90 Largest moon in the solar system
91 Got down
92 Discharges
94 Reasons for sneezin'
95 They might be backless
97 Fan favorite
98 Frequent Twitter poster
99 Thick hairstyle
103 For the case at hand
105 Hooded cloak
109 Home to the historic Moana Hotel
110 Connecticut city near New Haven
112 ___ speak

113 Kind of race
115 Dum-dums
116 In ___ (entirely)
117 Bit of advice before taking off?
118 Evasive basketball move
119 Brooding sort
120 Häagen-Dazs alternative

DOWN

1 Big name in Scotch
2 Appliance brand
3 Word before goat or state
4 Sporks have small ones
5 Suffix with crap
6 Bird bills
7 Now there's a thought!
8 Sign by a pool
9 Features of monarch butterfly wings
10 Add salt to, maybe
11 Santa ___
12 Former Buick sedans
13 "Victory is mine!"
14 Covered with water
15 Sleek fabrics
16 Closest to base?
17 Dry, as wine
20 Daze
27 Jessica of "The Illusionist"
28 Empty
33 Chocolate purchase
35 Language with six tones
36 180s
37 Dallas pro
38 Limit on what can be charged

39 "All right, let's play!"
40 Butcher's stock
42 Nickname for Springsteen
43 Comics superhero with filed-off horns
44 Joins forces?
45 Run off
46 Actor Wheaton
48 Prefix with -nomial
50 Joins forces
54 Insurance giant whose name begins with a silent letter
55 Spoke tediously, with "on"
56 Just for laughs
57 Marble marvel
59 Cuban province where the Castros were born
60 Found (in)
61 Nail polish remover
63 Trivia venue
65 Margarine container
68 Sign of wind on water
69 Range that's home to the Mark Twain National Forest
70 Unit of 74-Across
76 It stands for January
78 Raiders' org.
79 Big name in chips
81 Hamlet's plot in "Hamlet"
84 "To what ___?"
85 Bill
86 Italian castle town
87 Advance warning
88 Nancy Drew's boyfriend
89 "Finally!"

by Joel Fagliano

90 Roman Empire invader
93 Part of S.S.N.: Abbr.
94 Wrap tightly
96 Looks for purchases
98 Crested ___ (Colorado ski resort)
99 Like Santa's suit on December 26
100 Short-story writer Bret
101 The slightest margin
102 Shows nervousness, in a way
104 Taking action
106 Kids' character who says "People say nothing is impossible, but I do nothing every day"
107 What has casts of thousands?
108 Hair removal brand
110 Grate stuff
111 Potent venom source
114 "___-haw!"

ACROSS

1 Enjoy some rays?
6 Skip one's senior year, say
11 Off-kilter
15 Affectedly quaint
19 Plácido Domingo, for one
20 Was part of a crew
21 Colorful toys with symbols on their bellies
23 Stall
25 They may sit next to sofas
26 "God's in his heaven—__ right with the world"
27 Adjudge
28 Make out, at Hogwarts
30 Understand
31 Sounded
33 At risk of being offensive
38 Deputies
40 A pop
41 Oil-rich nation, for short
42 Prefix with -logism
43 Subtle sign from the distressed
47 Wasn't straight up
49 Holiday poem starter
50 Blade with no sharp edge
51 The "A" in TV's ALF
53 Director Lee
54 In the vicinity of
55 Tupperware feature
56 Very bad plan
61 Enjoys some rays
62 Auction units
63 Seat of Lewis and Clark County
64 Positive responses
67 "Vacation" band
69 Fake news items
70 It's said to cause a smile

71 Bash
72 Cosmic bursts
73 Seasonal cry (remember 43-Across)
77 TV show with the most Primetime Emmy noms
80 Per __
81 Lyft alternative
82 Farm refrain
83 Prince Philip's spouse, for short
84 West Coast law force, for short
85 House whose symbol is a red-and-white rose
87 Recipe that entails a lot of shaking (remember 56-Across)
90 Ben-__
91 Stick (out)
92 Campus grp. that organizes marches
94 Stay home for dinner
95 Play of Shakespeare (remember 23-Across)
100 Edy's onetime ice cream partner
103 Number two
104 Pro __
105 Computer menu heading
107 Color feature
108 Beethoven's "Archduke," e.g.
111 Not safe at home (remember 33-Across)
114 Racetrack display
115 Author Zola
116 Like horses and lions
117 Takes to court

118 Achievements of Henry Kissinger and Martin Luther King Jr., in brief
119 Links link them
120 Ticked off

DOWN

1 Patron of the Archdiocese of New York, briefly
2 It's bowed between the legs
3 Not calmed
4 Scout's magazine
5 Terrier's warning
6 Horror movie stuff
7 Grainy, in a way
8 Choice
9 __ sleep (a chance to dream)
10 1941 siege target
11 Leader in a red suit
12 Actress Jessica
13 Chicago airport code
14 Nanny around the house?
15 Ex-N.F.L. QB Tim
16 Perform a miraculous feat
17 Before, poetically
18 End of days?
22 Ballet support
24 Less ordinary
29 It dissolves in H_2O
32 River east of Tokyo
34 Home that sounds like two letters of the alphabet
35 Mushrooms, e.g.
36 Derrière
37 Flattens, for short
39 Sights in a Hooverville
43 Goofy drawing?
44 Sch. on the upper Hudson

45 Ancient land where the Olympics began
46 Important body part for a tuba player
48 "No ifs, __ or buts"
49 They're charged for rides
52 Certain Monday night entertainment
54 Hip-hop dance move
56 Holding charge
57 Chemical source of fruit flavor
58 "Hollywood Squares" win
59 Lose one's shadow, say
60 Dorm V.I.P.s
61 Sounded like R2-D2
64 Pretense
65 Quantity of garden tools
66 Like two-bed hospital rooms
67 The Castro in San Francisco and Chelsea in Manhattan
68 Stadium cheer
69 Trickster of Navajo mythology
71 Alum
72 Couleur du café
74 Below 90°
75 Component
76 Pasture
77 Co-star of Harrison Ford in "Blade Runner"
78 Ending with beat or word
79 Be flat
83 John Wayne movie set in Ireland, with "The"
84 That woman

by Victor Barocas and Andy Kravis

85 Shoulderless, sleeveless garment
86 Horse color
88 Saw no alternative
89 12 mins., in the N.B.A.
91 Marley of "A Christmas Carol"
93 They take 2–10 yrs. to mature
96 Fan publications, informally
97 Sporty car of old
98 Like a candle that's gone out, maybe
99 "Send My Love (To Your New Lover)" singer, 2015
101 Come onstage
102 Very thin
106 Knocks off
108 Rewards card accumulation: Abbr.
109 Debtor's letters
110 Stadium cheer
112 Old Parlophone parent
113 U.F.C. sport

ACROSS

1 Small house in the Southwest
7 Covert missions
15 Select
18 Wading birds
20 Light, catchy tunes
21 "Je t'___"
22 Cite
23 Pimp launches career in rap . . . BUT HAS AN EPIC FAIL!
25 Father of Paris, in myth
26 Apple buy-product?
28 Relax, with "out"
29 Assessed
30 Cabby saves prostitute . . . WITH HIS BLATHERING!
33 Labatt, for one
34 Composer known for mood music
35 Relinquish
36 Something coming off the shelf?
38 Tropicana products, for short
41 Floor
43 Guy makes a new best friend . . . WHO TURNS OUT TO BE A COMMUNIST!
50 Beverage called a "tonic" in Boston
51 Inclines
54 Enya's land
55 Appropriate
56 Retired pool shark returns . . . TO WIN FRENCH IMPRESSIONIST PAINTING!
60 "___ Revere, Engineer" (best-selling 2013 children's book)
61 Facial expression often accompanied by "Heh, heh, heh"
62 Big dipper
63 Pink-slip
64 ___ Equis (Mexican beer)
65 Chap gets life lessons from kid . . . WHO'S REALLY AN ANDROID!
70 One side in college football's "Big Game"
72 Blue
74 Bitcoin, e.g.
75 Utopias
78 Shoves (in)
81 West Coast officers track wisecracking detective . . . TO A BOVINE!
86 One with a role to play
87 Bullets, in cards
88 First "America's Funniest Home Videos" host
89 Glamorous Gardner
90 Friends gather for a funeral . . . AND COOK UP AN ENORMOUS STEW!
93 "Bali ___"
94 Lively tune
95 Symbolic bird in "On Golden Pond"
96 Recipe amts.
100 "Angel dust"
102 Kind of knot
107 Bog monster emerges . . . WITH A NEW LINE OF SNACK CRACKERS!
111 Shakespearean king
112 Auto safety feature to prevent skidding, for short
115 Man, for one
116 Greeting on Maui
118 007 gets fired . . . AND LANDS A JOB AS A SCOTTISH TAILOR!
121 Out early
123 Playing ___
124 "Spamalot" writer
125 Drained
126 Object of veneration by ancient Egyptians
127 Casualty of a crash?
128 One side of a ledger

DOWN

1 Goldfish, e.g.
2 Sidestep
3 Balkan capital
4 Mountaineer's tool
5 Skynet's T-800's, e.g.
6 One who's passed the bar: Abbr.
7 Parent's scolding
8 Praised
9 "___ Poetica"
10 Letters on a video surveillance screen
11 Trendy smoothie ingredient
12 Force on earth, in brief
13 Bussing on a bus, for short?
14 Two plus two equaling five, e.g.
15 High mark in Spanish class?
16 "Mon ___" (words of endearment)
17 Energetic
19 "Bon" time
21 Some
24 Color changer
27 Flick
31 Carpentry rod
32 Gift on a string
33 Spiner of "Star Trek: T.N.G."
36 Destined (to be)
37 Singer Sands
38 Goes (for)
39 In song, Jacob Jingleheimer Schmidt's first name
40 Mix and match?
42 ___ Gay (W.W. II plane)
44 Fifth sign
45 "___ Gang"
46 Grp. with the motto "Until every one comes home"
47 Gran Torino, e.g.
48 Part of a score, maybe
49 Dentist's directive
52 Lacking pizazz
53 "___ I" ("Same here")
57 Position sought by some M.B.A.s
58 Kind of shot
59 Olympics unit
66 Concern of an orthopedic M.D.
67 Howls
68 Org. that's found by accident?
69 Piece of chicken
70 Symbols on Irish euro coins
71 Video intrusions
72 Tracker's clue
73 Sole part
76 Astronomical event
77 Goodies in a goody bag
79 Swarm
80 Hindu honorific
81 Burger topper
82 Backtalk?
83 Miner's find

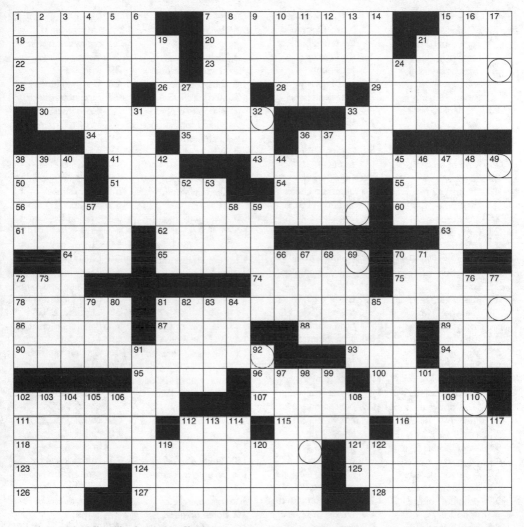

by Priscilla Clark and Jeff Chen

ACROSS

1 52-story Boston skyscraper, familiarly
7 Brass instrument with a mellow sound
15 ___ Malfoy, student at Hogwarts
20 Sorkin and Spelling
21 Kind of equinox
22 Puerto ___
23 "Stop! You're killing me!"
25 ___-garde
26 Give some lip
27 Uncut
28 More than willing
30 For whom the Lorax speaks
31 Internet home to "Between Two Ferns"
34 Latin for "womb"
38 Monsieur's mate
41 Y or N, maybe
42 Shakespeare character who says "This above all: to thine own self be true"
45 Actor Jason
47 Zugspitze, e.g.
50 A person skilled at deadpan has one
52 What "4" may stand for
54 French river or department
55 Beseech
56 Advert's ending?
57 Designer Geoffrey
58 Carrier to Karachi
61 Tugboat sounds
65 Decked out
67 Unimpressed response to someone's one-liner

72 ___ intolerance
73 Novo-Ogaryovo is the official one of the Russian president
74 Lavatory sign
75 Hawke of "Training Day"
76 Regrettable
79 Broadway's Hagen
81 "Roméo et Juliette" segment
85 Coin-toss call
86 Stand-up chain started in Los Angeles
92 Big engine additive
93 Log-in needs
94 Verbally assail
95 "Iglu," for "igloo": Abbr.
97 Cover over, in a way
99 Start limping
100 It might involve someone being "so poor" or "so old"
104 "___, amigo"
107 Count ___
108 Nail salon employees, at times
110 Its "reeds are a pain / And the fingering's insane," per Ogden Nash
114 Lipinski and Reid
115 "Jeez . . . lighten up!"
120 Be grandiloquent
121 To this day, Marie Curie's are still radioactive
122 Mystery
123 Lacoste and Descartes
124 Star of 1976's Oscar winner for Best Picture
125 Smoothed in a shop

DOWN

1 Some body art, for short
2 "Hilarious!"
3 Noteworthy times
4 Lobster traps
5 Med. professionals who take a pledge named for Florence Nightingale
6 Welcomes
7 Plaster
8 Condition for filmdom's Rain Man
9 Suffix with speed
10 "Oh, what the hell . . . I'll do it"
11 "Uh, you've told me quite enough"
12 Where Michael Jordan played coll. ball
13 Meadow call
14 Poet Ginsberg
15 "Game of Thrones" creature
16 Joan who quipped "A Peeping Tom looked in my window and pulled down the shade"
17 "Pick ___ . . ."
18 "Pretty please?"
19 Doing a pirouette, say
24 Poison ivy, e.g.
29 Some sneakers
30 Something carried onstage?
31 "Terrif!"
32 Fifth category of taste with a Japanese name
33 "Peter ___ Greatest Hits" (1974 album)
34 High hairstyle
35 Doughnut figures
36 Late '50s singing sensation

37 One of many scattered in a honeymoon suite, maybe
39 Light bark
40 Cry from Homer
43 Kind of port for a flash drive
44 Manage
46 Night vision?
47 Bowl
48 Maid's armful
49 Made an appeal
51 Hymn starter
52 Habitation
53 Around the time of birth
59 Chains
60 Car rental giant
62 Poet who wrote "Fortune and love favor the brave"
63 Org. that offers Prev✓ enrollment
64 ___ fly
66 One on the left?: Abbr.
67 Greatly bother
68 TV blocking device
69 Tops
70 Finish all at once, in a way
71 Things taken by government officials
72 "Sounds like a plan!"
77 "Don't be ___!"
78 ___ Walcott, Nobel Prize-winning poet
80 Patriots' org.
82 Bad state to be in
83 Mine transport
84 Modern party summons
87 Euros replaced them
88 Bustle
89 Grp. that puts on a show

by David Levinson Wilk

90 Fleets
91 Wall St. bigwigs
93 Like Mount Narodnaya
95 Empty
96 Brings a smile to
98 Like some angels and dominoes
100 Champion

101 Airport that J.F.K. dedicated in 1963
102 Erin of "Joanie Loves Chachi"
103 Locks up
105 Concoct
106 Bug
108 Jester

109 Feeling
110 Anthony Hopkins's "Thor" role
111 City NNE of San Antone
112 "My treat!"
113 "My stars!"
116 Cambodia's Angkor ___

117 Court org.
118 Skit show, for short
119 What makes you you?

PARONOMASIA

ACROSS

1 Like most seamen, supposedly
5 Writer who said "Women are meant to be loved, not to be understood"
10 Holiday celebrating the arrival of spring
13 Islam's final pillar
17 Non-irons
19 Two make a Hamilton
20 Handel's "Messiah," e.g.
22 Narrow passages for killer whales?
24 Kitchen nooks
25 Zodiac feline
26 Backs down
27 Fable about smoked salmon?
28 Kvetches
30 Balneotherapy site
32 "Yeah, right"
33 Raised some vegetables?
35 Decrease in the number of people named Gerald?
40 Hot Wheels maker
41 Are no longer
42 Mother ___
43 Gulager of "The Return of the Living Dead"
44 In amongst
45 Number of bits in a byte
48 Gradually diminishes
50 Abstract artist Mondrian
51 First mass consumer product offering Wi-Fi
53 Sticks for breaking things
54 Belts for a Chinese leader?
57 Chaney who was called "The Man of a Thousand Faces"
58 Oakland's Oracle, for example
60 Not budging
61 Cry from the mizzen top
62 Conveyance in "Calvin and Hobbes"
63 Overused
65 Storm harbinger, maybe
66 Gave a pick-me-up
69 Josip Broz, familiarly
70 Like many a campfire story
72 Responsibility lesson for a child
75 Inventors' diaries?
77 So-called "Island of the Gods"
78 Ordinary Joe
80 Impose
81 Afterthought indicator
82 Well-known Cuban export
84 Fancy collar material
85 Lao-___
86 Crucifixion letters
88 Guerre's opposite
90 MGM's lion, e.g.
92 Cloudophobia?
95 Opposite of a strong boil?
97 Pandora's release
98 Like Verdi's "La donna è mobile"
99 As-yet-undeciphered Cretan script
100 What brings the rocket to the pad?
104 Archaeologists' study
106 Managerial exec
109 Mark Twain farce about a painter who fakes his own demise
110 Jewelry for the oracle at Delphi?
112 Versatile
113 Subleases
114 Arafat of the P.L.O.
115 What Simon does
116 Classic British roadsters
117 Rank things
118 Trix alternative

DOWN

1 Not reporting as instructed, maybe
2 Induce ennui in
3 Fuss about "The West Wing" actor Rob?
4 Old English letter
5 Electricians
6 Several Russian czars
7 Resident of Riga
8 Cousin of a highboy
9 Part of a road test track
10 List heading
11 Runner Liddell depicted in "Chariots of Fire"
12 Pub container
13 It might pick up a passing comment
14 Contrived
15 Beverly Hills ___
16 Kid
18 Colorful shawl
19 Neighbor of Palisades Park, N.J.
21 Chanteuse O'Shea
23 Declining due to age
27 China's Chou En-___
29 Best
31 Early arrival
33 Service with more than a billion users
34 Recurring role for Stallone
35 Groks
36 Philatelist's item
37 Turn's partner
38 Hebrew leader
39 Wack
41 Small undergarments?
46 Like some sprains and champagnes
47 Rev
49 Carried cash around?
50 Schoolmarmish
52 Superman's birth name
55 Morales of "NYPD Blue"
56 Some Poe works
59 Mulligan
60 Un-to
62 Legal pause
64 "Come on in!"
65 Home, in slang
66 Buoyant cadences
67 "That is," to Caesar
68 At a frantic pace
69 ___ bulb
71 Wood often used for bow-making
72 Help with the harvest?
73 V.I.P. at the Oscars

by Matt Ginsberg

74 What's human, they say
76 Needle-nosed fish
77 Grocer's wheel
79 "___ de Lune"
83 Garfield's girlfriend in "Garfield"
86 Tepid approval
87 Small, biting fly
89 Lined with trees
91 Playwright Sean who wrote "Juno and the Paycock"
93 Lets out, e.g.
94 Step on it
95 All thumbs
96 Second and fifth
99 Career employee
100 G.I.s of concern
101 Cuba, por ejemplo
102 Drink disliked by Buzz Aldrin [true fact!]
103 Strangely enough, they're often even
105 Hershey chocolate
107 Doing the job
108 Shrek, for one
110 Voting affirmatively
111 Arctic explorer John

SEE 68-ACROSS

ACROSS

1 ___ aisle, part of a church
5 Prayer books
12 Bit of baloney
15 Rep
19 Two, in Toulouse
20 Neighbor of New York
21 Pesticide ingredient
23 Still a contender
24 Cousins of jaguarundis
25 City in Los Angeles County
26 Leave in the dust
28 European eruption site
29 Search engine failure?
30 Is able to translate what was heard on the wall?
32 Thwart
34 Choler
35 Not stay the course?
36 Gin, lime and soda combo
38 Things that are bought and soled
40 Arizona tribe
43 Scotland's longest river
45 River through Russia and Kazakhstan
46 Is expecting
48 Oddity
50 More in order
52 Dole (out)
53 Tactic in a war of attrition
54 It goes after go
55 Mattress tester's compensation?
61 Word after big or oil
62 Suggestion of what to do, slangily
64 Opposite of ennemies
65 Basics of education, briefly
66 Super superstar
68 Supercilious sort . . . or the title for this puzzle
72 A bushelful
73 Make faces in front of a camera
74 European capital named after a saint
75 "___ your head!"
76 Monster.com posting
77 Dress code requirement for the Puritans?
80 Peak in Suisse
83 City on the Erie Canal
86 Tops
87 Goads
89 Test prep aid
90 Dark beer
92 France's ___ Noël
93 What may follow a school period?
95 Connect, as picture with sound
96 Annual CBS awards broadcast, with "the"
97 Playoff matchup
99 Years ago
101 "Mudbound" director Rees
102 Actress Rowlands
103 Hoped-for conclusion by someone with sore knees?
108 Make a really long-distance call?
113 Rani's raiment
115 Matador's foe
116 Infamous Chicago bootlegger
117 Mediterranean resort island
119 "___ go bragh!"
120 Swimmers with flippers
121 Rufous ruminant
122 Census datum
123 Sp. miss
124 Follower of hi or lo
125 Slips into at a store, say
126 Louver

DOWN

1 "Hasta la vista"
2 Corral
3 Software package
4 Like high-quality olive oil
5 Nighttime event in the western sky
6 Business magazine
7 Resolve
8 Coarse, as language
9 Elvis ___ Presley
10 Engaged in arson
11 Request for aid
12 Pointless
13 Go over one's wardrobe?
14 Titanic's undoing
15 Burn a little
16 Went wild
17 Added numbers
18 Many mowers
22 Number of i's in "Sicilia"
27 Hula accompaniment, for short
29 With 29-Across, surprise in the mail
31 With 30-Across, is blunt
33 Khayyám and others
36 Left only the exterior of
37 Green of the L.P.G.A.
38 Fills
39 24 heures ago
40 Central command spots, for short
41 Sénat affirmative
42 Polish dumpling
44 Senate affirmative
47 Big brand of grills
49 Gunpowder holder
51 Overdue amount
56 Things that might be grabbed by someone in an argument
57 Authority on diamonds?
58 Uprightness
59 With 55-Across, big sleepover
60 What mos. and mos. add up to
63 French vineyard
66 Devilkin
67 Apt rhyme for "grr"
68 Everybody's opposite
69 New York Titans and Dallas Texans, in '60s sports
70 Mine, in Milano
71 Plains tribe
72 Lackadaisical sorts
74 Glaswegians, e.g.
76 Protrude
78 With 77-Across, red, blue and yellow
79 Welcome at the front door
81 "The Oblong Box" writer
82 Witch's home
84 Against
85 Electrical connection?
88 Like fried food vis-à-vis grilled food, typically

by Elizabeth A. Long

90 Fey's co-star in "Baby Mama" and "Sisters"
91 Simple variant of baseball
92 Part of Potus: Abbr.
94 Break, as a habit
96 QB's feat

98 Way out
100 Three-dimensional fig.
103 Wear down
104 Buenos ___
105 End of story?
106 With 103-Across, simple furniture style

107 Schubert's "Eine Kleine Trauermusik," e.g.
109 Lion queen in "The Lion King"
110 Prefix with dermis
111 Anchor

112 With 108-Across, not talking loudly on a cell, e.g.
114 "The King ___"
117 "D.C. Cab" co-star
118 Board hiree, for short

LETTER RECYCLING

ACROSS

1 Small flute
5 Tries to beat the buzzer?
10 Throws together
15 Airport waiter?
18 404 Not Found, e.g.
19 Energize
20 Not happy, to say the least
21 Kitchen brand
22 Historical period spelled using only the letters of 2-Down
24 Singer who once spelled her name with a "$"
25 Word before data or deal
26 Unlikely to be talked out of
27 "That wasn't nice!"
28 Revolutionary War hero spelled using only the letters of 13-Down
30 Website with a "Sell an item" option
31 Order to go
33 Enter the fray
34 Woman's name that sounds like its second and first letters, respectively
35 Fix
36 Snack items spelled using only the letters of 36-Down
38 Inner tubes?
40 Casual top
41 Ancient theaters
42 Prince of Shakespeare
43 Screw up
44 Fund-raising org.
45 Be annoying
47 Garment that's often plaid
48 Sukkot celebrant
51 Christmas drink
55 Geraint's wife, in Arthurian romance
56 What assayers assay
57 Butt's end?
58 Many an office worker's problem
60 It's imagined
62 TV demonstrator at the 1939 World's Fair
63 Page 1, e.g.
64 Oscar winner with four #1 Billboard solo hits
66 Bass player
67 When it comes to
69 You can lend one without letting go of it
70 Jewel case holder
73 Combo-meal entree
75 Spanish "Listen!"
76 Mound
77 Future stallion
79 Tin lizzies
80 Basket part
81 "That so?" reply
82 "See you later"
84 Basket part
85 Put the pedal to the metal
86 Word that might be helpful on a class reunion name tag
87 Rack site
89 Photog's purchase
92 What a press pass provides
95 Really impressive, spelled using only the letters of 39-Down
98 Chalked stick
99 Stern-looking
100 Many a year-end list
102 Alpo alternative
103 Drive-___
104 No-good, spelled using only the letters of 71-Down
106 Include without notifying others, in a way
107 Bygone deliverers
109 Cause of a tic, for short
110 "The Master Builder" playwright
111 Bagel topping spelled using only the letters of 89-Down
113 Penguins' org.
114 Group of stars
115 Temporary tattoo material
116 Writer Nin
117 Sun spot?
118 Track schedule
119 Much-abbreviated Latin phrase
120 "Aw rats!"

DOWN

1 It's comped
2 Historical period
3 Double a score
4 Therefore
5 Jamaican export
6 Was dateless
7 Muhammad's favorite wife
8 Young ___
9 Place to get pampered
10 Nanki-Poo's father, with "the"
11 Glacial ridges
12 Whole-grain cereal brand
13 Revolutionary War hero
14 Jamaican rapper ___ Paul
15 Shade of blue
16 Armpit, medically
17 Ones not up to par?
18 Grandfather of Alfred the Great
23 Aloft
28 Sarcastic response to a fail
29 Basil, e.g.
32 Word before "before"
33 Hypothetical
36 Snack items
37 Jackie of "The Tuxedo"
39 Really impressive
43 Holder of shells
44 "Hey!"
46 Approve another season of
47 Seaweed in Japanese cuisine
48 Amount of jam or jelly beans
49 Part of a motorcade
50 Berth places
51 "You and I have a deal!"
52 Roger in the Navy
53 Clandestine
54 Brand in the dairy aisle
59 Breakfast spots
61 Relish
65 Took back one's story
68 Cherry throwaway
71 No-good
72 Was mounted atop
74 Kind of medicine
78 In ___ of
83 Six things in some six-packs

by Will Nediger

85 Neighbor of a Montenegrin
88 Pep
89 Bagel topping
90 Slyly attracts
91 Gets back together
92 Extras

93 Nickname of Duke basketball's Mike Krzyzewski
94 Huggable
95 Challenge for a college-bound student, maybe
96 Medical inserts

97 ___ Creed (Christian statement of faith)
101 Actor Davis
103 Lead role in "Boys Don't Cry," 1999
105 Neeson of "Schindler's List"

106 Fostered
108 Ballot hanger
111 X
112 Dojo surface

CHARACTER BUILDING

ACROSS

1 Where Napoleon died in exile
9 Pursues, as a hunch
15 Assails with emails
20 Pauses for service
21 Demi with the 2012 hit "Give Your Heart a Break"
22 Droid with a holographic projector, informally
23 Equally pensive?
25 "Heaven forbid!"
26 Foldable beds
27 Witticism
28 Canada's largest brewer
29 Daschle's successor as Senate majority leader
30 Commit a peccadillo?
33 Mo. with Constitution Day
34 "___ calling"
36 Irish "John"
37 Part of E.S.L.: Abbr.
38 Shoot off
39 Break down, in a way
43 1980s–2000s Texas senator Phil
45 Beyond passionate
47 Perform the hit "Things I Should Have Said"?
52 Symbol over 9 or 0 on a keyboard, for short
53 Pet portal
54 Horror, e.g.
55 The Police frontman filming a shampoo commercial?

60 Golden State, informally
61 The night before, to a hard partier?
62 Whimsical
63 Bolted
64 "___ autumn, and a clear and placid day": Wordsworth
65 All-inclusive
66 Tying packages, securing helium balloons, etc.?
73 Lessens in force
75 Flirtatious quality
76 Throng
77 The Beatles showing absolute amazement?
81 Martial art with bamboo swords
82 Ketel One rival, familiarly
83 Selling point
84 Handholds while slow-dancing
85 "The Walking Dead" channel
87 Headey of "Game of Thrones"
89 Salon offering, familiarly
90 Important but sometimes ignored piece
93 First weapons used in a knife fight?
99 Yoga pose
101 Oxygen-reliant organism
102 Oh-so-handsome
103 Jungian souls
104 Disney bear
105 Surprising group of suspects?

108 Endorse digitally
109 "Baby, baby, baby!"
110 Lean fillet, as of lamb
111 "Walk Away ___" (1966 hit)
112 Enthusiastic consent
113 "The 15:17 to Paris" director, 2018

DOWN

1 Doesn't pay
2 ___ track
3 Metaphoric acknowledgment
4 Shared values
5 Performance for which one might grab a chair
6 Tridactyl birds
7 Blood type modifier, for short
8 Waste receptacle
9 Astronauts Bean and Shepard
10 Mag featuring "Fun Fearless Females"
11 Clair Huxtable or Peg Bundy
12 Browns
13 Nonprescription, briefly
14 Drama with many fans
15 Katey who played Peg Bundy
16 Parts of math textbooks
17 When duelers may meet
18 Beginning of the German workweek
19 Like chimneys
24 Truckload
28 Island veranda
30 Barfly

31 Kind of lily
32 School closing?
35 Snapchat posting, for short
38 One seeing ghosts
39 Including
40 Michael who wrote "The Neverending Story"
41 Things that clash in Washington
42 Pouty exclamation
44 "No ___"
45 Rap sound
46 The 48th star
47 Woodland god
48 Do with a pick, maybe
49 Briefly
50 The Theme Park Capital of the World
51 German border river
52 Quaint dismissals
53 Tech news website
56 Hypotheticals
57 Take with force
58 Bears ___ (national monument in Utah)
59 Messenger ___
67 Post-op stop
68 One releasing a dove in the Bible
69 Food truck menu item
70 Not tricked by
71 Advance look, say
72 Film for which Adrien Brody won Best Actor
74 "Park it"
78 "Honestly"
79 Verdant spot

by Byron Walden

80 Last Chinese dynasty
81 Not be serious
84 "___ Just Not That Into You" (2009 rom-com)
85 Relaxing
86 Catch in "The Old Man and the Sea"
88 Title family name in old TV
89 Hawthorne heroine
90 Snapped out of it
91 Out of control?
92 Showed shock
93 Cossack weapon
94 Crash into the side of, informally
95 Marshal
96 "You follow?"
97 Fancy soirees
98 Old record co. conglomerate
100 Strength
103 Celebrated boxing family
105 Edamame source
106 Alternative to café
107 ___ long way

IF FOUND, CALL . . .

ACROSS

1 Heading on a neighborhood poster
8 Radio personality Glenn
12 Bump, as from a schedule
19 Standing closet
20 Poison ivy soother
21 Huts
22 Anti-mob tool
23 Dryer buildup
24 "1984" superstate
25 "Get 'em!"
26 Power up?
27 High land
28 *Last seen riding in a basket. If found, call ___ [see 106-Across]*
32 Mix with
33 Fall off
36 Pizzeria chain, casually
37 Like a certain Freudian complex
39 Graduation attire
41 It goes around the neck
42 Doesn't just assume
44 *Last seen in the nursery. If found, call ___ [see 84-Across]*
46 One who can't keep weight off for long
50 Tempe sch.
51 Scream or bawl, e.g.
52 Like most holidays
53 Reverses, as a deletion
55 "Darn it all!"
58 It may hold the line
59 Toll rds.
61 Yokohama "yes"
62 Tijuana setting, informally
63 Postal abbr. for a rural address
64 *Last seen with a red-haired girl. If found, call ___ [see 119-Across]*
68 Drone, for one
69 Cyclotron bits
70 "Here's an idea . . ."
71 Some bygone theaters
72 Bleat
73 Confrere
74 Food cart offerings
76 One of the Marcoses of the Philippines
80 Alphabetically first "American Idol" judge across all 16 seasons
82 Go from bud to blossom, to a poet
84 Pretend
86 *Last seen chasing down clues. If found, call ___ [see 24-Across]*
90 Poet who wrote of Daedalus
91 ___-green
92 Theme song of Milton Berle
93 Forms, forms and more forms
96 Sash supporter
97 Any of the Baltic states, once: Abbr.
98 What's left on TV?
100 *Last seen being mocked by a cat. If found, call ___ [see 46-Across]*
103 Gambling mecca
104 Increase
105 Lilt
106 Proceed enthusiastically
109 Symbol gotten by typing Option+Shift+2
110 Hit straight to the shortstop, perhaps
114 Promo
115 War loser, usually
116 Declared
117 Storied journey
118 Puts the kibosh on
119 Algebraic variables

DOWN

1 Rowing muscle, for short
2 Iron Range product
3 Wee, to a Scot
4 Chests' places
5 Sudoku entry
6 Herb resembling spinach
7 Some kitchen appliances, for short
8 Adele's "Someone Like You," e.g.
9 Hebrew for "My God! My God!"
10 Idea
11 Etta of old comics
12 Sister of Ariadne
13 More hoarse
14 Snares
15 List-reducing abbr.
16 Prefix with play and place
17 Charlottetown's prov.
18 Checkpoint org.
21 Post
26 Discharges
28 43
29 Kind of dip
30 One-named Swedish singer with the Grammy-nominated song "Dancing on My Own"
31 It goes around the neck
32 Inn stock
33 The U.S., to Mexicans
34 Hallux, more familiarly
35 Stationed (at)
38 Clicking sounds?
40 Gold medal, to an Olympian
42 Repurpose
43 Dressy accessory
45 Boxing champ Roberto
47 Navel type
48 Cultural values
49 Where the engine is in a Porsche 911
54 A bit stiff
56 A bit cracked
57 Modest two-piece swimsuit
60 Sharply sour fruit
62 Ecosystem endangered by global warming
63 Up
64 Pacer
65 2000s corporate scandal subject
66 Heavenly sound?
67 Vagabond
68 Coddles
72 Marriage announcement
73 Some centerfolds
74 Golden Globe-winning actor for "Chicago"
75 Visit during a trip
77 Vision-correcting procedure
78 Big battery
79 Subtitle of Hawthorne's "Fanshawe"
81 Former part of the U.S.S.R.: Abbr.

by Matthew Sewell

83 Alternative to boeuf or jambon
85 [continued]
87 Love all around?
88 Actress Faye
89 Stop for now
94 Saw the sights
95 Ruffles
96 Moviedom
99 My word, maybe
101 Lures
102 Utah's ___ Mountains
103 Some greenery that's not grass
104 Parcel (out)
106 '60s Pontiac
107 Webster's Third competitor, for short
108 Scotland's longest river
110 Start of Yale's motto
111 Chicago terminal code
112 Double-back move
113 QB's tally

ACROSS

1 Big name in computer networking
6 Progressive rival
14 Aries
20 North Dakota-to-Michigan hwy.
21 Members of an Oklahoma tribe
22 Addressee of a waiter in a French restaurant
23 Exposes
24 Interrogate a founding father?
26 Uganda's Amin
27 One getting shooed
29 Bone: Prefix
30 Was wide open
31 Like the first man-made space satellite
33 What the earth and many political analysts do
36 They're added on bus. lines
38 "Sticks and Bones" playwright David
39 "There are no atheists in foxholes"?
41 Word aptly found in "controlled" and "marshaled"
43 Token in the game Life
44 Was a rat
45 Engaged in
46 Tremors?
50 Hershey brand
53 "From your lips to God's ears"
55 Frequent subject of paintings by Winslow Homer
56 Largest lake in South America
60 Charles de Gaulle's birthplace
62 Animal with a trunk
66 Interest's opposite
67 Kingdom in Tolkien's "The Lord of the Rings"
69 Email address ending
71 Suffix in Sussex
72 Comment by a Brit down to his last coin?
77 "We ___ the Champions"
78 Gardner of "Mogambo"
79 Joe of "Home Alone"
80 True
81 Instruments played on Mount Olympus
84 Expert
86 Words of resignation
88 Greek cross
90 "As you wish, Captain!"
92 Huck Finn possessive
93 One knocking out an opponent in the first round?
97 Russian council
99 Spanish snack
103 ___ Indianapolis
104 One of 100: Abbr.
105 Monarch who's fine and dandy?
108 Cries of surprise
110 Teeming
113 Veg out
114 Irish form of "Edmund"
115 Heinrich ___, "Die Lorelei" poet
117 N.W.A's "Straight ___ Compton"
119 More than a millennium
121 Indochinese language
122 Have a little ice cream delivered?
126 Like rope
128 Supermodel Bündchen
129 Birdie
130 With celerity
131 Kept others awake, maybe
132 Tip of a missile
133 More sound

DOWN

1 Picasso and Braque, for two
2 Dancer Duncan
3 Gone to great lengths
4 Middling mark
5 Like freelance work, often
6 Attys.' titles
7 Stops yapping
8 Sheik's land, for short
9 Presidential inits.
10 "Who's interested?"
11 Update, say
12 Terminate
13 English county
14 Response to an oversharer
15 Suspend
16 Catherine's husband in "Wuthering Heights"
17 Bishop's group, once
18 Ones moving with the aid of pseudopods
19 Seamstresses, at times
25 With vehemence
28 Ending of the Bible
32 Unappreciative sort
34 Metallic S-shaped piece
35 "___, sing America" (start of a Langston Hughes poem)
37 "Look Who's Talking Too" and "2 Fast 2 Furious": Abbr.
40 Basic French question
42 Number for two
46 Sentient ones
47 Words that can't be heard, for short
48 Western wear
49 Strong bond?
51 Publisher Arthur ___ Sulzberger
52 Song woman who's asked "Darlin', won't you ease my worried mind?"
54 Subject of the mnemonic "Men Very Easily Make Jugs Serve Useful Needs"
56 Taj ___
57 Mimic's activity
58 Not so common
59 Medieval weapon
61 Suffix with trick
63 Pope who excommunicated Elizabeth I
64 Judas's question to the Lord
65 Change the color of again
68 More trendy
70 TV's "Growing Up ___"
73 Some gametes
74 Accumulation
75 Things with colons inside them
76 Kind of leap
82 Abbr. that's sometimes doubled or tripled
83 Nordstrom rival
85 Term for a hole in Swiss cheese
87 1979 exile
89 It'll take you for a ride

by Daniel Raymon

91 Prefix with -graphic
93 Hard-shell clams
94 Mark the beginning of
95 Unsatisfying answer to "Why?"
96 Bagel variety
98 British sports automobile
100 Kind of harp
101 Atonement
102 Nuisance
105 Trophy alternative
106 Navy petty officer: Abbr.
107 The so-called "Flying Kangaroo"
109 Curl one's lip
111 Informal sleep option
112 People: Prefix
116 Man's name that comes from an English noble
118 Some summer wear
120 Ser : Spanish :: ___ : French
123 Iraq War danger, for short
124 A.C.C. powerhouse
125 Rumpus
127 F.D.R. job-creating prog.

29 FOLLOW THE SUN

ACROSS

1 Government policy chief
5 Assented
12 Not empirical
19 Not natural-looking
21 Sometimes hard-to-find shirt opening
22 Drunkard
23 Onetime co-host of "The View," informally
24 Contest once hosted by Bob Barker
25 Makes reference (to)
26 Catastrophic event that can be caused by a gigantic earthquake
28 "Fer sher"
29 Folds, as a business
30 Headed for
34 Abbr. on mil. mail
36 French painter of ballerinas
40 Injunction
42 How Hercule Poirot likes to address Hastings
43 Money in Malmö
45 Headstone inits.
46 Stag
48 Ones in rocking chairs, stereotypically
50 Smartphone feature
53 Cherry variety
54 Start to many bumper stickers
55 Response to pointing out a resemblance between two people
56 Hollywood labor groups
59 See 71-Down
60 Plant stalk
62 Crank (up)

63 Chipotle choice
65 Nitwit
66 180s
67 2015 hit spinoff of "Despicable Me"
68 How someone in awe might describe himself
70 Pretty cool, in slang
73 One of the Big Four accounting firms
74 Deft touch
75 Placeholder letters
78 Better now
80 Trivia fodder
81 All ___
83 Rough shelter
84 Hannah who coined the phrase "the banality of evil"
86 Largest city in the Baltics
87 Planets like ours, in sci-fi
88 Hue lighter than lime
91 Per ___ (yearly)
92 Vintage film channel
93 Goody
95 Like St. Augustine, among all U.S. cities
97 College, to a Brit
98 Amérique
101 Immigrants' class, for short
102 Only words on the front of the Great Seal of the United States
104 Really fresh
106 Its hub at JFK was designed by Eero Saarinen
108 Hubbub
110 Artistic, chatty sorts, it's said
113 Draft
117 Testify
119 "I got the check"

120 Ancient, undeciphered writing system
121 Towel fabric
122 Relatives of asters
123 Tony who won a Tony for "Angels in America"
124 "It's a deal!"

DOWN

1 E.M.T.'s training
2 Speed along
3 Print ad come-on
4 Sit on the throne
5 International conglomerate whose name means "three stars"
6 Cable news host Melber
7 Gchats, e.g.
8 Some A.L. players
9 Response to a surprising claim
10 "That's something ___!"
11 Voyager
12 Medieval Spanish kingdom
13 Sport last played in the Olympics in 1936
14 Was awesome
15 Occupied
16 Funny
17 Riddle-me-___
18 Qtrly. check recipient, maybe
20 "Stars above!"
27 "___ soon?"
31 Smear
32 Writing in a window?
33 Paranoid sorts, in slang
35 Pushes back
37 "Mamma Mia!" setting
38 In a light manner
39 Outbreaks

40 Anthropomorphic king of Celesteville
41 "Still ___" (Julianne Moore film)
43 Rios, e.g.
44 Decisive assessment
47 Intl. Rescue Committee, e.g.
49 R&B singer with the hits "So Sick" and "Mad"
51 Tempe sch.
52 Things in restaurant windows
57 Sac fly result
58 Outlay that cannot be recovered
59 Some corsage wearers
61 Grand Lodge group
64 Ready . . . or red, maybe
65 "Let's keep this between us"
67 Wasn't kidding about
68 Stunt at the end of a powerful performance
69 Informal assent
70 Go back on one's word?
71 With 59-Across, some works of Tennessee Williams
72 Big ___ (the drug industry)
74 Biter
75 Moment of liftoff
76 Dangerous toy
77 "Same here"
79 Legal vowelless Scrabble play
80 Herculean act
82 Bit of art pottery
85 Preface to a heart-to-heart conversation

by Finn Vigeland

89 End of a George Washington address?
90 Safer alternative to paintball
91 If you're lucky
94 Candy brand owned by Hershey
96 Word before and after "no"
99 Salt-N-Pepa and Ben Folds Five
100 Branch of Islam
102 Rakes in
103 Not taken seriously?
105 Tiniest change
107 Popular gaming console that sounds like two pronouns
109 It's a long story
110 "Keep movin'!"
111 Info for a chauffeur, perhaps
112 Yahoo alternative
114 "Yuck!"
115 Grp. of connected computers
116 + of a 43-Across
118 Manhattan part . . . or a suburb near Manhattan

1 + 1 = 5

ACROSS

1 Hardly
8 Chemicals proscribed by '70s legislation
12 Like some legal damages
20 2018 N.C.A.A. football champs
21 "I know the answer!"
22 Final song in "Fantasia"
23 Excited sort
25 Chinese restaurant chain
26 Actress Green of 2006's "Casino Royale"
27 Tasteless
28 7½-hour exam, for short
29 Component of a summer cloud
30 One doing the lord's work
32 Something you hope people have when they leave?
34 Bee ___
35 Business bigwigs
39 Caught morays
40 What a spoiler spoils
42 Crush
44 Heroic figure in "Star Wars" films
49 "I need everyone's help!"
54 "Geez, that was tiring!"
55 Rumpus
56 Many a cereal box toy
57 Speckled horse
59 Big name in nail polish
60 Bathtub accessory
61 Rating for "Game of Thrones" and "House of Cards"
62 Area for filming in Hollywood
65 ___ favor
66 Org. that oversaw F.D.R.'s Federal Project Number One
67 Haw's go-with
68 Patriotic song lyric before "Mind the music and the step"
71 Regulation followers, in brief
72 Shorn animal
73 An ace has a low one
74 Relatives of channels
75 Gallic gal pal
76 Dumbbell curls build them, for short
77 Aides: Abbr.
80 ___ Rios, Jamaica
81 Cry to a prima donna
82 Had
83 Hero
85 Natural disaster of 2012
88 Magician known for debunking paranormal claims
91 IV bag contents
92 Big ___, nickname of baseball's David Ortiz
93 Fetch
96 Photo-editing option
98 4-Down personnel, informally
100 Item in a sink
102 Lasting, unpleasant memory
105 Match (with)
106 Move to solid food
108 Something used in a pinch?
112 Social ___
113 Stretchable wrappers
115 1988 crime comedy rated 93% positive on Rotten Tomatoes
117 Spanish 101 question
118 They may be loaded in a casino
119 Device many use in bed
120 Massé, e.g.
121 On the double
122 Go down

DOWN

1 Deceptive moves
2 Partner of well
3 Cockpit devices
4 "Enemies: A History of the ___" (2012 best seller)
5 Delhi dignitary
6 Country whose total land area is less than .01% forested
7 Retailer with a star in its logo
8 Flaky entree
9 A, B, C or D
10 Brothel
11 ___-crab soup
12 Vatican jurisdiction
13 Eye part
14 Call from behind a counter
15 The "Home Alone" boy, e.g.
16 Things to shoot for . . . or shoot at
17 Ryan of "The Beverly Hillbillies"
18 Embassy issuances
19 Big ___ Conference
24 Sermon topic
28 Señora, across the Pyrenees
31 Reddish-purple
33 Prefix with liter
34 Have an exclusive relationship
36 Nutrient in lentils and liver
37 X
38 Pathetic
40 Make easier to plow, in a way
41 Makes a connection
43 Pfizer competitor
45 Dieting units: Abbr.
46 Helen Reddy's signature hit
47 Malleable
48 Tougher
49 Like a fictional Casey
50 Have as a housemate
51 "I wanna look!"
52 ___ Zero
53 Leafy vegetables
58 Acknowledge without words
62 Irish Spring, e.g.
63 Pueblo ancestors
64 It's lit
68 "Totally, bro"
69 Four-letter island name with three syllables
70 Some expensive gowns
75 Associate of Athos and Porthos
78 ___ Fridays
79 "___ in the Rain"
81 Certain bra spec
84 Big heads
86 ___ ipsa loquitur
87 Hot state
89 Each
90 Goal for a tailor

by Sam Ezersky

94 Beethoven's Third
95 Typewriter formatting aid
97 Consent (to)
98 Ballroom dance in duple time
99 City near Biscayne National Park
100 Touches, as with a tissue
101 "This is SO frustrating!"
103 Poet who wrote "For the Time Being" and "Another Time"
104 Figure on a poster
105 Bench presses build them, for short
106 Well thought?
107 Prefix with -derm
109 Kept in the loop, in a way
110 Prudence
111 Whoops?
114 French possessive
115 Billboards, e.g.
116 France's ___ du Bourget

31 TRIPLE SPOONERISMS

ACROSS

1 Anesthetic of old
6 Forcefully remove
12 Very good, as a job
18 Purple candy's flavor, often
19 Sea-dwelling
21 Things a spy may have many of
23 Stares slack-jawed
24 What caused the nosebleed on the playground?
26 Sponsor of U.S. Olympic swimmers
28 Ball hit for fielding practice
29 Burro's call
30 Tagline in an ad for Elmer's Glue-Ale?
35 Holiday song closer
36 Bygone channel that aired "Veronica Mars"
37 Chill in the cooler
38 Finish filming
40 Gets up
43 Bernadette of Broadway
45 Succumb to sleepiness
50 High-flown, as writing
52 Big ox
53 Discreet attention-getter
57 Lash with a bullwhip
58 Deliberative bodies
60 Description of a yeti?
63 Parodied
65 Capacitate
66 Tip jar fillers
67 Novice parasailer's fear?
73 Ingredient in a Roy Rogers
74 Coarse
75 What a Möbius strip lacks
76 Containers for electric guitars?
80 They're easy to take
85 Unfamiliar
86 Quite a few
87 It hangs around the neck
89 Sandwich with Russian dressing
90 One-room apartment, to Brits
92 Motifs
95 Like the questions in 20 Questions
96 Very worst
99 "Law & Order" actor Jerry
101 Sealer for sailors?
102 Drawbacks
106 Best place to buy a platter of fruit-flavored sodas?
111 Square footage
112 Bishop's headgear
113 Paradisiacal
114 Mend fences after Caesar's civil war?
120 Maker of PowerShot cameras
122 Apathetic response to "What's new?"
123 Leave behind
124 Something to live by
125 Market offerings
126 Trick-taking game
127 "Napoleon Dynamite" star Jon

DOWN

1 Easter ___
2 It's a bunch of garbage
3 Discovers by chance
4 Pentathlon items
5 Complete policy overhaul, in D.C.-speak
6 1987 action film originally given an X rating for violence
7 Winter driving hazard
8 Shell game object
9 Cooper's wood
10 Game with 108 cards
11 Small scraps
12 Hedgehog predator
13 Second, or worse
14 Quibble
15 Dresses
16 There's enormous interest in it
17 Nut in pralines
20 Caddie's selection
22 ___ terrier
25 From scratch
27 Fizzler
30 Lays down the lawn?
31 Classic seller of compilation albums
32 Seek moolah from
33 Alphabet ender
34 According to
39 Cal ___
41 Setting for a period piece
42 Instrument whose name means "three strings"
44 What shopaholics do
46 "The Martian" star
47 Long-armed climber, for short
48 Joins
49 Own (up)
51 Kick out
54 Dance akin to the jitterbug
55 Prized Siberian animal
56 Bathroom floor, often
59 Podcast that won a 2014 Peabody Award
61 Detectives run them down
62 More rare, perhaps
64 Resonator guitar
67 John Kennedy ___, author of "A Confederacy of Dunces"
68 Charlton Heston title role
69 Aids in golf course maintenance
70 Irrefutable point
71 Play at maximum volume
72 R&B's ___ Brothers
73 Sideways scuttler
77 Cutlet?
78 "Life Itself" memoirist Roger
79 Swahili for "lion"
81 Actor's last line, maybe
82 Stayed sober
83 Rules for forming sentences
84 Mock sound of disinterest
88 Exhausted
91 Tufted songbirds
93 Sweetie
94 Multiplex count

by Patrick Berry

97 Dark meat options
98 Jimmy's "Late Night" successor
100 Deceived
102 "High Hopes" lyricist Sammy
103 Snacks in stacks
104 Opposite of o'er
105 "Frida" star Hayek
107 Spanakopita ingredient
108 Ones who grasp elbows in greeting, by tradition
109 "How revolting!"
110 Drum kit component
115 Lab coat?
116 FISA warrant objective
117 Genetic macromolecule
118 Unmatched
119 One of the Three Stooges
121 Winner of the most medals at the 2018 Winter Olympics: Abbr.

32

PREPOSITION PROPOSITION

ACROSS

1 Sound of a dud
5 Personnel overhaul
12 End of the block?
15 Pitcher's feat, slangily
19 Peace activist Wiesel
20 Rear seating compartment in old automobiles
21 Replaced someone on a base
23 Wagers for a gym exercise?
25 Big name in luxury S.U.V.s
26 Successfully persuades
27 At the most
28 Sub
30 Opposite of stiff
31 Figures on slots
33 Bad thing to see under a truck's hood?
35 Small breather?
38 Customer service worker
40 "Man and Superman" playwright
41 Anxious feeling
42 Wastebasket or folder, maybe
43 Avoided trans fats and refined sugars, say
47 Part of NASA: Abbr.
48 Unrecruited athlete's bottleful?
52 ___ al-Hussein (Jordanian royal)
53 Private eye
55 Word after flight or credit
56 "Zounds!"
57 ___ dish
58 It's not in the bag
61 Intake in many an eating contest
62 Makes drunk
63 Certain note passer, for short
64 Timely entrance?
69 Kitty
70 "Here's the thing . . ."
72 Lawn coating
73 Grueling workplace, so to speak
75 Man first mentioned in Exodus 2
76 Something removed at a T.S.A. checkpoint
78 Purple smoothie flavorer
80 German "you"
81 Caught in ___
82 Understudy's delivery?
85 Nonsense singing
88 Closet rackful
90 Suffer from a lockup
91 Zeros
93 "Fight, fight, fight for Maryland!" singer, familiarly
94 Duke of ___, character in "The Two Gentlemen of Verona"
96 Reaches by plane
97 Scam alert?
101 Paragons
103 Hoppy brew
104 Info provider
105 Optimist's credo
106 What an A.P. class likely isn't
110 Throws at
112 Fight clubs?
115 Serving to quell violent protests
116 Free, as a seat
117 Web links, briefly
118 Trickle
119 Certain baseball positions: Abbr.
120 Lunchtime errands, e.g.
121 ___ Classic (cable channel)

DOWN

1 Juices (up)
2 Something a chimney sweep sweeps
3 Permeate
4 Gossips
5 Pennzoil competitor
6 Low-cost lodging
7 Playwright Chekhov
8 Bags that might have drawstrings
9 Startled squeals
10 Neighbor of Oman, for short
11 Press, as a button
12 Vertical, to a sailor
13 Saying "Eww!," say
14 Make hard to read
15 Org. that's nearly one-fourth Canadian
16 Speak before Parliament, e.g.
17 Comaneci of Olympics fame
18 Time in Tokyo when it's midnight in New York
22 ___ salad
24 App customers
29 10/
32 Scene
33 Founder of Philadelphia
34 Strong strings
35 Sister
36 Man ___ mission
37 Soundtrack for a brawl?
39 Proceed well enough
42 Story featuring divine intervention
43 ___ premium
44 Compositions often chosen for encores?
45 Seuss title character
46 Sad, in San Juan
49 Department
50 Small dam
51 Smoking or stress
54 Forfeits
57 Hits with snowballs
58 Nonexpert
59 Portrayer of Mr. Chips
60 Ball support
61 Something "shaken" in a trick
62 The Ravens, on scoreboards
65 Take too much of, briefly
66 Call for
67 "To repeat . . ."
68 Self-absorbed
71 Hope that one may
74 Doesn't go on at the right time
76 Exit
77 Gives birth to
78 "Eso Beso" singer
79 Doctor treating patients
82 G.I. reply
83 Any of the Galápagos
84 Singer known for her 85-Across
86 Skill

by Alex Bajcz

87 Chinese menu name
89 More likely to escalate
92 Member of a four-time Stanley Cup-winning team in the 1980s
94 Emcee's item
95 Spring river breakup
96 Certain Summer Olympian
97 Gyro holders
98 Barely ahead, scorewise
99 Interior decorator's asset
100 Brisk paces
102 Gracias : Spanish :: ___ : German
105 Avid about
107 Some Nikons, for short
108 Go "Ow, ow, OW!"
109 Professional grp.
111 Apt rhyme of "nip"
113 Card game cry
114 Some doorways

33

PLUSES AND MINUSES

ACROSS

1 Bedbug, e.g.
5 "Police Line—Do Not Cross" material
9 Gay ___
14 Blemish for a straight-A student
19 R.p.m. indicator
20 Having gone tit for tat
21 Florida city whose name ends with two state postal abbreviations
22 Humiliate
23 Makes eye contact before undressing?
26 Hoosier hoopster
27 Expatriate
28 Wide-eyed type
29 "What ___ thou?"
31 One of five permanent members of the U.N. Security Council
32 One reading up on infant care, maybe
34 Equilibrium
36 Minor setback
38 Butts
39 Parent wearing your Superman costume?
42 Year abroad
43 The sun, for one
44 "Party Up (Up in Here)" rapper, 2000
45 Bugs's cartoon pursuer
46 Org. with evening meetings
47 Book after Jonah
49 "Get ___"
51 Root beer brand since 1937
54 Script suggestion about starting the fight scene?
60 A.F.L. partner
61 The "A" of I.P.A.
62 Ocean buildup
63 Willa who wrote "My Ántonia"
65 Mean-spirited sort
68 Richard Gere title role
69 Eat a little here, a little there
70 Greek god of sleep
72 Take for granted
76 Early Chinese dynasty
77 Black ___
78 Ballet choreography?
84 Sport
86 RR ___
87 Widening of the mouth?
88 Broody genre
89 Racy film
91 FEMA offering
94 Cartoonist Thomas
95 Beaut
96 Was harder for the bronco buster to hold on to?
101 High flier
102 Firstborn
103 University of Illinois city
104 Lumbering, say
106 In days of yore
107 "Same with me"
109 Subjects of an apartment restriction
111 Actresses Field and Hawkins
113 Rarity in a Polish name?
115 Like the digit "0" in 2018?
118 Iowa senator elected in 2014
119 ". . . but I could be wrong"
120 Reynolds of "Deadpool"
121 James who was nominated for a 1967 Grammy for "Tell Mama"
122 Hives, e.g.
123 Forte's opposite
124 Old flames
125 Balance

DOWN

1 All-too-common V.A. diagnosis
2 Corroded
3 Fall guy
4 Loses intentionally
5 What the classics stand
6 "Selma" director DuVernay
7 Southernmost Ivy
8 Hyphen's longer cousin
9 Agricultural locale that's weed-friendly?
10 Down's counterpart: Abbr.
11 Trail mix bit
12 Title city in a 1960 #1 song
13 "Don't panic"
14 Event for Jesus described in Matthew 3:13–17
15 Kegler's org.
16 Popular Mexican folk song
17 Depletes
18 It's a wrap
24 "Uhh . . ."
25 Positioned
30 Lambaste
33 Auto repair chain
35 Boxcars half
37 Looped in, in a way
38 Skipper, informally
40 Places for conductors
41 Kind of tide
43 Breakfast order at a diner
48 Giggle syllable
49 The New Yorker cartoonist Chast
50 Tip of the tongue?
52 Number between nueve and once
53 Put out
55 Make
56 Politician inducted into the Automotive Hall of Fame
57 Trunk
58 Tally, in Britain
59 Vituperated
64 Orbitz booking
65 Grub
66 Build up
67 Fickleness of life
71 Demeaners of the #MeToo movement, say
72 Part of a stockyard
73 Dungeons & Dragons, e.g., for short
74 T-shirt size: Abbr.
75 First name on the Supreme Court
76 Monsoons
79 Draws
80 Treeless plain
81 Put on an act?
82 February birthstones
83 1899 gold rush destination
85 Be absolutely awesome

by Ross Trudeau

90 Makes potable, in a way
91 Wall St. worker
92 Probably will
93 Supergiant in Cygnus
96 A state of rapture
97 Notable whose name is an anagram of GALORE
98 Some arm bones
99 Journalist Fallaci
100 Emotionally developed
101 ___ whale
105 Bacon runoff
108 Cockeyed
110 Boundary between the earth and the underworld, in myth
112 R.B.I.s or H.R.s
114 The "e" of i.e.
116 III or IV, maybe
117 When doubled, a 2010s dance craze

ACROSS

1 Projects
5 Nowhere close
11 Former first name on the Supreme Court
15 Delight
18 Supercollider bit
19 Online tracker
20 Country whose capital lent its name to a fabric
21 "___ reading too much into this?"
22 Meadows filled with loos?
25 Originally
26 Bar that might be dangerous
27 Ax
28 Be agreeable
30 Negligent
35 Old letter opener
37 Blotto
38 Where sailors recover from their injuries?
42 No longer edible
43 Square figure
44 Actor Paul of "There Will Be Blood"
45 Lead-in to -tainment
46 Quashes
48 Chart again
50 Checkpoint offense, for short
52 Gusto
55 Goings-on in accelerated classes?
61 "My man"
62 Subject for The Source magazine
63 Sch. of 30,000+ on the Mississippi
64 Bill's support
65 It dethroned Sophia as the #1 baby girl's name in the U.S. in 2014
67 Home for a Roman emperor
69 Onetime Bond girl ___ Wood
71 "So obvious!"
74 Common core?
75 Like
76 Prime-time time
80 Dog that doesn't offend people?
87 Come down hard, as hail
88 Barnyard male
89 First name on the Supreme Court
90 Dreyfus Affair figure
91 Subject for Ken Burns, briefly
93 Burg
96 Went by air?
99 Dorm monitors
100 Cry of devotion from a non-academy student?
105 Source of the line "They shall beat their swords into plowshares"
106 Things that may be rolled or wild
107 Soprano Tebaldi
108 Some fasteners
110 They aid in diagnosing A.C.L. tears
112 Funny face?
116 Old White House nickname
117 Morning zoo programming?
123 Panama City state: Abbr.
124 Substantive
125 "Don't doubt me!"
126 Clue
127 Divinity sch.
128 Chatty bird
129 Provider of aerial football views
130 Actress Kendrick

DOWN

1 Best Picture nominee with three sequels
2 Pac-12 school that's not really near the Pacific
3 Completely, after "in"
4 Like wet makeup
5 Media watchdog grp.
6 Sister co. of HuffPost
7 Hundred Acre Wood denizen
8 Agrees to
9 Lord's domain
10 Fixation
11 Slice for a Reuben
12 Things that have slashes
13 With nothing out of place
14 "What other explanation is there?!"
15 Former "Today" show host
16 Word before pan or after Spanish
17 Investment figures
20 GMC truck
23 Like poor months for oysters, it's said
24 Mentally wiped
29 Stiff
31 Sch. with an annual Mystery Hunt
32 Words of compassion
33 Stuffed
34 Weak period
36 "Fifty Shades of Grey" subject, briefly
38 Symbol of China
39 Onetime Blu-ray rival
40 Blue-green
41 Albright's successor as secretary of state
42 Craft shop item
47 "The Sweetest Taboo" singer, 1985
49 Combo bets
51 Absolutely harebrained
53 Astonishment
54 Cryptanalysis org.
56 Queens player, for short
57 Pledge
58 ___ Poly
59 Green org.
60 Caesar dressing?
66 Some neckwear
67 Italy's ___ d'Orcia
68 Laid up
70 Second U.S. feature-length computer-animated movie, after "Toy Story"
71 Modern subject of reviews
72 Row maker
73 Elite court group
77 Ecuadorean coastal province known for its gold
78 Micronesian land
79 Some future execs
81 Inclined to stress?
82 Gas brand with a torch in its logo
83 Druid's head cover
84 Studio sign
85 Ransack
86 Boca ___
92 2007 female inductee into the National Soccer Hall of Fame

by Peter Wentz

94 Hex
95 Our, in Tours
97 "Uncle Tom's Cabin" girl
98 Stave off
100 Rice dishes
101 Of service
102 Gore's successor as vice president
103 Green-skinned god of the underworld
104 Harley-Davidson competitor
109 "___ Against Evil" (IFC series)
111 Totally awesome, in slang
113 Role in "Thor," 2011
114 Islamic spirit
115 Second letter after 118-Down
118 Second letter before 115-Down
119 Word with camp or care
120 L.L.C. alternative
121 That: Sp.
122 Dr. ___

35

LET'S PLAY TWO!

ACROSS

1 Perpendicular to the ship's middle
6 "Let's do this!"
13 Larger of Mars's two moons
19 Proof of purchase for some contests
21 Maines of the Dixie Chicks
22 Out of date?
23 *Underwater mine?*
25 Some end-of-season announcements
26 ___ Plus (grooming brand)
27 "Insecure" star Issa
28 Comparison middle
29 Peaceful protest
30 *Get a copy of a 1965 #1 Beatles hit?*
37 South America's ___ Picchu
39 Left-winger
40 U.N. worker protection agcy.
41 "___ Music's golden tongue / Flatter'd to tears this aged man . . .": Keats
42 Actor Milo
43 Minute Maid Park player, informally
45 Formed for a particular purpose
47 Sultan Qaboos's land
48 Something to be defended
50 *Rather poor ambassador's skill?*
53 School in development?
54 Hat, informally
56 Bomb with the audience
57 Brand with an arrow through its logo
58 Grp. getting a pay cut?
59 "Roll Tide!" school, for short
62 Rolled ___
65 Prefix with warrior
66 Formerly known as
67 *Reason a computer program wouldn't open?*
70 Some touchdown scorers, for short
73 Zippo
74 "Am ___ sensitive?"
75 Existed
76 Thanksgiving serving
77 Things folded in the kitchen
80 "Cinderella" mouse
82 Big-eared animal
84 Past
85 *Incredibly hard puzzle?*
90 One with a confession to make
92 Consume
93 Responds wistfully
94 First name in fashion
96 Impressive hole
97 "___ reconsidered"
98 Padre's hermano
99 Prefix with pressure
100 "Eww!"
101 *Link a quartet of supermarket employees?*
109 Aid for a tracking shot
110 Jumpy sort, for short?
111 Vehicle that often rolls over, in brief
112 ___ mater
115 Angry Shakespearean cry
117 *Something you're not allowed to do in math?*
121 Mistakes
122 Bit of nonsense in a #1 Ella Fitzgerald hit
123 Not ruling out
124 Gadget for lemons
125 Goes back and forth (with)
126 A cylinder has two

DOWN

1 Band with a symmetrical logo
2 Bath toy
3 Pizzeria order
4 Some lawyers' cases
5 Kind of biol.
6 Picks up later in life?
7 Red ___ (sushi fish)
8 Irish icon, for short
9 Ankle bones
10 Relating to the pelvis
11 Prefix with communication
12 Hair-raising cry
13 Pigtail, e.g.
14 Many a ". . . For Dummies" book
15 Transmitting
16 Comic who acted in "Ocean's Eleven"
17 Smelling of mothballs
18 Part of O.S.: Abbr.
20 Original home of Paddington Bear
24 Moves effortlessly (through)
29 Streetside hangouts
31 Draw back in fear
32 River that rises in the Cantabrian Mountains
33 Player/coach Jason of the N.B.A.
34 K–12
35 Constellation between Ursa Major and Ursa Minor
36 Kids' rhyme starter
37 Big name in pain relief
38 Onto land
44 Code on a bag to Chicago
45 Annually
46 Like a space cadet
47 1847 novel of the sea
49 "Finlandia" composer
51 Rollickingly funny
52 "Time was . . ."
55 Feature of a millpond
60 "You couldn't possibly mean me!?"
61 Oil field?
63 Kind of job
64 ___ Bird, 10-time W.N.B.A. All-Star
67 Bite-size, say
68 Teaching positions can be part of their work
69 Chest protector
70 "La La Land" actor
71 Rolls out of bed in the morning?
72 Messy treats
73 Fluorine's atomic number
77 "Way to go!"
78 Purple flowers
79 Longtime Walter Berndt comic strip
81 Spot for wallowing
83 All-out attack
85 Stylish
86 Cry at a happy hour, maybe
87 Cry of excitement
88 "Well, Did You ___?"

by Brendan Emmett Quigley

89 Gate
91 Did some documentary work
95 Bolivian capital
102 0%, in the dairy aisle
103 Highest-level
104 Nice forecast
105 Population classification
106 Settle down for the night
107 Sam who sang "Twistin' the Night Away"
108 Corn syrup brand
113 Tiny bit
114 They always come with mayo
115 Flat-topped hat
116 Heat
117 Keyboard key
118 ___ minimum
119 Anthem contraction
120 One rampaging in 2018's "Rampage"

36

LOVE AT FIRST SITE

ACROSS

1 Arcade hoops game
7 Some TV ads, for short
11 Went through channels?
15 Hitter's hitter
18 "The Simpsons" or "Futurama"
19 Litter's littlest
20 To whom Brabantio says "Thou art a villain"
21 Singular
22 Good name for a deep kissers' dating site?
25 Vittles
26 A shroud of secrecy, idiomatically
27 Endlessly starting over
28 Performances at Paris's Palais Garnier
30 Manning with the second-longest QB starting streak in N.F.L. history
31 Numerical prefix
32 "Ish"
34 Monster slain by Hercules
35 North Carolina university
36 Victor's shout
39 It's all in the head
41 Member of a southern colony
43 Actor whose first and last names look like they rhyme, but don't
47 Slice of a timeline
50 Fruit drink
51 Good name for a dating site full of hot dudes?
54 Obsolescent high school course, informally
56 No.1 pal
57 Good name for a dating site of massage therapists?
59 In amazement
61 Emerald or aquamarine
63 Revolting sorts
64 Kitty-cat, e.g.
65 Carbo-loading dish
67 Patty alternative?
70 IV checkers
71 1988 top 10 hit for Tracy Chapman
73 George ___ University
75 Swamps
76 Good name for an extreme sports dating site?
79 Be traitorous to
82 Burger topper
83 Good name for a non-monogamist dating site?
85 Big Apple cultural site, with "the"
88 Alway
89 Southernmost of the Lesser Antilles
91 Napa Valley vintner Robert
93 Grannies
95 Previous name for an athletic conference now with 12 members
98 Comparable (to)
99 Sky-blue
101 Performer in makeup, typically
105 Certain layers
106 ___ Aviv
107 UTEP team
109 First things to go into jammies

112 "Trading Spaces" host Davis
114 Neat as ___
115 Good name for a dating site for lovers of natural foods?
118 Ad
119 Big loss
120 John of the Velvet Underground
121 Tot's wear
122 Junior
123 Lincoln Logs and such
124 Something taken on a field?
125 Ones passed on a track

DOWN

1 [Avoid watching this in front of the boss]
2 Sped (along)
3 Had a table for one
4 Chinese leader Xi
5 Rainbows, e.g.
6 "That doesn't impress me much"
7 Immediately
8 Natural light beam
9 One of the Brontës
10 Group dance with stomps and claps
11 Instrument plucked with a mezrab
12 Cools one's heels
13 Back in time
14 Like early Elvis recordings
15 Good name for a carpentry dating site?
16 The rite place?
17 Thompson of "Selma"
21 "Toodles!"
23 Noggin
24 Chairman and ___ (common title)

29 Ones to watch
31 Back-of-newspaper section
33 Poetic tribute
35 Org. with a flower logo
37 "Just ___ suspected"
38 1940s vice president Wallace
40 Enthusiastic
42 Not new
44 Chaperones, usually
45 Lincoln's home: Abbr.
46 "I'll return shortly," in a text
48 Swing time?
49 German interjections
52 "That's mine!"
53 '
55 Dignified lady
56 Model Page known as "The Queen of Pinups"
58 Naval officer: Abbr.
59 Geronimo, for one
60 Good name for a "High Noon"-themed dating site?
62 Hit hard
65 ___ Bread (cafe chain)
66 NPR host Shapiro
68 "2 funny!!!"
69 "To Live and Die ___"
71 Visage
72 Player of Robin Hood in 1991
74 Like child's play
75 Nautical title, informally
77 Whole lot
78 Prefix with center

by Neville Fogarty and Erik Agard

80 Ginormous
81 Lowly workers
84 O.T.C. O.K.'er
85 Command of Captain Jean-Luc Picard
86 Satanic look
87 Cookie holder
90 Movement
92 Statistician's grouping
94 "___ you the clever one!"
96 Gum ingredient
97 Titter
99 Stockpile
100 Nada
102 Certain computer whiz
103 Deep defenses
104 Long span
108 Put in order
110 Camping menace
111 Digitize, in a way
112 ___ colada
113 Real lookers?
116 Down Under hopper
117 Gather around, as an idol

37

RHYMES, SCHMYMES

ACROSS

1 Picnic annoyance
8 Cold quarters
13 Racetrack informant
20 Like okapis and giraffes
21 Sit pensively
22 Cry from a survivor
23 Conversation over a few whiskeys?
25 Wear
26 Pose
27 Mario Vargas Llosa's country
28 Strummed instrument, for short
29 Where butter and cheese are produced
30 ___ buddies
31 Moreover
32 Org. for drivers
33 Return to base
36 2015 Verizon purchase
38 Filth covering pecans and such?
45 Borodin opera prince
46 Fasten, in a way, with "in"
48 Asian holiday
49 Tush
50 Venison spread?
53 Relics, to Brits
55 "You betcha!"
56 Very beginning?
58 Give a leg up . . . or a hand
59 Lose one's coat
60 Casting need
61 Notwithstanding
63 Brings on
64 Sprayed in the face
67 Hardly a dolt?
68 Powerful scents
69 Made-up
70 Virus fighters
71 Director Wenders
72 Unnamed character in Camus's "The Stranger"
73 Ground cover?
74 Connections
75 Buds come in them
80 Office's counterpart
83 Avoid a jerk?
85 Mozart's Don Alfonso and Leporello
86 Shout with an accent
88 Gathered intelligence (on)
89 It has lots on the internet
90 Break up with an "unbreakable" Ellie Kemper character?
93 "Black-ish" network
94 Part of a kit
95 It may be found next to a spade
96 Sashimi option
98 Ready for battle
100 DNA building block
105 Restroom sign
106 "What's Going On" singer, 1971
107 Tampa Bay N.F.L.'er
110 Beats in the race
111 Puts a stop to sentimentality?
114 Term for a word that isn't in the dictionary, but maybe should be
115 Subject of una serenata
116 Subject of the 2006 documentary "When the Levees Broke"
117 Promenades
118 Rehab program
119 Plug

DOWN

1 Cake with rum
2 Hovering craft
3 Understand
4 Industry, for short
5 Treat on a stick
6 Stuns, in a way
7 Intruded (on)
8 Watson's company
9 Cavity filler
10 Be a witness
11 Exude
12 Loving verse?
13 Some pageant wear
14 Brought charges against
15 Daddy
16 Criticize severely
17 Part of a makeshift swing
18 ___ after
19 Depend
24 "Just pretend I'm right"
29 Singer of high notes
30 Scottish accents
33 Dusted off, say
34 James who won a posthumous Pulitzer
35 Says, informally
37 "When the Levees Broke" director
39 High ___
40 Publisher in a robe, familiarly
41 Algonquian Indians
42 Open, as a bottle
43 Prince and others
44 Some drink garnishes
46 Fish whose name sounds like the past tense of 46-Across?
47 Greets silently
51 Begets
52 Take back
54 3–3, e.g.
57 Site of one of the Seven Wonders of the Ancient World
61 Professional fixer, for short
62 Uses Gchat, e.g.
63 Scornful sound
64 H. G. Wells villain
65 Four-time Australian Open winner
66 Picasso, e.g.
67 Recent arrival
68 Personalized music gift
69 Backyard shindig, informally
70 Perfect score, or half of a score
71 Smart remarks
73 Zooey of Fox's "New Girl"
75 Long, narrow pieces of luggage
76 Modify
77 Where Hemingway wrote "The Old Man and the Sea"
78 Old Chrysler
79 ___ terrier
81 Parties

by Will Nediger

82 Pastor role in "There Will Be Blood"
84 Keeper of the books, for short
87 Japanese appetizer
91 Lifts
92 Everything
94 Appear that way
97 101 course
99 ". . . I'll eat ___!"
100 Order (around)
101 May or Bee
102 Prevent from clumping, say
103 In conclusion
104 Sway
107 Random data point
108 ___ Reader
109 Powerful politico
111 & 112 Coupled
113 "Collage With Squares Arranged According to the Laws of Chance" artist

ACROSS

1 New Hampshire's is 21 kilometers long
6 Simultaneously
13 Actress Rivera
18 Layer of the earth
19 Knight in a medieval romance
20 Monopoly pieces
22 21
25 But nevertheless
26 Chicken choice
27 Practices crystal gazing
28 LAX listing, for short
29 Where the Bactrian camel is native
31 Leave unsaid
32 Scenery chewers
33 Former Nebraska senator James
34 21
40 One might be cast in a Harry Potter film
41 Famous writer who entered West Point at 21
42 Alias of rapper Sean Combs
43 Sadat and Arafat, e.g.
47 Polling abbr.
48 Certain dumbbell weight: Abbr.
51 21
59 What a hungover person might have had
60 Who said "The opposite of love is not hate, it's indifference"
61 Line of work: Abbr.

62 Crunchy sandwich, for short
63 Pick, with "for"
64 Prefix with cycle
65 Replicas
70 Doing evil
74 21
76 Moreno and Hayworth
77 B&B
78 Old British firearms
79 What "you know you make me wanna" do, in a classic R&B song
82 Loos
83 Dirección toward sunset
87 21
96 "Out of Africa" author Dinesen
97 21st-century currency
98 Competitor of Allure
99 ___ bean
100 The Stones' "Aftermath" and "Flowers"
101 The U.S.S. Maine sank in its harbor
103 "M*A*S*H" actor David Ogden ___
105 Agent, informally
106 21
110 Action hero Steven
111 Shape of every Baha'i temple
112 Component of natural gas
113 Without smiling, say
114 "Workers of the world, unite!" and others
115 Hurdles for aspiring D.A.s

DOWN

1 Pens
2 Erstwhile
3 Raiders' org.
4 One covered with food stains, say
5 Hellion
6 Transport "to Sugar Hill way up in Harlem"
7 Sad, in French or Spanish
8 "___ that somethin'?"
9 Bit of a scolding
10 End of an illness?
11 Fu ___
12 Memory trace
13 Inferior in quality
14 Harleys, e.g.
15 Suffix with señor
16 Sent an important message, once
17 In sum
18 Settlers of the Yucatán Peninsula
21 Summer Olympics host after Atlanta
23 Showcase
24 Something a sea star can regenerate
30 So much fun
33 Nonpoisonous, as mushrooms
35 California town whose name is Spanish for "the river"
36 Put in (for)
37 Sets of points on graphs
38 Davis of old Hollywood
39 He lost to Dwight twice

44 Time span with a tilde
45 Little girl, in Italy
46 Parts of "at" symbols
48 Big hits
49 It starts with E, in two different ways
50 State whose capital is 21-Down: Abbr.
51 Clowns
52 Twist open
53 Brand of wafers
54 Dossier contents
55 Lots
56 You, in Yucatán
57 Italian city where St. Valentine was born
58 Movers and shakers
66 White's co-author of "The Elements of Style"
67 Query from Judas
68 Witty zinger
69 Guardian Angel Curtis ___
70 Capital of Belarus
71 Unfriend?
72 Otherwise
73 Start for every Perry Mason title, with "The"
75 Old civil rights org.
79 Guzzles
80 Unlike dial-up internet service, informally
81 How one might wish
84 Ogle
85 Bars
86 Tick away
88 Almost

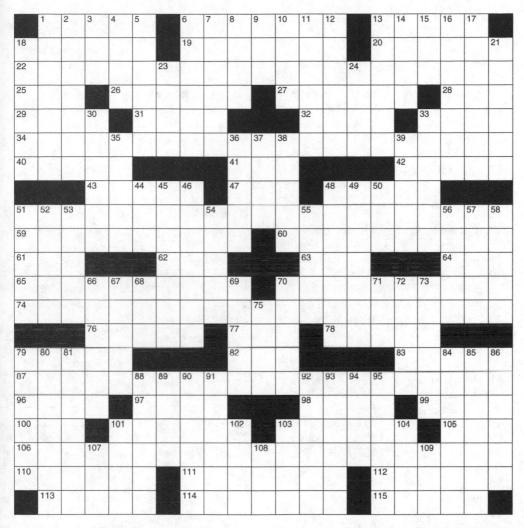

by Andrew Chaikin

ACROSS

1 Drawing tool
8 One not acting alone
14 Literally, "great O"
19 Ackbar's rank, in "Star Wars" films
20 Relating to an eye layer
22 What fan fiction is not
23 Writing tip #1
25 Accessory
26 Plant anew
27 Lo ___
29 So
30 Contractor's guidelines
33 Writing tip #2
38 Yearn for
39 Unlike the wind
40 Lead-in to guess or game
41 Got up there
42 Balneotherapy site
45 Bi- and bi-?
48 Train part
49 Writing tip #3
54 Relating to a major vessel
55 Hexagonal state
56 Invalidate
59 Restaurant chain with a flag in its logo
62 Band aids
65 Make suitable for indoors, as a plant
67 Home of Ithaca, Athens and Olympia
68 Writing tip #4
74 They go from town to town: Abbr.
75 That, in Tijuana
76 Ed.'s request
77 Cell parts
78 "Uh-huh"
80 German auto co.
82 Flew off the handle
85 Writing tip #5
93 Bill Clinton or Barack Obama
94 ___ group (structure found in proteins)
95 Old English letter
96 Shoot the breeze
97 Turn on
101 4,840 square yards
103 Cylinder-shaped pasta
104 Writing tip #6
109 Regarding
110 Large Hadron Collider org.
111 Hoity-toity sort
112 Became adept in
114 1983 Michael Keaton title role
116 Writing tip #7
123 Operative
124 Less watertight
125 Energetic pooch
126 Graph parts
127 Knights' needs
128 Primes

DOWN

1 Give the ax
2 Poem of homage
3 2005, to Cato
4 Ring bearers, maybe
5 Bring in
6 Droops
7 It "knits up the ravell'd sleave of care," per Macbeth
8 Doctrines
9 Atop, poetically
10 RR stop
11 Up to
12 Jungian inner self
13 Knocked to the ground
14 Andean tuber
15 Like the movies "Brian's Song" and "Sharknado"
16 Circumvention
17 It uses the PageRank algorithm
18 Irritates
21 Classic camera brand
24 Prefix with liberal
28 Vice President John ___ Garner
30 Digitize, in a way
31 Bounce along, in a way
32 Anticipatory days
34 Gala
35 Where to find some very wet sponges
36 Gives in confidence
37 Gosling of "La La Land"
42 Tried
43 Favorite
44 Santa ___, Calif.
46 Templeton from "Charlotte's Web," e.g.
47 Visibly awed
50 "Me neither," formally
51 Refuse to talk, with "up"
52 Conductance quantities
53 Like a good proof
57 "Makes sense"
58 ___ Day (June event, informally)
59 Not needing a cane, say
60 Commanded
61 Syria's Bashar al-___
63 Person of note?
64 Fee-free spot, briefly
66 Unruly hair, metaphorically
69 Jacob's twin
70 Composer of many patriotic tunes
71 Conveyor part
72 Course part
73 Something tacky to hang on the wall?
79 Stroke of luck?
81 Bill Clinton or Barack Obama, informally
83 It's mined, all mined!
84 Stayed on the shelf
86 Homework lover, maybe
87 Military stints
88 Like some audiobooks
89 Romance writer Roberts
90 "Yikes!"
91 When repeated, an old sitcom catchphrase
92 Leave in

by Tom McCoy

97 Character that goes "waka, waka, waka . . ."
98 Exceed
99 Wriggled
100 Punitive
102 Goes in
103 Gently towel
105 Peace signs
106 W. W. II danger
107 Cape ___
108 Early days
113 Patella site
115 Much of W. Va.
117 Mike's confectionery partner
118 Dungeons & Dragons piece
119 Like William Carlos Williams's wheelbarrow
120 Actress Peeples
121 Ron of the Dodgers
122 '17 and '18

ACROSS

1 Zip along
7 Example of 22- and of 65-Across
12 Conscience-stricken
19 Opposites of alphas
20 It may be grand
21 "Hah!"
22 7- and 112-Across
24 Flashing lights
25 What scouts gather
26 Intentions
27 Donkey's call
29 Naval engineer
31 Example of 65-Across and 39-Down
33 Subsides slowly
37 Org. for ex-G.I.s
40 Diddley and Derek
41 Farewells in Florence
42 Take temporarily
44 First lady before Bess
47 116-Across and 96-Down
49 Levin who wrote "A Kiss Before Dying"
50 Silver, for example, in the opening to TV's "The Lone Ranger"
51 Torah receptacles
52 A professional may need one to practice: Abbr.
53 Work unit
54 Intimates
55 Wash'n ___ (towelette brand)
56 Caribbean land whose capital is St. George's
59 It'll knock you out
60 Ricochet
62 Ambition for an actor
64 In view
65 7- and 31-Across
67 "So long," for short
69 Part of a machine assembly
71 Like Odin or Thor
72 Titter
73 Some scratchy attire
74 "Sprechen ___ Deutsch?"
75 Lowest points
76 Car for which you "Listen to her tachin' up now, listen to her whine," in a 1964 hit
78 Land in the Seine
79 "I cannot tell ___"
81 "Nuh-uh!"
82 Film critic Christopher
83 112-Across and 96-Down
86 Dress adornment
87 Lathers (up)
89 Not esos or estos
90 Coiled killer
91 Nikon product, for short
92 "___ Rebel" (1962 #1 hit)
93 Example of 34-Down and 108-Across
94 Dimes, essentially
97 Straight
100 "Othello" traitor
101 Milky gems
105 Admit
108 93- and 116-Across
112 Example of 83- and 22-Across
113 "Little Women" author
114 Ruined
115 Dead Sea Scrolls sect
116 Example of 108- and 47-Across
117 "See ya!"

DOWN

1 Desert crossed by the Silk Road
2 Gulf state
3 Celebration
4 Writer/critic James and family
5 Animal with luxurious fur
6 Org. with a "3-1-1" rule
7 Twenty-one words
8 Give ___ all
9 Damage
10 Blight victim
11 Film again
12 Money in the bank, e.g.
13 This and that
14 Razor brand
15 Example of 39- and 34-Down
16 Lang. heard in Haifa
17 Before, to a bard
18 ___ Moines
20 Bugs about the trash
23 Toil
28 Competitor of Petro-Canada
30 Scrub, as a mission
31 Squealer
32 They may be high in a fallout zone
34 93-Across and 15-Down
35 When repeated, a Polynesian getaway
36 What trees do in fierce storms
37 Is on the brink
38 Passed quickly
39 31-Across and 15-Down
41 Len of stage and screen
42 They're often pulled at night
43 13½" gold-plated figure
45 Hall of fame
46 A mere stone's throw from
47 Upscale London retailer
48 Fatty acid compound
55 One of a pair of best friends in Greek legend
56 Heights of achievement
57 Witherspoon of "Legally Blonde"
58 Fussed over, as a grandchild
60 Like some diplomats
61 AOL alternative
63 Skeptical response
65 Dudes
66 Puts forward
68 Holt of NBC News
70 Part in an animated film
72 "Well, look what I did!"
75 Lightly bite
76 Word of wonder
77 "Really!"
79 Ear: Prefix
80 Den denizen
84 ___ the Explorer
85 Guide to studying the night sky
86 What "Mc-" means in a name
88 Richard Strauss opera
90 Sired, biblically

by Charles M. Deber

93 Is disposed
94 Need for a professional designer
95 ___ toad
96 Example of 47- and of 83-Across
98 Excited cry in a casino
99 Highest score in baccarat
100 Privy to
102 ___ Barksdale, drug dealer on "The Wire"
103 Jay who preceded Jimmy
104 Big bunch
105 Juice drink
106 Fleur-de-___
107 ___ Palmas, Spain
109 90° bend
110 Obama health law, for short
111 Old, clumsy ship

SILENT TREATMENT

ACROSS

1 Chimp relatives
7 Free spot, for short
10 Mouth pieces
14 Pac-12 team
18 Asian plumlike fruit
19 Rihanna's 2016 ___ World Tour
21 Puma alternative
22 QB Tony
23 Reversals of reversals in sentences?
25 Ribald
26 Making the honor roll, e.g.
27 Org. involved in an annual open house
28 Directional suffix
29 Shell containers
31 Railroad name starting in 1832
32 Golf ball's path
33 Result of waves hitting rocks
35 "Don't worry about me!"
37 With 73-Across, a symbol of Massachusetts
38 Laundry unit
40 Small egg
41 Donates shelter to some beavers?
44 Bedding in a horse's stall
46 Name that's Hebrew for "my God"
47 Relative of "POW!"
48 Crop-damaging rodent
49 "Don't give up!"
51 New pony
53 One following the dotted lines?
57 Soup, black bread and, for the wealthy, meat?
62 Neutrogena dandruff shampoo
66 John or James
67 "What nerve!"
68 ___ Raton, Fla.
69 Gear for a hike
70 Part of E=mc²
73 See 37-Across
74 Not quite leaders of the pack
75 Social Security fig.
76 Based on theoretical deduction
78 Like concrete that's shaped in advance
80 Road sign silhouette
81 Kings and queens bringing their steeds to a halt?
84 Nelson who wrote "The Man With the Golden Arm"
86 James who wrote "A Death in the Family"
87 Freddy once hailed as "the next Pelé"
88 Husband to Emilia in "Othello"
90 Golfer Ernie
92 Tiny bit
94 Popeye creator E. C. ___
98 "Excuse me, but my partner's and my kids go first!"
102 "___, Escher, Bach" (Pulitzer-winning book)
104 Tackle box item
105 When repeated, "All right, that's enough!"
106 Up (for), paradoxically
107 Better than normal
110 Gchat notes, e.g.
111 Medical professional on TV
113 Part of a classic diner sign
115 "Listen up, Luis!"
116 WSJ competitor
117 Fantasy game role
118 Icelandic saga
119 Feast consisting entirely of Hawaiian foodstuffs?
122 Flight destination?
123 "Enough!"
124 Word with pink or cow
125 Illinois college town
126 James of R&B
127 Ring ___
128 Sot's woe
129 Like elves' ears

DOWN

1 Cronies
2 Plant disease whose two words differ by only one letter
3 Amphibious auto
4 Essence of an idea
5 Powerful winds
6 Lead-in to phonic
7 Greek god depicted on the cover of "The Wind in the Willows"
8 Onetime rap moniker
9 Clothe
10 Tomb raider ___ Croft
11 "The Terrible" czar
12 When repeated, plea to a stage magician
13 Powers to decide
14 Goad
15 "Ugh, that hits close to home!"
16 "Shoot over your response"
17 Very serious
20 Part of las Filipinas
24 Scoundrel
30 Popular rapper with a feline-sounding name
34 Bacteria-battling drug
36 Intoxicating Polynesian drink
39 Cloud's purpose
42 Hurt
43 #1 Presley hit
45 Court orders
47 "Ugh!"
50 Big fashion inits.
52 Follows, as advice
54 One might represent a representative
55 Sleazeball
56 ___ culpa
57 Frothing at the mouth
58 Lyric poem
59 Who has ever won a debate over the internet?
60 Start of the Marines' motto
61 Honoring grandly
63 Did so-so at school
64 Digital currency
65 Hangs in there
71 Singer India.___
72 One of 56 in 1776
74 Some Mardi Gras wear
76 S. Amer. land
77 Inlets
79 Genetic material
82 "Oh, boohoo!"

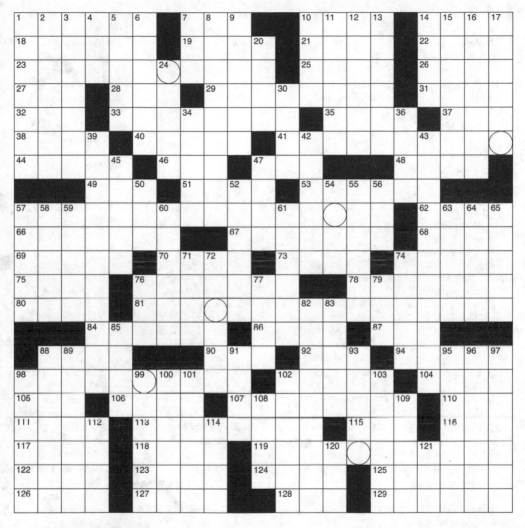

by Sam Trabucco

83 Gettysburg general
85 Head of an estate
88 "Hmm . . . it's escaping me"
89 "If all else fails . . ."
91 Exam for future attys.
93 Warehouse
95 Native of Conakry

96 Little raider
97 Athlete's time off
98 Single shot awarded for being fouled while scoring, in basketball lingo
99 Straight
100 Had because of

101 Start of a Spanish count
102 Clear one's head?
103 Confines due to injury
108 Qualifying words
109 Facsimile, for short
112 It follows epsilon
114 Fuzzes

120 Photo ___
121 Stat for Lou Gehrig or Manny Ramirez

42 CROPPED

ACROSS

1 Weary
6 Flaky stuff
10 Deal watcher, informally
14 Like most grapes
19 ___ bear
20 "Because Freedom Can't Protect Itself" sloganeer, briefly
21 Finished
22 British politician Farage
23 Rummage (through)
24 Rummage (through)
25 Southern bread
26 Crept furtively
27 Tree-damaging pest accidentally introduced to the U.S. in 1996
31 Ache
32 One likely to have lots of perks
33 Neither good nor bad
34 "Casablanca" woman
35 "Olé! Olé! Olé!," for one
37 Eddie with the #1 country hit "Every Which Way but Loose"
40 The "doll" in Ibsen's "A Doll's House"
44 Southwest tourist destination
48 Having a variegated, changing pattern
50 Lost
51 Tech company founder Michael
53 Tie up
54 Matey's cry
55 Sword go-with
57 Residence of the Japanese imperial family for more than 1,000 years
59 Baseball no-nos
60 Life is a bad one
61 Request
63 Outdoor game for the very young
67 Yearbook sect.
68 Constitution holder
70 Some notebooks, in brief
73 Second-largest city in Vermont
74 Give
75 Give a damn
76 Rehab procedure
80 Singer Rimes
81 High
83 Ham-handed
84 Swiss river to the Rhine
87 Skirt option
89 Hold forth
90 MCAT subject
93 "Seinfeld" character
95 Don
96 Salve
98 Dieter's salad order request
99 Church area
101 Pair on a slope
103 Kitty
104 Gatekeeping org.?
107 Canful in a cupboard . . . or a hint to parts of six answers in this puzzle
112 ___ friends
114 Three-time N.H.L. All-Star Kovalchuk
115 Rice-based drink
116 Actor Quinn
117 Big name in organized crime, once
118 Come together
119 "You said it!"
120 Alarm
121 Like those who really have guts?
122 Latin 101 verb
123 Titian's "Venus of Urbino," e.g.
124 Cheerleaders' practice

DOWN

1 Sunscreen option
2 Good quality in a model
3 Puckish
4 Lion in "The Lion King"
5 Spy's attire, stereotypically
6 Like Robinson Crusoe
7 Desktop sight
8 Hard shoes to run in
9 Often-doubled cry at a play
10 "Sure thing!," jocularly
11 Shakespeare's stream
12 Former Haitian president Préval
13 Loan shark, for one
14 Starts
15 The Wildcats of the Big East Conference
16 Feverish fit
17 Base ___
18 Animal on Michigan's flag
28 Be apprised (of)
29 Where Sanyo and Panasonic are headquartered
30 Slugs
35 Beat handily
36 Many a character on "The Big Bang Theory"
38 Science class, informally
39 Personal commitment?
41 Birthstone after sapphire
42 Game played on a map
43 Does something
44 Observes Ramadan
45 Else
46 Manual's audience
47 Cunning sort
49 Lift things?
52 Minnesota's state bird
56 Tennis great Tommy
58 Bricklaying or pipefitting
62 GPS display: Abbr.
63 ___ acid (wine component)
64 Brenda's twin on "Beverly Hills 90210"
65 German digit
66 Video game count
68 Adjoining
69 Fertile soil
70 ___ Games
71 Island south of the Cyclades
72 Commemorative meal with wine
75 Round up
76 Frisbee, e.g.
77 Singer heard in the first "Lord of the Rings" movie
78 Work day by day, say
79 Bush and Gore, in 2000
80 Do House work
82 Relaxed
84 Formerly

by Jacob Stulberg

85 Vodka or gin: Abbr.
86 Codswallop
88 Petroleum byproduct used to make synthetic rubber
91 Violet shade
92 Join together
94 Like some points
97 Leaf producer
100 Texas A&M athlete
102 Former SeaWorld performer
104 ___ wave
105 Traffic headache
106 Dancer de Mille
107 November imperative
108 They can be brown or blonde
109 Ta-tas
110 Gave one's blessing to
111 "Well done!"
112 Give it ___
113 Surround, as fans might an idol

THE LONG AND WINDING ROAD

Note: When this puzzle is done, read the letters along the shaded path to get another example of the theme.

ACROSS

1 Major tenant of Rockefeller Center
6 "Young Frankenstein" role
10 Theater drop
15 Nuke
18 CBS's "Kate & ___"
19 Turner of "Peyton Place"
20 Bad thing to bring one's family
21 Wealthy: Sp.
22 "With the Beatles" song written by Smokey Robinson
26 In all seriousness
27 Gen ___
28 Emulated the tortoise and hare
29 One of seven in the Book of Revelation
31 Ladies' men, in older usage
33 Gulf state: Abbr.
36 Monastery head's jurisdiction
39 Domesticate
43 Intimate
47 Zombie or flaming volcano
48 "Yuck!"
51 Part of U.N.L.V.
52 "Let's go!," in Baja
53 Meditation leader
54 Altar exchange
56 Bus. need that most lemonade stands don't have
57 Some Japanese watches
58 Big ___ (some sandwiches)
59 Edgar in "King Lear," e.g.
60 It might help you get to Carnegie Hall, for short

61 Riga resident
62 Garden party?
63 Record shop stock
64 Talk, talk, talk
65 "The Time Machine" race
67 Something you might lose a little sleep over?: Abbr.
68 Delany or Carvey
69 Whopper
70 Last Hebrew letter
71 Capital bombed in 1972
74 Grade school subj.
75 Audio problem
78 Harrison's successor
79 African antelope
80 Message from the Red Cross, maybe
81 Cinematic composer André
84 Triumphant cry
85 Its state quarter has a lighthouse
86 Luxuriant
87 Charge, in a way
88 Spanish letter between ka and eme
89 Piece org.?
90 Silverwork city in southern Mexico
91 "Strangers and Brothers" novelist
92 Move quickly
94 1943 penny material
95 Merchandise: Abbr.
96 Structure used in extreme sports
102 "Antennae"
106 Raised a ruckus
108 1977 Warhol subject
111 Filmmaker Guy

116 "Revolver" song that Paul McCartney described as "an ode to pot"
119 They go in locks
120 Ancient
121 Footwear for a run
122 Like a good scout
123 Fifth qtrs.
124 Résumé listing
125 It used to be made of lead
126 Les ___-Unis

DOWN

1 One side of a vote
2 Link studied at Ancestry.com
3 Coterie
4 Part of an old-fashioned swing
5 Zigs or zags
6 Napoleon's partner on "The Man From U.N.C.L.E."
7 "Wonder Woman" star ___ Gadot
8 Shade of black
9 Fury
10 Onetime JFK sight
11 1968 movie based on "Flowers for Algernon"
12 Indy 500 winner Bobby
13 "___ roll!"
14 Blue
15 Penny, mostly
16 Zenith
17 "The Gold-Bug" author
21 Certain tribute
23 Most watchful
24 Living thing
25 "___ & the Women" (2000 Altman film)

30 "Hey Jude" song that mentions every day of the week but Saturday
32 "Yikes!"
33 Solvers' shouts
34 What TSA Pre✓ helps people avoid
35 "A Hard Day's Night" song that Lennon called McCartney's "first 'Yesterday'"
37 Strongly worded attack
38 Panther or puma
40 "With the Beatles" song playing in the E.R. when Lennon died
41 Tiki bar cocktail
42 Houdini feat
44 George of "Star Trek"
45 Bunches
46 Try out
48 "Sgt. Pepper's Lonely Hearts Club Band" song whose title is followed by "where the rain gets in"
49 Twin Cities suburb
50 Sacrosanct
55 Pommes frites seasoning
59 Slowly fade away
65 Like names on trophies, often
66 "I can't hear you!"
68 Extra-special
71 End of a shift
72 Disc jockey Freed
73 Hair-razing name?
75 Bigger than big
76 Beans, e.g.
77 ___ teeth

by Patrick Blindauer

80 The highest form of flattery?
82 Tommy Hilfiger alternative
83 Old movie theater lead-ins
90 Kitchen shortening
93 "___ a wrap"
97 Latin 101 word
98 Theater sections
99 Lose it
100 ___ dish
101 Pastoral poem
103 Came (from)
104 Pacific ___
105 Bob or weave
106 Lacquer, e.g.
107 Contents of some envelopes: Abbr.
109 Officially go (for)
110 Black as night
112 Circulatory block
113 Slangy greeting
114 "___ first you don't succeed . . ."
115 Congers and morays
116 Melted mess
117 Olive ___
118 Cape Horn, for one

ACROSS

1 Relieves
9 "You ___!"
15 Noted brand once owned by a utopian colony in Iowa
20 Theodore, for one
21 Display no talent for
22 Like boots
23 Deadliness
24 Make lots of people stop in their tracks?
26 Heartbeat
27 Bite stopper
29 When Juno Beach was attacked
30 Herb in absinthe
31 Be watchfully ever-present
34 Flub
36 Obtain through trickery
37 Roughly equal
39 "Austin Powers: The Spy Who Shagged Me," e.g.
40 Demanding
41 One of the singing Carpenters
42 Unnecessary extras that don't cost much?
44 One may be circular
47 Neighbor of Turkey
48 Did some farm work
49 Sharp
50 Lugosi of film fame
51 Cry of Pontius Pilate
53 Company behind the Falcon 9 launch vehicle
56 Grad student headaches
57 Ancient Greek vessel

59 Diamond stat
60 Mountain in the logo of Yerevan State University
61 Sweetheart, in slang
63 Brother who's a criminal?
67 Subject of the photo "Guerrillero Heroico"
68 Trembling, say
70 Friend of Huck
71 Hectic scramble
73 Cirrus clouds, e.g.
74 King of the Titans, in Greek legend
77 Movie starring Michael J. Fox as a lycanthrope
80 French press alternative
81 Look ecstatic
82 Neighbors
84 How Bilbo Baggins traveled
85 Currency with notes in denominations of 1,000, 5,000 and 10,000
86 Annoy actors Keaton and Crabbe?
89 Clog clearer
90 On again
91 Green
92 Scotland's ___ Islands
93 Doomed
96 Soprano Fleming
97 Cold treat eaten with a spoon
98 Strapped, say
99 ___ relative
100 Boris Pasternak heroine
102 Org. that might come pounding at the door
105 Safety worry?

108 Home to some flying monkeys
111 Heals
112 "Am I the only one thinking this . . . ?"
113 Hollywood resident, e.g.
114 Said "C-O-L-O-U-R," e.g.
115 Kind of acting
116 Made fun of mercilessly

DOWN

1 Doesn't just sit there
2 Flat, e.g.
3 With 44-Down, half-dozen real estate agents?
4 Longtime news inits.
5 "Breaking Bad" channel
6 One escorting
7 Log
8 Terrier named after a Scottish island
9 Real pal, for short
10 Bit of jewelry with a pendant
11 Attached with a knot at the end
12 Not nebulous
13 Nebulous
14 Downed
15 Climbs
16 ___ sauce (macaroni and cheese ingredient)
17 Word after sing or string
18 Post on a banister
19 Perplex
25 Off the beaten path
28 Plain dwelling?
32 Part of a concert that many people impatiently sit through

33 Moving vehicle
35 Some infrastructure
36 Name for a cat
37 Depression Era refugee
38 Stash hunter
39 Hebrew name that means "his peace"
40 Annotation on Santa's list
42 About which you might ask "One lump or two?"
43 Theme in "To Kill a Mockingbird"
44 See 3-Down
45 Name on the Saudi flag
46 Refuse
48 Not engaged
50 It has two cups
52 LP players
54 Teaser
55 ___-Bakr (father-in-law of Muhammad)
56 Like Mork
58 Put in a crypt
60 Aconcagua's range
61 Like most Judd Apatow comedies
62 In flames
64 One may be polyatomic
65 Ripe
66 "Golden Boy" playwright
69 Pokémon Go, for one
72 Posh
74 Yogurtlike beverage
75 Whole lot
76 "Gymnopédies" composer
78 Africa's ___ Chad
79 James who wrote the best seller "A Million Little Pieces"

by Will Nediger

81 City next to Gulfport
83 Cut at a slant
86 Selfish demand
87 Discover
88 City on the Italian Riviera
89 Sign of a hit
90 What jets may do midair
92 Word often said to lack a rhyme
93 Contents of drives
94 Do better than
95 Mother-of-pearl
96 Size again
97 Candid
99 Nasdaq alternative
101 "C'est la vie!"
103 Paleontologist's find
104 Polo brand
106 Cook who's entrepreneurial
107 ___ talks
109 It might get your feet wet
110 Stadium cry

45

ACROSS

1 Five Norwegian kings
6 Nighty-night wear
9 Bird bills
13 Fancy-schmancy
17 Bottoms
19 O.K., in Okinawa
20 First name in courtroom fiction
21 Bee-fitting?
23 Overcome an embarrassment
25 Carolina ___
26 Kind of question
27 Med. school subject
28 Traditional Chinese forces
30 Male duck
31 Author Anaïs
32 ROFL alternative
33 Palm piece
34 Polish rolls
35 Get off at Grand Central, say
37 Like most things in "Ripley's Believe It or Not!"
38 Bring home the bacon
39 Nary ___
40 Make brighter, as a fading tattoo
41 Mufflers and such
45 "Anyhoo," e.g.
47 Architect Gehry
48 "Thanks ___ God!"
49 One challenged by a sentry
50 Couturier Cassini
51 U.S. rebellion leader of 1841–42
52 Alternative to wind
54 Rhett Butler's final two words
56 Like some thinking

58 "My ___" (1979 hit by the Knack)
60 Nail polish brand
61 Places to get looped
64 As a joke
67 Dried (off)
68 "Hidden Figures" actor
72 One of 16 works by Brahms
73 Roasted: Sp.
74 Slept with, biblically
76 Kvetch
77 "___ Just Seen a Face" (Beatles tune)
78 DVD button
79 ___ an independent (eschewed the party label)
81 Geneva and Beirut
82 "Miss Julie" opera composer, 1965
85 19th-century French landscapist
86 Weisshorn and others
87 "Beowulf" and others
88 Bottle for oil or vinegar
89 Excuse for not turning in homework
92 Nursery rhyme destination
95 Ersatz
96 Quarrel (with)
97 Singer DiFranco
98 Actor Gillen of "Game of Thrones"
99 What you should do "if symptoms persist"
101 Artist who designed costumes for "Ben-Hur"
102 Twosomes

103 12.01, for carbon: Abbr.
104 Ignorant
106 Hang
107 Fifth-century pope known as "the Great"
108 Son of, in Arabic names
109 Company lover?
110 Captain von Trapp's betrothed
111 Met soprano Berger
112 Cpl., e.g.
113 Captain Nemo's creator

DOWN

1 Ashore
2 Actress Kazan of "My Big Fat Greek Wedding"
3 Reasons to say yes
4 Word-before Cong or Minh
5 Mister, in New Delhi
6 45 player
7 Resident of Tatooine in "Star Wars"
8 It's Irish for "We Ourselves"
9 Orange avenue in Monopoly
10 Picking up a quart of milk, say
11 Recipe direction
12 Hong Kong's Hang ___ Index
13 Nice thing to hit
14 Having an effect
15 Rope fiber
16 It might absorb a blow
18 Frustrate

22 Discouraging words
24 Gorilla watcher Fossey
29 "It's on me!" . . . or a hint to this puzzle's circled letters
32 Shipping route
34 Scott of "Joanie Loves Chachi"
36 Partially edited version of a movie
37 Erodes
38 Bedazzles
40 Elementary school trio, briefly
41 Actor Reeves
42 "___ first . . ."
43 Gold rush city of 1899
44 Boomers' offspring
45 Plant
46 Bush or Clinton, collegiately
47 Oral tradition
48 Fly-fisher's line joiner
51 French nobleman
53 Shield border
54 Whizzes
55 Bunny chasers?
57 1970s TV cool dude, with "the"
59 Rushed
62 "Life According ___" (Emmy-winning documentary)
63 Pai ___ (Chinese gambling game)
64 "Victory!"
65 Place to pray
66 Ran off
69 Awful idea
70 No longer fast?
71 Hosp. staffers
75 D.C. athlete
78 Whizzes

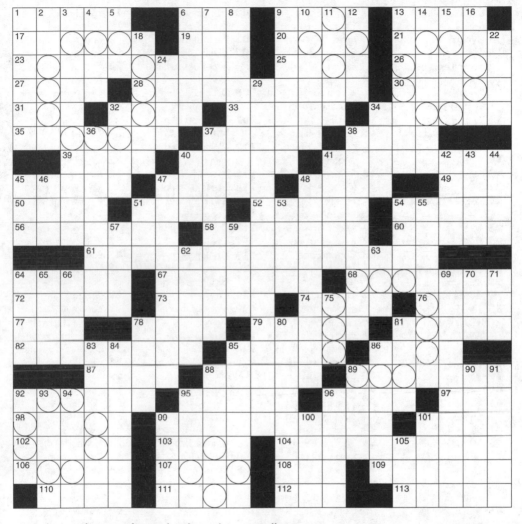

by Andrea Carla Michaels and Pete Muller

ACROSS

1 Top
5 Wears
10 Pioneer in computer chess
13 Channel setting on many airport TVs
16 Gets cheeky with?
18 Act on a sudden itch to be hitched
19 Fit for service
20 It may be seeded
21 Even (with)
22 Roger who battled 13-Across
23 Utter
25 Cut, Paste and Print
27 Degree in math?
28 Mountain ___
29 Copse makeup
30 Title character in a 1943 French novella [6]
35 Zap
37 Pedagogic org.
39 Vote for
40 Pacific capital
41 N.F.L.'s Jaguars, on scoreboards
42 Sugar suffix
43 1990 Literature Nobelist Octavio ___
44 Toner cartridge contents
46 Is from ancient Rome?
47 The Big Pineapple [4]
50 Rhyme scheme ending a villanelle
52 French word between two surnames
53 Intl. commerce grp.
54 Banded gemstones
55 Bert who sang "If I Only Had the Nerve"
57 Poor People's Campaign organizer, for short
59 Frequent Bosch setting
60 Capital accumulation
61 Dance craze of the 2010s
63 "___ and animals are free" (party slogan in "1984")
65 "___ Mine" (George Harrison book)
66 Like some lawyers' work [4]
67 Musical talent
68 Cartographer
71 Try to sink one's teeth into
72 Cheap cooking implement
76 Like, forever
77 Steely Dan's best-selling album
78 Naval noncoms
80 E'erlasting
81 ___ one-eighty
82 Bleeping government org.?
84 Trophy figure
86 "Why are you looking at me?" [4]
88 Where It. is
89 Inverse trig function
91 Agcy. that oversaw plants
92 Ones "from Mars"
93 Inits. in some parlors
94 American-born Jordanian queen
95 "Shoo!"
98 Org. behind the Human Genome Project
99 Lewis ___, 1848 Democratic candidate for president
100 11th-century campaign [4]
103 Put in stitches
105 Like the Salt Lake Bees baseball team
106 Decoration for an R.A.F. pilot
107 "Will you let me have a taste?"
112 Clothing associated with Hillary Clinton
115 "Same here"
116 Like many pools and highways
117 Cooperation
118 They begin trading, for short
119 Frankincense, e.g.
120 Singer of a famous bath time song
121 Crooked
122 Barack Obama's mother
123 Sturm und ___
124 Garner

DOWN

1 Like some radios
2 "Born Sinner" rapper J. ___
3 17,000+-foot peak near the Equator [4]
4 Guarantee
5 Make airtight, in a way [4]
6 Others of ancient Rome?
7 Band member's time to shine
8 In public
9 Monster's moniker
10 Healthy [4]
11 "Don't ___ hero!"
12 Nightshade family member [5]
13 Prized possession [5]
14 Home of the Gallatin Sch. of Individualized Study
15 Take home
17 Unit around one foot?
19 Spending
23 Mich. Neighbor
24 Mater ___
26 One doing routine office work, informally [5]
31 "Wasn't that fantastic?!"
32 Long
33 Move to protect the king, say
34 Praises highly
35 At all, in dialect
36 Me.-to-Fla. route
38 Color of el mar
45 Butt
48 Flowers native to damp woods
49 "Please, I'll handle it"
50 Totally LOL-worthy
51 Dave of jazz [4]
56 Supermodel Lima
58 Certain fire sign
59 Like the Greek god Pan
62 Flip out
63 One leading the exercises, for short? [4]
64 Singer Bonnie
66 Sandwich inits.
68 Having as ingredients
69 Guinea pig relative
70 Fruity spirit [6]
73 Vain, temperamental sort [7]
74 Long range
75 Bright lights
77 Band member's main squeeze? [4]
79 ___ song
82 1940 Disney release [3]
83 Swamp swimmer

by Caleb Madison

85 Woman who took a "roll in ze hay" in "Young Frankenstein"
87 Pulling off bank jobs [5]
90 Teddy Roosevelt targets
96 Much-swiped item
97 Short trailer
99 Borgia who was an illegitimate son of Pope Alexander VI
101 Took a breather
102 Message from the marooned
104 Noah of "ER"
108 Grp. with a mission
109 "Sure, sign me up!"
110 Predecessor of Rabin
111 What's lost in "Paradise Lost"
112 Rabbit's foot
113 It's inspired
114 Original "Veronica Mars" channel

ACROSS

1 Little bit
4 Chickenhearted
9 Spur-of-the-moment
13 "Word just got out . . ."
19 Funny Gasteyer
20 Offer a thought
21 Shakers' movement?
22 Loren of "Marriage Italian-Style"
23 Top limit, for short
24 Flaunt a loose dress at a soiree?
27 Text changes
29 Mideast royal name
30 Fair-hiring letters
31 Vogue rival
32 Overstuff
33 Title of a fashion industry seamstress's tell-all?
38 With 53-Across, goethite, e.g.
39 N.F.C. North rivals of the Bears
40 Support under a tank?
41 "Enrol," for "enroll": Abbr.
42 Ones who fix toys?
43 Grub
44 Flapper wrapper
45 Ideal
49 Chipper greeting
51 Cellphone chip holder
53 See 38-Across
54 Personal guide
56 What some wrap dresses are?
60 D.C. summer setting
61 ___ pants
62 Plot at home, maybe
63 Fantasy writer Michael
64 "___ who?"
65 Exercise with keys
66 Way off base?
67 Unwanted pressure
69 Bit of a grind
71 Get the gold
72 Author Michael ___ Dyson
74 "Frozen" snow queen
75 Mars vehicle
76 Scatter
77 Like a model's hairstyle?
81 Calendario opener
82 Argentine article
83 Northern Indiana county or its seat
84 Kind of pressure
85 Souls
88 French possessive
89 Bundle
92 Shiner
95 Boating aid
96 Civil War inits.
97 Ding maker
98 Kind of street
99 Takes fashion photos using an unorthodox camera angle?
104 More limited
105 "Keep it ___"
106 Bylaw, briefly
107 Plane-related
108 N.B.A. notables Korver and Lowry
109 Shorten some couture dresses?
115 Bach's Partita No. 6 ___ Minor
116 Resistant (to)
117 Swift ending for a bad stage performance
118 Chill-inducing, say
119 Writer/critic Hentoff
120 Got the impression
121 Uneasy
122 Ground breaker
123 Chicago rumblers

DOWN

1 Last Scottish king to die in battle
2 How you might do something dumb
3 Preferred means of arriving at a fashion show?
4 Some rescues
5 Subj. for CNBC
6 Putin's peace
7 Stain that's hard to remove
8 Keeps from proceeding
9 Loses
10 Order member
11 Klingons, e.g.
12 Tower with many eaves
13 Suffix with 105-Across
14 Christmas threesome
15 Banned supplement
16 Not worth ___ of beans
17 Go through
18 Historical trivia
25 Vandals
26 ___ party
28 Decagonal
33 A butter alternative
34 Actress Vardalos
35 Little Boy, e.g., informally
36 Got out of
37 Stud site
44 Dust jacket part, usually
45 Revenue source for a magazine
46 Inspects a fashion designer's offerings?
47 One who says "I'd like to have . . ."
48 AOL alternative
50 Food prep class at school
51 Very short climb
52 Chilling, so to speak
54 Ruins as a dog might
55 Food in the field
56 Cantina treats
57 Top of the world
58 Quattro minus uno
59 Edict
67 "Take it!"
68 Nutmeg State collegian
70 Cry of exasperation
73 Warlords, e.g.
78 Medium-to-poor
79 Ideal
80 Drunk's problem
84 Cop's target
86 Cans
87 One may be tipped
89 Goes through
90 Creator of an ancient pyramid scheme?

by Isaac Mizrahi and David J. Kahn

91 Ring around the collar
93 Place for cannons
94 Winter apples
96 Holiday scene
97 You, once
99 Some Latinas: Abbr.
100 Pitch
101 Like some floors
102 Order member
103 Long-winded
108 Leg bender
110 Advantage
111 ___ Xing
112 Put in, as hours
113 Glass on public radio
114 Suffix with fact

48 ANCHORS AWAY!

ACROSS

1 "Cease!," on the seas
6 "What nonsense!"
9 Walk on the edge?
13 Luminary
17 Clubs with strobes
19 Hieroglyphic bird
21 ___ O's (chocolaty cereal brand)
22 Asian territory in the game Risk
23 Roll out
24 Sailing vessels that Cap'n Crunch might commandeer?
27 Cuzco builders
29 Tetris piece
30 Testing times
31 Heavily armored vessels getting married?
35 Smelter input
36 Whiskey distiller's supply
37 "The plot thickens!"
38 Candy in collectible containers
39 Mideast monarchy
43 Numbers on right-hand pages
45 Resells ruthlessly
47 Speaker on a car's dash
48 Polished
49 Fruit mentioned in the "Odyssey"
51 Equal
52 Actor Stephen
53 Split, e.g.
54 Kids' game in which small vessels attack each other?
59 Rio maker
60 Flood survivor
61 ___ Gold, chief of staff on "The Good Wife"
62 Often-quoted chairman
63 A large amount
66 Fishing vessel that can pull only half a net behind it?
70 Bruce of "The Hateful Eight"
71 Messenger ___
72 Rare craps roll
73 Incapacitate, in a way
74 Growth ring?
76 Recreational vessel that's never left the harbor?
84 1997 action film set on a plane
85 X amount
86 Isaac Newton, e.g.
87 Brings up
89 Bad at one's job
90 P, to Pythagoras
91 Revolver, in Roaring Twenties slang
94 Use scissors on
95 Governess at Thornfield
96 Berkeley institution, briefly
97 In place of
98 It brings people together
99 No. of interest to some recruiters
100 Luxury vessel with a pair of decks, both of which need swabbing?
106 Malodorous mammal
109 A&M athlete
110 Matisse who painted "La Danse"
111 Cargo vessel full of iPads?
114 Mown strips
117 "Game of Thrones," e.g.
118 Blackens
119 Staple of Shinto rituals
120 Second story?
121 Rub out
122 Not needing a cane, maybe
123 Deadhead's hits?
124 Foolish

DOWN

1 Kick in
2 Struggle
3 Ambitiously sought
4 Noninvasive medical procedures
5 Flashlight : U.S. :: ___ : U.K.
6 Consequential
7 Addis ___
8 Lookout point
9 "You Send Me" singer, 1957
10 Coffee holder
11 Works on as a cobbler might
12 Libertarian pundit Neal
13 Head honcho
14 It may end on a high note
15 D.C.'s National ___
16 Chicago-based fraternal order
18 Mezzanine access
20 They hang around the rain forest
25 Return from a trip to the Alps?
26 Pharma watchdog
28 Surveillance aid
31 Coat in a cote
32 Fire
33 Longtime retailer hurt by Amazon
34 Coverage provider?
40 Femme's title
41 Choice for an online gamer
42 Star of "Kinsey," 2004
44 Is downright terrible
46 Actress Téa
47 Beauty
48 Under goer?
50 Biathletes do it
52 Uncreative creation
53 Forming spiral patterns
55 Holy Week follower
56 ___ State (Alabama's nickname)
57 Measure of purity
58 Cheer with an accent
63 "___: A Love Story" (1998 George Burns book)
64 Like soubise sauce
65 Coat of arms element
67 Flock female
68 Vogue or Elle
69 Ehrich ___ a.k.a. Houdini
70 Chops up
75 Elephant ___ (pastry)
77 It may help remove a curse
78 Hold an assembly
79 Revival movement prefix
80 Not mainstream

by Patrick Berry

81 Bellyacher
82 Quits, informally
83 Nonsensical talk
88 Prep for a match
90 Dilapidated dwelling
91 Manhandles, with "up"
92 Like the Gemini flights
93 Way out
96 Wares at fairs
97 "Around the World in 80 Days" protagonist
101 Nonpermanent sculpture medium
102 Flower with rays
103 Vichyssoise vegetables
104 Single
105 Dialect of Arabic
106 Entry ticket
107 Iridescent stone
108 Women's Open org.
112 Go astray
113 Roulette bet
115 Cool, in the '40s
116 Roguish

ACROSS

1 Bit of a Bollywood soundtrack
5 Hawaiian giveaway
8 Home of van Gogh's "The Starry Night," informally
12 Walgreens competitor
19 Greek warrior of myth
20 Person from Calgary or Edmonton
22 Source of material for a baseball bat
23 Magic trick performed at 78-Down
25 Company accountant's responsibility
26 Concern for wheat farmers
27 Nickname for an Oxford university
29 Puzzle-loving group
30 Sugar found in beer
34 Mouselike rodents
36 Sometimes-stinky pair
39 Adds to
43 Agcy. that cares what airs
46 Mauna ___
47 Magic trick performed at 119-Across and 104-Down
49 Burden for Jack and Jill
50 Female org. since the 1850s
52 Lee of Marvel Comics
53 Pals around (with)
54 Coca-Cola brand
55 ___ duck (Chinese entree)
57 "Carmina Burana" composer Carl
59 Grant-making org.
60 Like most doors
61 Followed closely, as a set of rules
63 Zest source
65 Feudal vassal
67 Magic trick performed at 123- and 124-Across
71 Word repeated before "everywhere"
72 Online "Very funny!"
73 Basic gymnastics flips
76 Comic Aziz of "Master of None"
79 "Is that true about me?"
81 Movies with big budgets and no audience
83 At the proper moment
84 Simple percussion instrument
85 Greenish-blue hues
87 Musical based on Fellini's "8½"
89 Ready to take part
90 Escape maker
91 Magic trick performed at 55-Across
94 Blue, on some maps: Abbr.
95 Onetime White House nickname
96 Apt anagram of IS A CHARM
97 Eight-line poems
99 Hullabaloo
100 Four-string instrument
102 Kind of jar
105 Crisp fabric
109 Tequila source
113 "Whenever you want"
115 Magic trick performed at 15-, 16- and 17-Down
119 Skinny sort
120 Hydrogen has one
121 Architect Saarinen
122 Swiss and others
123 First name in jazz
124 Bad: Prefix
125 Prohibitionists

DOWN

1 Go gaga
2 Not quite closed
3 Bunch of friends
4 Truisms
5 ___-di-dah
6 QB Manning
7 Arabic for "son of"
8 Advertising icon who wears a single earring
9 Missouri River native
10 Hurt badly
11 Latin years
12 Output of N.W.A or DMX
13 "This ___ test"
14 Herbs related to mints
15 English lengths
16 Baseball's Hank
17 Physicist Bohr
18 Crème ___ crème
21 They can be inflated or shattered
24 Lesley of "60 Minutes"
28 Manipulative type
31 Lane in Metropolis
32 12:50
33 Schindler of "Schindler's List"
35 Officers below capts.
36 Relief carving
37 Shout of pain
38 Talkative birds
40 "Yuk!"
41 Relative of pop?
42 Place from which to withdraw deposits
43 Long tooth
44 Give as an example
45 Wearing, with "in"
48 Prefix with structure
49 Décor of many dens
51 Onetime honor for cable TV shows
54 Mozart title character
56 Part of P.E.I.
58 Some dental work
60 Titter
62 South American monkey
64 Old war zone, briefly
66 Tangled up
68 Ill-defined situation
69 Offspring
70 Front
74 Director of 1957's "12 Angry Men"
75 Looks like
76 Name on some boxes of film
77 Neophyte, informally
78 Provide part of a coverage policy for
80 ___-pedi
82 "Mirabile ___!" ("Wonderful to state!")
85 Reproves
86 Dweller in a virtual "City"
88 Great Lakes city
91 Greek X
92 J. Crew competitor

by Eric Berlin

93 New York archbishop Timothy
96 Furs from rabbits
98 Got a move on, with "it"
99 "I would ___ surprised"

101 Stand-up comic Williams
102 Like the Spanish nouns "gato" (cat) and "perro" (dog): Abbr.
103 Literary collection: Abbr.

104 Vaccine holder
106 Run away
107 Tumbled
108 Stuntman Knievel
110 The New World: Abbr.
111 Be inconsistent

112 Book of Mormon book
114 Fannie or Ginnie follower
116 Suffix with dull
117 Small dog
118 Entrances

ACROSS

1 Matisse, e.g., stylistically
6 H. H. Munro pseudonym
10 XXX
14 Back up on disk
18 Cons
19 Juicy
20 Seats by the orchestra pit, perhaps
21 Film excerpt
22 Re: ___ (suitor's subject line)
25 25, 27, 29, etc.
26 The first pope, to French speakers
27 Words before fat and lean, in a nursery rhyme
28 The Gabor sisters, e.g.
29 Re: ___ (stingy date's subject line)
34 Hairstyle rarely seen in the military
37 Apply to
38 Formally chooses
39 The crystal in some crystal balls
41 Carrier to Seoul, for short
42 The lowest of the low
44 Catering staple
45 Re: ___ (song lyricist's subject line)
49 Part of a locust tree
53 Place to say 9-Down
55 Help
56 Quenched
58 World leader who proclaimed "Women hold up half the sky"
59 Bathday cakes?
61 Kind of diagram
62 Dwellers on the Arabian Peninsula
65 Re: ___ (film director's subject line)
69 Re: ___ (sales agent's subject line . . . with an attachment)
72 Peanut butter choice
73 Municipal regs.
75 Prefix with liberal or conservative, but not moderate
76 Slippery sort
77 One is usually set by a chair
80 Purpose
81 Talk smack about
85 Baseball exec Bud
88 Re: ___ (duster's subject line)
91 Tony winner Hagen
92 $$$$, on Yelp
94 "Selma" director DuVernay
95 Greek gods' drink
97 "Down," at a diner
100 Pithy observations
103 Best-of-the-best
104 Re: ___ (prison librarian's subject line)
108 Hansen of a 2016 Broadway hit
109 Sidney who directed "12 Angry Men"
110 Actress Arquette
114 The Destroyer, in Hinduism
115 Re: ___ (celebrity physician's subject line)
119 Mark Zuckerberg when founding Facebook, e.g.
120 Eliminated by a ref's decision
121 Heavenly hunter
122 Monastery figure
123 European capital
124 Repair shop figs.
125 Stuff
126 Simple, as a question

DOWN

1 Online help
2 "Are you some kind of ___?"
3 Lone Star State sch.
4 Guest
5 Perfume compound
6 Inspector Clouseau's employer
7 "A Navel" artist, 1923
8 Wine-and-cassis drink
9 See 53-Across
10 Dalmatian, e.g.
11 Lilylike plant
12 Tot's "Lemme up on your shoulders!"
13 Old-fashioned gunfight locales
14 Like the people who invented golf
15 Astronaut after whom Buzz Lightyear was named
16 Couch potato
17 Some home printers
19 Title Seuss creature
23 "Stop!," to a cop
24 Lowly worker
30 Bugged
31 Short and detached, in music: Abbr.
32 Surefire
33 Expert on meters and feet
34 An official color of the Miami Dolphins
35 Roll up
36 Tirade
40 Den, often
42 Gucci or Givenchy, e.g.
43 The first "A" in Reddit's A.M.A.
46 Mesmerized
47 "You bet!," in Yucatán
48 Radiuses' neighbors
50 Marriott competitor
51 Third one's a harm?
52 Wine's aroma
54 China setting
57 Doofus
60 Novelist Seton
61 Mesa ___ National Park
63 Moaning Hogwarts ghost
64 Not even close
65 The Red Baron and others
66 Northern Montana tribe
67 Poker player's tic, perhaps
68 ___ Python
70 Depose
71 Cubbie or Card
74 From the top, to a musician
78 Sierras, e.g.
79 Want ad letters
80 Take the heat from?
82 Motorcade unit

by Ruth Bloomfield Margolin

83 Lee of Marvel Comics
84 Storied also-ran
86 Apple product discontinued in 2017
87 Tennis's Steffi
89 Through with
90 Like some training

93 Quarantine
96 "Is that even possible?"
97 Must pay
98 Main forces?
99 See the world
100 Tea times: Abbr.
101 Ransom note writer

102 Deseret News reader, e.g.
105 "Turn up the A/C!"
106 Must have
107 Paris's Musée d'___
111 Fleet on Fleet Street
112 With 117-Down, Mesabi Range output

113 Regarding
116 Thick coat on a cold day?
117 See 112-Down
118 Small inlet

ACROSS

1 Way around London, with "the"
5 E.R. V.I.P.s
8 Haunted house sound
13 Backflow preventer in a drain
18 Brief, as a visit
20 Sub
21 Oscar role for Vivien Leigh
22 Astonishing March Madness success, e.g.
24 He denied Christ three times
25 Device with a Retina display
26 The opposition
27 "Madame X" painter John Singer ___
29 23-Across, literally?
33 Cozy
35 Actor ___ Buchholz of "The Magnificent Seven"
36 Epitome of simplicity
37 Sour
39 Spicy fare?
41 "Where America's Day Begins"
43 Made an impression?
45 Iron: Fr.
46 Get ready to be dubbed
50 Machine-gun while flying low
52 Stereotypical oil tycoon
54 Remains unused
56 Sweets
58 Take both sides?
60 Word on a jar
61 Muskmelon variety
65 Bombs developed in the 1950s
66 Some airport figures, for short
67 Eminently draft-worthy
68 Pitch
71 Wiped out
72 Middling
73 Plenty sore, with "off"
74 Heat
76 Antiparticle first observed in 1929
78 Noon, in Nantes
79 Disaster film?
82 Singer Simone
83 Doomed
85 N.B.A. Hall-of-Famer Thomas
87 Ladies' shoe fastener
91 Staff openings?
92 By way of
94 Wine bar order
96 Elusive
97 ___ Lenoir, inventor of the internal-combustion engine
100 Location of Waimea Valley
101 What one will never be, in golf
102 Tended, with "for"
104 Comedian's stock in trade
106 118-Across, literally?
110 Africa's oldest republic
112 Result of some plotting
114 Bingo square
115 Old Russian ruler known as "Moneybag"
116 Detective in a lab
122 Frisbees and such
123 Like spoiled kids
124 Metallic element that's #21 on the periodic table
125 Like many concept cars
126 Gregor ___, protagonist in Kafka's "The Metamorphosis"
127 Snack food brand
128 Latin years

DOWN

1 Sign of nervousness
2 Sea urchin, at a sushi bar
3 Declare verboten
4 Break off a romance
5 Takeaway, of a sort
6 When a baby is expected
7 1904 world's fair city: Abbr.
8 Utilities, insurance, advertising, etc.
9 Loosely woven fabric with a rough texture
10 Try to find oneself?
11 ___ quotes
12 What a designated driver takes
13 Candy that fizzes in the mouth
14 New Hampshire
15 Gives stars to
16 Have no existence
17 Line usually on the left or right side
19 Tonto player of 2013
20 ___ characters (Chinese writing)
23 Murderer of Hamlet
28 Tuna, at a sushi bar
29 Doesn't keep up
30 Go up against
31 Facial feature of the Bond villain Ernst Blofeld
32 Jargon
34 Runs for a long pass, say
38 One component of a data plan
40 What the prefix "tera-" means
42 Contributed to the world
43 56-Down, literally?
44 "Don't you ___!"
47 Line judge?
48 Home to the National Border Patrol Museum
49 Teacher's unit
51 Funny Tina
53 Bubkes
55 60-Down, literally?
57 Stay
59 Setting eschewed by Hawaii: Abbr.
61 Capturer of some embarrassing gaffes
62 "The Iceman Cometh" playwright
63 Hospital sticker
64 Handling well
69 Winner of four 1990s–2000s golf majors
70 1953 Leslie Caron film
75 Other: Abbr.
77 Networking assets
80 "Ta-ta!"
81 Former world capital called "City of Lights"
84 Shift+8
86 "Everybody's a comedian"
88 Certain cheap car, informally
89 Mathematician Turing
90 Apt rhyme for "fire"

by Jeff Chen

93 Asked for a desk, say
95 That the sum of the numbers on a roulette wheel is 666, e.g.
98 Uganda's Amin
99 Marsh birds
102 Showing politesse
103 Lower
105 International package deliverer
107 Desi of Desilu Productions
108 Show a bias
109 Nintendo game princess
110 Lens caps?
111 Where fighter jets are found: Abbr.
113 "Gangnam Style" hitmaker
117 ___ pro nobis (pray for us)
118 Sch. in Fort Collins
119 The dark side
120 Symbol on the flag of Argentina or Uruguay
121 "Eww, stop!"

ACROSS

1 Mayhem
9 Bowfishing need
14 Happy event after a split?
19 Really happening
21 "Don Juan" girl
22 Prince of ___
23 *Law enforcer with the Coast Guard
25 "___ we lucky?"
26 Nat ___ Wild (cable channel)
27 More decisive
28 Place for stars
30 Buffet heater
33 *It passes on some bits of information
37 What the last letter of 107-Down stands for
38 Very puzzled
40 Record collection?
41 Constellation next to Corona Australis
42 ___ Jahan, leader who commissioned the Taj Mahal
43 ___ Jorge (part of the Azores)
44 Little sucker?
48 *Philosopher who wrote "Out of the crooked timber of humanity, no straight thing was ever made"
53 "Works for me"
54 Company known for combining expertise?
55 Presidents Taft, Ford, Clinton and both Bushes
59 Remain
60 What the Tower of London was for over 850 years
63 Adhere (to)
64 Utter, as a sound
65 One put in bed?
66 *Celebrities working for the U.N., perhaps
71 Disposition
72 International fusion restaurant chain
73 Hall-of-Fame Bruin
74 Tater
75 Common Korean surname
76 Low-quality bank offerings whose acronym suggests stealthiness
79 A little teary
83 Peevish
85 *Certain photo poster
88 Island nation that was once part of the Spanish East Indies
89 TV's NBA on ___
91 Tribe that gave its name to a state
92 Grp. of people puttering around?
93 Tow truck
96 You might pass one in a race
98 Onetime Yankee nickname
99 *Business bigwigs
103 Seep through
105 Like a bogey
106 Tie up quickly?
108 Cleveland athlete, familiarly
109 Educator Montessori
110 Sex appeal . . . or a hint to the answers to the six starred clues
117 Main force
118 Bring to a full amount
119 Bratty
120 Big instrument in electronic music, informally
121 Pillow covers
122 Washington newsmaker of 1980

DOWN

1 Start to call
2 U.N. workers' grp.
3 Handle in the entertainment industry
4 Solar system model
5 Home testing kit target
6 Early seventh-century year
7 Very long spans
8 In a mischievous manner
9 Actress Woodard
10 Big seller of outdoor gear
11 Ocasek of the Cars
12 Call with a charge?
13 Geniality
14 Crystal jewelry company with a swan in its logo
15 Some patterned floors
16 Fox Islands dweller
17 ___ Elise Goldsberry, 37-Across winner for "Hamilton"
18 Poly- follower
20 TV producer Michaels
24 Cheese often served with olives
29 Hebrew name meaning 62-Down
30 Unadventurous
31 Crooner with the autobiography "It Wasn't All Velvet"
32 U.S.S. Missouri's resting site
34 Person who's dreaded?
35 Publisher of the magazine America's 1st Freedom, for short
36 Prefix with system
39 ___ Bo (workout system)
42 Golf's Slammin' Sammy
45 It helps keep things straight
46 First sign of spring
47 Wacky tobacky, in part
49 Lingo
50 One-third of a B-52 cocktail
51 "___ iacta est" ("The die is cast")
52 First phase
53 Draft status?
56 Mastered, British-style
57 Conversation fillers
58 "___ me?"
61 Take responsibility for something
62 Safari sighting
65 Site of biblical destruction
66 Davis of "Thelma & Louise"
67 Heat center of old?
68 War on Poverty prez
69 Things displayed by mannequins
70 "The Lady of the Camellias" author, 1848
71 Dot on a screen
76 One suffering from numbness, maybe
77 Unit of petrol
78 Browning vessels
80 Do make-up work?
81 Plants with bell-shaped blooms
82 Pokémon card transaction
84 Penn State symbol

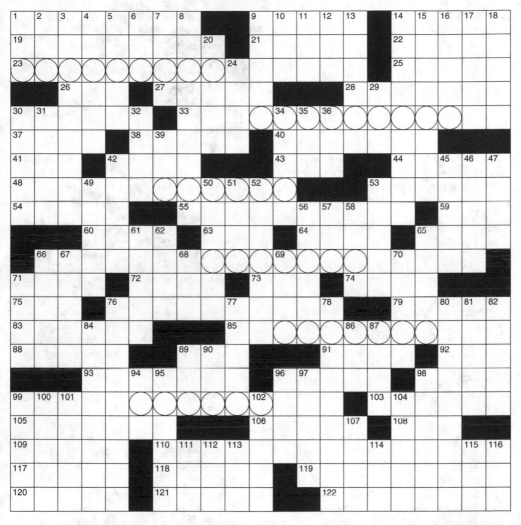

by Andrew Zhou

ACROSS

1 "Watch yourself out there"
7 Comic Sweeney
12 ___ All-Star Race (annual event since 1985)
18 Getaway for meditation
19 Rub oil on
21 Fruit dessert
22 Spin class activity?
24 City with one of the SUNY schools
25 That craft
26 TV host Gibbons
27 What Siri runs on
29 SC Johnson product with a lightning bolt in its logo
30 Wireless data and messaging company
32 Number of appearances in a grain holder?
38 ___ Tomé (African capital)
39 Stuck at a ski lodge, say
41 Wallops
42 Like long chances
44 River near the start of an alphabetical list
45 Primordial universe matter
47 What people sing when they don't know the words
49 Au courant, once
50 Storms that don't offend?
53 Actress Christina
55 God, to Hebrews
57 Staple of Hawaiian cuisine
58 Mammals with webbed feet
60 Business with a guestbook
62 French 101 verb
63 Appropriate rhyme for "cache"
65 Robust
66 RC, for one
67 Left college athletics, maybe
69 Lesley of CBS News
71 Nonsense
73 Second hand: Abbr.
74 Loads
76 2016 Disney hit
78 George who founded Industrial Light & Magic
79 "___-hoo!"
80 Position on a steamship
82 Schedule inits.
83 Europe's largest lake
84 Region of ancient Egypt
86 Makes a quick map of an Egyptian peninsula?
89 Very, in Veracruz
90 Sequel to a sequel to a sequel to a sequel
92 Action at a bris
93 Popular website that explains the news
94 Lille women: Abbr.
95 Not debut
97 Mint
99 War su ___ (boneless chicken dish)
100 Opening performers that are all mimes?
104 Orchestra tuner
107 Brand with a rabbit symbol
108 "___ little confused"
109 It has a lock, stock and barrel
111 Take in
113 Citroën competitor
116 Rod-and-reel event in old Vietnam?
121 North and South Korea, e.g.
122 Nurse's outfit
123 Indian appetizer
124 Prince Edward's former earldom
125 Belief
126 High as a kite

DOWN

1 Big party
2 Photorealist painter Richard
3 Order to a pool hustler to suck up some broth?
4 "So vast is ___, so narrow human wit": Alexander Pope
5 Do not
6 Run the show
7 Rapper with the music streaming service Tidal
8 Take out, as wine bottles
9 "Haha"
10 Due east on an old clock dial
11 Common female middle name
12 Smoking or ___
13 Black church inits.
14 Spot on a fern frond
15 TBS late-night show
16 Room with a slanted roof
17 All systems go
20 Cry to kick off the weekend
21 "Down goes Frazier!" sportscaster
23 Relating to the abdominal cavity
28 Surg. locales
31 Nonstandard verb from Popeye
33 Pastoral poet
34 "___ & Stitch"
35 Common opening bid in bridge
36 Argument
37 Fruit with greenish-yellow rinds
40 TV's "Tales From the ___"
42 Suddenly start, as in fright
43 Strands, as a base runner
44 German lament
46 Workplaces with a need for speed
48 Government group on offspring?
50 Felon, to a cop
51 Drink holders
52 Greyhound stop: Abbr.
54 Plotting (with)
56 Alicia of "Urban Legend," 1998
59 Ex-isle of exile
61 Denies
63 Play alone
64 Jerry Lewis, notably
66 "Oh, fudge"
68 Snare drum sound
70 Rebel in "Henry IV, Part 1"
72 Jai ___
75 Green-lit
77 Green
80 Tornado warning
81 Raised, as a flag
83 Laissez-faire
85 Pre-practice tests?

by Brendan Emmett Quigley

87 Lush's favorite radio station?
88 Drowse
91 Santa makes millions of them every Christmas
94 French month
96 Ingredient in an Aunt Agatha

98 Blinking light
99 Attacks
100 Cast about
101 Chemistry Nobelist Joliot-Curie
102 Understudy's study
103 Ticket
105 Ignorance, so they say

106 Nerve-racking
110 Think tank, e.g.: Abbr.
112 "Heavens!"
114 It may be pulled after a wrong turn
115 Old law
117 Do something
118 Heat

119 Heater
120 H.R. offering for employees

ACROSS

1 Naval engagements
8 Setting a world record, e.g.
12 "The Hallucinogenic Toreador" artist
16 Evidence in an arson investigation
19 "No point arguing with me!"
20 Some rounds
21 "The only beauty that never fades," per Audrey Hepburn
23 Fancy French shellfish dish
25 Beer parlor
26 "Then again . . . ," in a tweet
27 Collection of Hindu aphorisms
28 Palindromic bird
30 It's got you covered
31 Tennis's Novak Djokovic, by birth
32 Rex Tillerson's alma mater, for short
34 Proteins responsible for mad cow disease
35 Special ___
37 It's got you covered
39 Carved emblem
41 Keys for Keys?
44 German pronoun
46 South American plains
48 Tikkanen who won five Stanley Cups
49 All together, as a family
51 Classroom item
54 Schoolboy
55 More chichi
57 Get a bite?
58 Team finale?
60 Hot spot, both literally and figuratively
63 Roman philosopher who wrote "All cruelty springs from weakness"
67 Buenos ___
69 Central Park's SummerStage, e.g.
73 At the limit, with "out"
74 Save from disaster
76 The same as
78 "Homer and ___ Exchange Cross Words" (2008 episode of "The Simpsons")
79 Music genre for Weezer or the Shins
83 Catch like Spider-Man
85 Child's seat, maybe
86 Tech overseer
91 Reason to stop reading
93 Stranded cellular stuff
94 ___ plane
95 Addis Ababa's country: Abbr.
96 Claim deposits
97 "I rock!"
100 Backup group for Gladys Knight
102 Mahmoud Abbas's grp.
103 Quarter deck?
105 Tiny conductor of heat or electricity
108 Email best not replied to
112 Mulled wine ingredient
113 Extra periods at TD Garden
114 Mythical beast with goatlike features
115 Jazzy Fitzgerald
116 Premise of the film "Freaky Friday"
118 Some positives and negatives
121 Welcoming diners at midnight, say
122 Singer India.___
123 Adds water to
124 Director Anderson
125 Surveys
126 "Darn it!"
127 A good place to start

DOWN

1 Grain containers
2 Theatricalize
3 National ___ Day (last Friday in April)
4 Football formation
5 007, for one: Abbr.
6 ___ monkey
7 Cocky walk
8 Copyright concern
9 Symbol for a break
10 ___, amas, amat
11 Taquito wrap
12 What may grow with interest
13 Barley wine, e.g.
14 Burton of "Reading Rainbow"
15 "Totally understood"
16 Blessed
17 Frequent director of De Niro
18 Pigment in red blood cells
22 "Star Wars" droid
24 Letters on N.Y.C. trains
29 Together
33 Swiss folk hero with a crossbow
34 Dig for answers
36 After-dinner drink
38 Speed skater Karin who won eight Olympic medals
40 Scratch
41 Celestial object that emits radio waves
42 Drawn
43 Poisonous snakes
44 Anthropomorphic hedgehog of gamedom
45 "Don't mind ___!"
47 Elbow-benders
50 ___-pah-pah
51 Pair
52 "Excuse me"
53 Kidney-related
56 Dark time, in poesy
59 Wrap-up
61 1, 1, 2, 3, 5, 8, 13 . . . , e.g.: Abbr.
62 Less mendacious
64 Like the Dalai Lama
65 One of the Borgias
66 Evolves
68 The Philippines' ___ Sea
70 Author Rankin
71 1428 ___ (horror film address): Abbr.
72 The N.B.A.'s Curry, informally
75 Singer James
77 Baja bear
80 Vermin
81 Straight: Prefix
82 Signer of many a permission form
84 Congress, with "the"
86 ___ wolf
87 Not level
88 Old outdoor dance sights
89 Place to try patatas bravas
90 Actress Lena
92 "Relax!"

by Mark MacLachlan

95 Trusts and ___ (law school class)
98 Authority
99 Gertrude who swam the English Channel in 1926
101 Brand of note?
102 Teen driver's acquisition
104 The New Yorker piece
106 Western tribe
107 "Turn! Turn! Turn!" band, with "the"
109 One-named philosopher
110 Paul ___, Microsoft co-founder
111 En ___ (as a group)
112 Boast
113 Bullfight chorus
117 Homophone for the atomic number of oxygen
119 Altar constellation
120 St. Pierre, par exemple

ACROSS

1 Tennis world since 1968
8 St. Louis Arch, e.g.
15 Gasoline may make it go
20 Impersonated
21 Performing, perhaps
22 Change of locks?
23 "Try not to miss Bangor and Lewiston"?
25 "___ de Lune"
26 Player of TV's Det. Tutuola
27 Publication read by drs.
28 Kind of torch on "Survivor"
29 Private eye, slangily
30 Where Spartacus was from
32 Rite for a newborn Jewish boy
34 2:00 in New York vis-à-vis St. Louis?
36 Chopper topper
38 "___ 'em, boy!"
40 Fifth wheel
41 Part of a full house
43 Haunted house sound
45 Duds
47 Be sociable, say
50 Whistler from two Eastern states?
53 Financial institution whose parent company is Canadian
55 Name in a Salinger title
56 Cheers after a go-o-o-oal!
57 Quaint store descriptor
59 Just beat
60 Put away

61 ___-equipped
62 "I'm such a klutz!"
64 Sportscaster Al
68 "We shouldn't sell our Fort Wayne home"?
72 How a B.L.T. might come
73 Rice-A-___
74 Public image, briefly
75 Farm female
77 Reebok rival
78 Navy commando
80 It means "farmer" in Afrikaans
82 Hydroxyl compound
83 Airbnb offering
86 "Sooner this, Sooner that . . . can't you talk about any other subject?"?
89 Imparter of umami taste, in brief
90 Exact look-alike
93 Resort near Snowbird
94 Middle-___
95 Big 2016 film set in Polynesia
96 Cab alternative
98 Follows
100 Deal another blackjack card to a young Salem woman?
104 Take from the top
106 "Consider it done"
110 Tomorrow
111 Architect Saarinen
113 Some young 'uns
115 Grammy-winning singer of "Shepherd Moons"
116 A-lister

117 Midwest state secedes and will join the United Kingdom?
120 Whale food
121 Place
122 Direct route
123 Overused
124 Directed
125 Having braids

DOWN

1 Footnote abbr.
2 Take stock?
3 Fragrant compound
4 Pitted fruit
5 Icelandic letter
6 Powerful engine
7 Cruising
8 Be successful
9 The slightest amount of
10 Oscar-winning foreign film of 2005 set in South Africa
11 Tiny-scissors holder
12 Nutsy
13 Competing with
14 Thirst
15 Firmly in place
16 Have a connection
17 Turbaned teacher
18 Loathing
19 Like some myths
24 "You'll have to pay for me"
29 Stylish
31 Unit of firewood
33 "Freedom ___ free"
35 Commercial lead-in to Pen
37 Walter ___, Dodgers owner who moved the team from Brooklyn to L.A.

39 Submits, as a phone report
41 Previous incarnations
42 Part of a recovery effort
44 Writer of "The Gnat and the Bull"
46 ___ Conference
47 Added up
48 City just east of LAX
49 Vintage Jaguars
50 Apology start
51 Oktoberfest music
52 First-rate, in British slang
54 Buyer of a dozen roses, maybe
58 Former parent co. of Gramophone and Parlophone records
61 Ideology
63 Again, in Mexico
65 Getting help getting clean
66 Dijon darling
67 Avoid puddles, say
69 Pointer's pronoun
70 Sister of Helios
71 Ancient fortuneteller
72 In the 70s, say
76 Yellowstone grazer
79 Unadon fish
81 Armchair accompanier
82 Things painted in the spring
84 So darn cute
85 Like some fertile soil
87 Status
88 They may block passage
91 Start to form?

by Alan Arbesfeld

92 Single, for one
95 Art ___, longtime Cleveland Browns owner
97 Pressure indicator on a map
99 Iger's predecessor at Disney
100 Hardly sophisticates
101 Sluggish
102 Actress Shire
103 Quattro + tre
105 Fabulist's confession
107 Diarist Nin
108 Jeff ___, leader of the Electric Light Orchestra
109 Got on board
112 Licentious sort
114 Word with ceiling or financing
117 C.I.A. forerunner
118 Tour de France time
119 "Who'da thunk it?!"

THAT'S ONE WAY TO PUT IT

ACROSS

1 Draw in
8 Tight garment
14 Come before
21 Stingy sorts
22 Blogger's pick for a pic
23 Utility worker
24 Falling down
26 Mean
27 Very: Ger.
28 Earth goddess
29 G.P.A. killers
30 "Sprechen ___ Deutsch?"
31 Robert of "The Sopranos"
32 Speeding ticket
37 Prep for the runway, maybe
40 Ball ___
41 Besmirch
42 Emotionally demanding
43 Climbing Mount Everest, e.g.
45 Be Kind to Editors and Writers Mo. [for real!]
48 Notable features of Stockholm and Amsterdam
51 It "exists when one goes against one's conscience," per Pope Francis
52 Fire places
55 D.C. lobby for seniors
57 Locale for two of the Quad Cities
58 Egyptian cobra
61 Lying
66 Heat, as to soften metal
67 "u r hilarious!"
68 How scallops are often prepared
69 French horticulturist after whom a variety of fruit is named
72 Cause of insomnia, maybe
74 Design detail
77 Google ___
78 Run too far or lift too much
81 Go over in blackjack
84 In working order
87 Layoff
94 Old sitcom character who was 229 years old
95 Utah's ___ Canyon
96 Get 29-Across
97 Railway offshoot
98 "So that's it!"
99 Florae and faunae
101 Down
103 Mariners
105 TWA competitor
108 Classic Jag
110 Who "can't buy you love" in an Elton John hit
113 "There, there"
114 Tax increase
120 Cheers in un estadio
121 Canon camera
122 Take off quickly
123 "If I ___ penny for every . . ."
124 Some WSJ topics
128 Summer Olympics host after Barcelona
130 Dead
133 Custom-fits
134 Took off quickly
135 Pasta recipe phrase
136 Show contempt for
137 At the scene
138 "We should avoid doing that"

DOWN

1 New Testament book
2 Pilgrims' pronoun
3 Radio host John
4 Life in the big city, to some
5 Bee: Prefix
6 Dance with a kick
7 John Irving protagonist portrayed by Robin Williams
8 Wine holders
9 Spermatozoa targets
10 Dance party enthusiast
11 Wooden
12 Worries no end
13 Five-point rugby play
14 Stripes mismatch, traditionally
15 Amazon, e.g.
16 Oklahoma City-to-Tulsa dir.
17 Develops (from)
18 Charlotte ___, Virgin Islands
19 Very last part
20 Pep
25 André ___, 1947 Literature Nobelist
30 Narrow waterway
33 Part of an accusation in Clue
34 Laker named to the Basketball Hall of Fame in 2016
35 Small anatomical container
36 Landing post-E.T.A.
37 12 cc, maybe
38 Country star Church
39 Alternative to a name: Abbr.
44 Draw, as a scene
46 Ratcheting wheel mechanism
47 Adjust with Photoshop, maybe
49 Japanese drama
50 Knocks over
53 Even
54 Trauma reminder
56 School support grps.
58 Corona, for one
59 Repeated cry at a dance class
60 Most profs
62 Mother-of-pearl
63 Out in court
64 Boost the horsepower of
65 Dish served with chopsticks in a bowl
69 Florida beach city, informally
70 Like the head of a tennis racket
71 Lowly worker
73 Bit of wind
75 Those, in Tijuana
76 Complaining fish?
79 "Hots"
80 "Creme sandwich" introduced over a century ago
82 Animal depicted in Edwin Landseer's "The Monarch of the Glen"
83 Work, work, work
85 Air-conditioner fig.
86 Entrap
88 Army NCO
89 Alien autopsies, crop circles and the like
90 Liquid-___
91 Pet food with a paw print logo
92 Where to accent "Laotian"
93 Pinstriper
99 Store blowout
100 Suffix with brew

by Robert Fisher

102 Underbrush clearer
104 Occasionally
105 W.W. II shipping worries
106 Oman's leader, e.g.
107 Antarctic penguin
109 Officially prohibit
111 Lamb, e.g.

112 It goes up to about 1700
115 Aquarium fish
116 Swelter
117 Holiday celebrations
118 Holy Roman emperor called "the Great"

119 Country rocker Steve
125 One of the Ivies
126 Not conned by
127 Let stand, editorially
129 Neither's partner
130 U.N. observer since '74

131 Day-in-and-day-out pattern
132 D.C. summer setting

ACROSS

1 Agcy. for Kennedy and Reagan
4 Push
9 Positive quality
14 Provider of directions, for short
17 Penne ___ vodka
19 Around
20 Claw
22 "Intriguing!"
23 Aquaman's favorite singer?
25 The Human Torch's favorite band?
27 ___ Edberg, two-time U.S. Open tennis champion
28 With child, informally
30 Nicely muscled
31 Canine warning
32 Feminine hygiene product
33 Seashore feature
34 Oriental, e.g.
35 The Hulk's favorite band?
38 Does 110, say
40 Sculptor/collagist Jean
41 Staff
42 Number between cinque and sette
43 Mama ___ Elliot
44 Iceman's favorite band?
48 Bermuda, e.g.
50 Sweetly sing
52 14-pound unit
54 Australian friend
55 The Flash's favorite singer?
58 Adamant refusal
60 Animator's frame
61 "Your" of yore
62 Bit of progress
64 "Seriously?"
66 Front of a vessel
68 Magneto's favorite band?
70 Quaint agreement
71 Comment advising you to set your sights a little lower?
73 Low tie
74 Response to "You have something on your face," maybe
75 List-ending abbr.
76 Gobbles (down)
78 Spider-Man's favorite band?
83 Smell ___ (sense something fishy)
85 Like Hägar the Horrible
87 ___ Martin
88 "Enough already!"
89 Batman's favorite rapper?
91 Revivalists, for short
93 Not only that but also
95 Singer Sumac
96 The Avalanche, on sports tickers
97 Make do with a lesser option
99 Thor's favorite rapper?
101 Actress Thurman
102 32° Fahrenheit, in Celsius
103 Parisian street
104 ___ volente (God willing)
105 Old-fashioned provider of directions
107 Completely set
109 Sir and madam
112 Electro's favorite singer?
114 What the musical artists in this puzzle would form if they all performed together?
116 Decompose
117 Let breathe, as stinky shoes
118 Tangent line?
119 Princess Fiona, after sunset
120 One begins "Thou still unravish'd bride of quietness"
121 ___-turvy
122 Chocolate cup inventor H. B. ___
123 Pained cry

DOWN

1 Things the police may keep on suspects
2 Narrow cut
3 [legally covering our butts here]
4 Clickable item
5 Boom ___
6 Remit in advance
7 Digital greeting
8 "Stay in your ___!"
9 Approximately
10 Untroubled
11 Divine bovine?
12 Timeline sections
13 Wee bit
14 Destined for greatness
15 Opening in cosmetology?
16 Molt
18 Woodard with four Emmys
21 Covalent bonds of a carbon atom, e.g.
24 Things sailors spin
26 Late afternoon hour
29 Some economic figs.
32 Tournament bridge players, typically
35 Stick-to-it-iveness
36 Santa ___, Calif.
37 Speak out against
38 City by the Bay, informally
39 "Why, you little . . ."
43 Several quarter turns?
45 Jay with jokes
46 Starting squad
47 Speak up, and then some
49 ___ Brand, two-time N.B.A. All-Star
51 Boo-boo
53 Good trait in a housemate
56 "Jeez, wasn't expecting that!"
57 For rent
59 Test for fit
63 Song with the lyric "A loko e hana nei"
65 Things equestrians have on hand?
66 ___ dish
67 What 14-Across will do if you miss a turn
68 Fruit salad ingredients
69 "___ bon"
71 Pup grown up
72 Uptown
74 "___, won't you blow your horn?" (old lyric)
77 Cold summer treat
79 Puerto Rican city that shares its name with an explorer
80 System of roots?
81 Part of a so-called "grand tour"
82 Trade barbs or blows
84 Like some saws and bobsleds
86 Supplication

by Erik Agard and Alex Briñas

90 "What did Delaware?" "I don't know, but ___" (classic joke)
92 University in North Carolina
94 "Feel me?"
98 "___ fugit"
99 Gooey chocolate treat
100 Public transit system
103 Be economical with
105 Lead-in to -centric
106 Stepped
107 Italian dear
108 Victim of a revolution
109 What the upright yoga pose vrikshasana simulates
110 It's worth a little more than a dollar
111 Violently send out
113 Stridex target, informally
115 Mag personnel

ACROSS

1 M.I.T. Sloan grad, often
4 Raven's cry
7 Steal, slangily
11 Bridge work?
18 Office restoration
21 "Didn't expect to see you here!"
22 Generally
23 Interns at a cemetery?
25 Start of a class field trip, maybe
26 Had a bead on
27 New Left org.
28 Features of Utah's Capitol Reef National Park
30 Instants
31 Endorse
32 ___ Court (London district)
34 Series ender in London
35 Start over in cards
37 Lead-in to much
38 Take to social media following a good round of golf?
41 Work at, as a trade
42 Chickadee, e.g.
44 Brown ermine
45 Ready-to-___
46 Crown
47 Have-not
49 Emmy-winning show of both 1976 and 2017, in brief
50 One sending flowers, say
52 One holding flowers
53 Brain readings, for short
55 Sounded sheepish?
58 Speed demon
61 Pacts between packs?
65 Rage
66 Does penance
68 Corp. manager
69 "More than I wanted to hear!"
70 "Not nice!"
72 Original Beatle Sutcliffe
73 Ones sharing quarters at the most macho fraternity?
77 Aviary parts
78 Places to cool one's jets?
80 Adventurer in Grouchland
81 Big tablet
83 Nozzles into blast furnaces
85 One of 17 on a Monopoly board: Abbr.
87 Policy at a wedding's open bar, maybe
90 Switch on the radio
92 Nabokov novel
93 Excel
95 It led to a 1773 protest
97 Amazon peril
98 Stylish underwear?
101 Mess maker
102 Ill feeling
104 It doesn't mean "lots of love"
105 Euphoric
106 Smears, as a reputation
107 Svelte
108 Excite
110 Camping gear retailer
111 See 48-Down
112 Homie
114 Things swapped at a convention of supermarket owners?
118 "Just about done"
119 Citrus hybrid
120 Starter supply for making bourbon
121 "Slow down, tiger!"
122 Fifth-most abundant element in the universe
123 Court org.
124 Director Ang

DOWN

1 It decreases with acceleration, for short
2 Get closer to, as the heart of the matter
3 It's played on the road
4 Rep
5 A myrmeke of Greek myth is a giant one
6 City near where Chopin was born
7 Actor Hamm of "Mad Men"
8 *cough*
9 Bit from Sunshine Biscuits
10 Yap
11 Catches
12 Big Ten powerhouse, for short
13 Mouths off to
14 Slipped up
15 Social gatherings where fruit drinks are served?
16 Bluejacket
17 Samantha of 96-Down
19 Drawn
20 California ball club
24 Some bars in the Caribbean
29 Over-and-above
31 "Park it!"
32 Diminutive suffixes
33 Paleolith
35 Fixes, as a bath area
36 Caustic soda
39 Haymaker?
40 Some feet
43 Presumptive assertion
46 Something a shooter shoots
48 With 111-Across, cinnamon candy
50 "Same here"
51 Speak to, with "with"
54 "Hurry up!"
56 Q.E.D. part
57 Places to hibernate
58 Unconsidered
59 Kofi Annan's middle name
60 Take attendance in a magical forest?
62 Routine problem, for short
63 Horns in on?
64 Something kept close to the chest
67 Watches via Netflix, say
71 Modern-day circus
74 Onetime govt.-prescribed nutritional figure
75 Home of Berkshire Hathaway
76 Sloth, for one
79 Extra product
82 Another name for hopscotch
84 Country rocker Steve

by John Guzzetta and Michael Hawkins

86 Complete
88 Spacious and splendid
89 "The Departed" director
90 Court org.
91 Where the Missouri River begins
93 Be extravagant
94 Ones holding down things?
96 Station for 17-Down
98 Call for
99 Cork-popper
100 Early record label
103 Like much mouthwash
108 Not just think
109 ___ grounds
111 Part of un día
112 Bully in "Calvin and Hobbes"
113 Long ___
115 The Bengals, on scoreboards
116 Place to soak
117 "That's all ___ wrote"

ACROSS

1 Signs off on
4 Bei Bei and Bao Bao
10 Mike's place
16 Barnyard bleat
19 Remained unused
20 Morphine, for one
21 Still
22 Pitches
23 Facebook Status: "2016 Summer Olympics and a day trip to one of the new Seven Wonders of the World!"
26 Bobs and buns
27 Tea party girl
28 "Repeat . . ."
29 Valuable china, e.g.
31 Facebook Status: "Across the pond! And front-row seats to the Henley Royal Regatta!"
35 "King ___" (1978 hit)
37 "Above" and "beyond," e.g.
38 Island ring
39 Chill out
40 Okapi feature
42 Salad green
43 Lily who played Ernestine
46 An arm or a leg
47 "___ it the truth!"
48 Dough dispenser
51 Facebook Status: "Yes! Retail therapy at the largest shopping spot in the U.S.!"
54 Cyberaddress
57 Van Susteren of cable news
59 Campbell of "Scream"
60 Second-___
61 ___ Miguel (largest island in the Azores)
62 Use part of
64 Sicilian erupter
67 "Am ___ believe . . . ?"
68 Analogy connector
69 TV host Geist
70 Facebook Status: "Ahhhh . . . Sun and surf in Cancún, Mexico! Bring on the unlimited piña coladas!"
72 Battle of the Atlantic craft
74 "Sleep ___"
75 Old United rival
77 One crossing the line?
78 Eminence
79 Call, as a game
80 "Live With Kelly and Ryan" co-host
82 Gusto
84 10-time French Open champ
85 Born
86 Facebook Status: "Hej from København! This statue turned 100 years old in 2013 but is still a beauty!"
90 Double-O sort
91 Cows and sows
93 Top that may have a built-in bra
94 Exam administered on the forearm
96 Fleur-de-lis, e.g.
98 Bad place for a frog
100 Captained
101 ___ room
104 Praying figure in Christian art
105 It can be smoked
106 Facebook Status: "10-9-8-7 . . . Ringing in the New Year with 1,000,000 of my newest, closest friends!"
110 Excessive regulation
112 Swahili "sir"
114 Neuter
115 QB Manning
116 Facebook Status: "History abounds! Neo-Classical architecture surrounded by gorgeous cherry blossom trees. Next stop . . . the White House!"
121 Sch. with the mascot Mike the Tiger
122 Anatomical ring
123 Recording studio effect
124 JFK posting
125 Place of Bible study: Abbr.
126 In an uncivil way
127 Wife, to Juan
128 Oedipus, for one

DOWN

1 Its official name is Academy Award of Merit
2 "The Prophet" author Gibran
3 Shoot (for)
4 Brainteaser
5 Well-put
6 Niggling detail
7 Morse word
8 Elite group
9 Classic blazer fabrics
10 Mani-___
11 Dingy part of a kitchen?
12 Just-passing mark
13 Con
14 ___-friendly
15 Wife on "The Addams Family"
16 Facebook Status: "Vegas, baby! And who would believe I'm standing next to Beyoncé and Katy Perry!"
17 Very cute, in slang
18 Judge
24 Seal the deal
25 Where the Santa Ana and Long Beach Fwys. meet
30 Tip off
32 For 17+ viewers
33 "When pigs fly!"
34 Lightsome
36 Tongue-lash
41 Crater's edge
44 Muscat resident
45 Unheard-of
47 Get the better of
48 Damaged over time
49 Workplace newbie
50 Facebook Status: "Nosebleed seats - but home-field advantage! GO GIANTS!!!"
52 Ultrasound target
53 Cousin of 15-Down
55 Bad joint
56 How Mark Twain is often quoted
58 Bias
63 Russian "invader" of the 1980s
65 Olympics airer since 1988
66 Bowl over
68 Speck
70 Challenge to prove you're human
71 Critic Roger
73 Alabama and Kansas, for two
76 Quick thinking
78 Schedules
81 Start of a drill, maybe
83 Saunter
86 Still partly open, as a door
87 Punk offshoot

by Tracy Gray

88 Mazda two-seaters
89 Roadside bombs, for short
92 This answer ends in "T," e.g.
95 More on the mark
96 Some edible fungi
97 "Otherwise . . . !"
98 Prime setter, informally
99 Cassiterite, e.g.
102 Less strict
103 Spawn
107 Flowing locks
108 Chipotle rival
109 You might take it to go
111 Arequipa is its second-largest city
113 Fay of "King Kong"
117 Rival
118 Series honor, for short
119 Workplace inits.
120 Half a couple

ACROSS

1 Lecterns
6 Some looping online animations
10 No. 2's
13 Canine supporters
17 It's all an act
19 Actor Epps
20 "Abracadabra!"
22 "The Lion King"
24 Pool divider, or a further hint to 22-Across
25 Wine often served with dessert
26 College department that might offer paid studies, informally
27 "Who, me?"
28 Majestic
29 Get excited about crosswords, say, with "out"
30 Hockey feint
31 Hallmark.com offerings
34 Bond, for one: Abbr.
35 Fig. on a master's application
37 Geometry test directive
38 Maître's domain
41 Suffix with legal
42 "Jerry Maguire"
45 Box a bit
46 Hunter in the night sky
47 Feature of Chairman Mao's cap
51 Reaction to a bad joke
52 They're often cross-bred with apricots
53 Smart-alecky
54 American pale ___
55 Bozo
56 Get up

57 Judge's seat
58 Neural conductor
59 Carnival, say, or a further hint to 42-Across
61 Musical score marking, or a further hint to 101-Across
63 Full house, for one
64 ___ mater
65 Ideas spreading virally
66 Duel tool
67 Blue Devils' org.
68 Hephaestus' forge is said to be under it
69 Uninspired
70 Satiated
71 What I may turn into
73 Coin at an arcade
74 "The Merry Drinker" painter
76 "The Force Awakens"
79 Traffic-monitoring org.
82 Herb pronounced differently in the U.S. and U.K.
84 Appears
85 Item with the words "Member Since"
87 White House extension?
88 George Takei's role on the U.S.S. Enterprise, in brief
90 Small beam
91 When Macduff slays Macbeth
92 They're first in the draft
95 "Sure"
96 Brunch offering
98 Where Samson slew the Philistines

99 F-150s or Thunderbirds, or a further hint to 76-Across
101 "The Dark Knight"
104 Onlooker
105 Ills
106 "Friday I'm in Love" band, 1992
107 Caviars
108 Defib locales
109 "In that case . . ."
110 Language in which the first four cardinal numbers are ane, twa, three and fower

DOWN

1 Sci-fi weapons
2 Symbol of strength
3 Stonehenge priests
4 McKellen who played Gandalf
5 City south of Seminole, Okla.
6 Singer with the 2012 #1 hit "Somebody That I Used to Know"
7 Apple desktop
8 New Year's Eve figure
9 Mrs., abroad
10 Ad ___ tax
11 Daring thing to wear with polka dots
12 ___ Gabriel Mountains
13 Big gust
14 Eponymous Israeli gun designer
15 Get by
16 Refine
17 What metathesiophobia is the fear of
18 Kind of penguin

21 Splat preceder
23 Out of whack
27 Connoisseur
30 Capital of Qatar
32 Some salmon
33 Get old
36 $100 bills, in slang
37 Study
39 Turn over
40 Yiddish cries
43 José, Bengie and Yadier ___, catcher brothers with five World Series rings among them
44 Redundant-sounding engine parts
45 Like the 1-to-7 balls
48 Prepared for takeoff
49 Stag
50 Actress Russo
51 Like trampolines
52 ___ ballerina
53 Got one's feet wet?
55 Harry's wizarding foe
56 Never-before-seen
57 Candy heart message
58 Suisse peaks
59 A fish . . . or to cook it, in a way
60 Have nutritious foods
61 Pariahs
62 Flinching, typically
65 Play up
68 K-12
69 What "w" is in Welsh, at times
72 Window fixtures, for short
73 Get ready to drive
74 Most cozy
75 "Preach!"

by Ross Trudeau

77 Publishers
78 ___ Productions, company behind TV's "Dr. Phil"
79 Look onto the street, say
80 First family after the Garfields
81 Counsel
82 Endangered ape
83 Opposed (to)
86 Multicolored
87 Choose
89 Jazz pianist McCoy ___
90 Artist's base
93 Coolers in coolers
94 Camera option, for short
97 Loafs around a deli?
100 "___ had it!"
101 The U.S. joined it in 1917: Abbr.
102 Quizzical utterances
103 Fun, for short

ACROSS

1 Popular web portal
4 Sweet stuff
11 Braggadocio
18 "Well, well, well!"
19 Coming
20 Slant in columns
22 1992 movie based on an "S.N.L." sketch . . . or, diverged: Modus vivendi
24 Railroad line?
25 "Out!"
26 Suffix with host
27 Like pins-and-needles feelings
29 Mystiques
30 Defunct org. in which Donald Trump owned the New Jersey Generals
32 "Adios!"
33 "Prince Valiant" son
34 "We're doomed!"
39 Computer mouse action . . . or, diverged: Event for RuPaul
44 Less friendly
45 Blue-roofed eatery
47 Gambols
48 Time to remember
49 Erstwhile Fords
50 "The Simpsons Theme" composer Danny
52 Many a frat pledge
53 Become bored (of)
54 ___ mother
55 Scarcely
56 Freudian "will to live"
58 Better, to an impatient boss
60 Spots likely to smear
63 Italian novelist Morante

66 Destroys, in gamer-speak
67 1916 Frost verse . . . or, diverged: Start of a saying about meaning well
71 "Star Wars" nomad
73 Opposite of "da"
74 Put a cover on
78 Molson rival
80 "No ___!"
82 Heads overseas?
83 Coral, e.g.
84 A long way off
85 Part of a treasure chest
89 Another form of "Jehovah"
91 Big swig
92 W.W. II org. whose insignia featured Athena
93 Prepare, as leftovers
95 Fill-up filler
96 Cassava, for one
97 Bring someone home . . . or, diverged: Common high school offering
100 Frigid
102 From l. to r.
103 Proscriptions
105 Chill out
106 "Button" that's plainly visible
109 Showy debut
110 A germophobe might have it, for short
112 Acronym for the four major entertainment awards
115 Artist with the third most Top 40 hits in the 1960s, behind Elvis and the Beatles

117 Nissan S.U.V.s . . . or, diverged: Emotional appeal
120 Hit 2007 Will Smith film
121 Some potatoes
122 Comic strip cry
123 Establish, as rules
124 Gratiano's love in "The Merchant of Venice"
125 Line in the sand?

DOWN

1 Does course work?
2 Bygone title
3 Expression of shock at someone's actions
4 Go after for redress
5 Try to induce a bigger purchase
6 Rookery cries
7 Symbols of density
8 Beyond, to bards
9 Sea dogs
10 Went for a whirl
11 Vegas casino robbed in "Ocean's Eleven"
12 Without purpose
13 Supermodel Carangi
14 Armless coats that may bear coats of arms
15 Overflow (with)
16 Fabulist
17 Russia's ___ Sea (arm of the Arctic Ocean)
20 Hungarians
21 Activist youth org.
23 Snacks
28 Ball brand
31 La Dame de ___ (Eiffel Tower nickname)
33 Sacred crosses
34 1946 femme fatale film

35 Santa's reindeer, e.g.
36 Monumental support
37 TV band
38 "Word on the street is . . ."
40 Deadly cobra
41 Wilson of "The Office"
42 They might be giants
43 Kind of review
46 The usual
50 Actress Sommer
51 "Keep out" sign
53 Burgs
55 Bygone Apple app
57 ___-pitch
59 Autobahn autos
61 Feuding
62 Syndicate head
64 Online ticket exchange
65 Chem. neurotransmitter
68 Sheriff's asst.
69 "Them's the breaks, I guess"
70 ___ Industries (oil and gas giant)
71 "Aladdin" villain
72 Summers back in the day?
75 "How Deep Is Your Love" group
76 "Introduction to the Analysis of the Infinite" writer
77 Cool again
78 God, informally
79 Gender-neutral possessive
81 Lummox
86 Philip ___, first Asian-American film actor to get a star on the Hollywood Walk of Fame

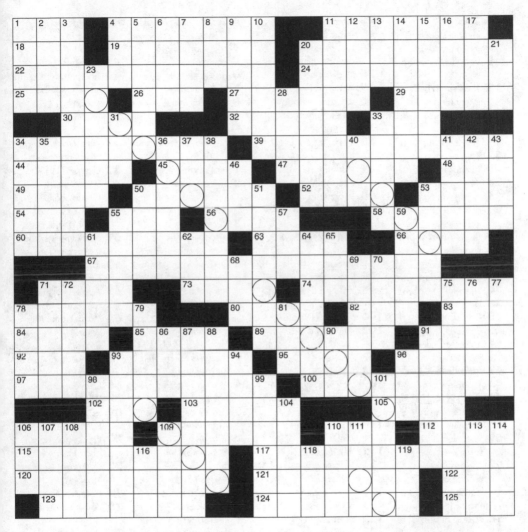

by Natan Last

"S-Q's Me!"

ACROSS

1 Philbin's onetime morning co-host
8 Equality-promoting org.
12 Those who believe everything has a spirit
20 Off base
21 Small songbird
22 Patronized a restaurant
23 Prodigality?
25 Emmy-winning actor on "The West Wing"
26 Spinny pool shot
27 Direct (toward)
29 Part of many German names
30 "Ready?" response
33 Hog seller?
38 Chefs' hats
40 Corp. budget item
41 1969 self-titled jazz album
42 Salad alternative
43 Trouble maker
46 Depend (on)
48 Letters of warning on internet sites
52 Radiologist's tool, for short
53 Cigar City, so-called on account of a former major industry
54 A part of Life?
55 Irritate
56 Suffix with market
57 Mr. Magoo biopic?
62 Actress Thurman
63 N.Y.C. subway letters
65 High school sweethearts
66 "___ said . . ."
68 Birthplace of Emily Dickinson
71 Sloppy sort
72 Roadblock
73 Canadian coin, informally
74 Like rebate coupons, typically
78 "How cool!"
79 Actor Kilmer
80 Cuckoo or dodo?
83 Locale for a flock
86 Nonreactive
88 Abbr. in a military title
89 Dark times, informally
90 Trickster
91 Mariner's org.
92 Small
93 Resembling down
95 General ___ chicken
96 Buccaneer's quaff
98 Was on a crowded bus, say
100 Soprano Renata
102 Prepares cube steak?
107 Altar sites
108 A/C stat
109 Gay who wrote "Frank Sinatra Has a Cold"
110 "I ___ talking to you!"
112 The "E" of E.D.
114 All-day gripe sessions?
121 Like a rope in tug of war
122 Northern Iraqi
123 Alter ego on "The Simpsons"
124 Tightwads' opposites
125 Hungers
126 Questionable

DOWN

1 Ones in a mess, informally
2 Question: Abbr.
3 Pot-au-___ (French stew)
4 Basis of the plot of "Gone Girl"
5 Like Corinthian columns
6 Bacilli shapes
7 Habiliments
8 Cobbler's tool
9 Vineyard designation
10 ___ Cayes (Haitian port)
11 Not related?
12 Gilbert who wrote "Love and Death on Long Island"
13 Rosetta Stone discovery site
14 In a senseless way
15 Deranged, in slang
16 Polish movie named Best Foreign Language Film of 2014
17 Work out
18 Henry VII's house
19 Lee who co-created the Avengers
24 Not an elective: Abbr.
28 Flower colored by Aphrodite's blood, in myth
30 "You know who this is"
31 "A Visit From St. Nicholas" poet
32 Ways out of embarrassing situations?
34 Polished
35 It may have a ring to it
36 Enero a diciembre
37 Civil rights activist Guinier
39 Laker legend with a size 22 sneaker, informally
44 Something absolutely necessary
45 Fast-paced two-player card game
47 Munchies, say
49 Enumerations of things to be sat on?
50 Is plenty angry
51 Song words before "the World" and "the Champions"
53 Like pre-1917 Russia
55 Green shells
58 Animal with a flexible snout
59 Early title for Julius Caesar
60 Brightest star in Orion
61 Apollo 11's Eagle, for short
64 What Lionel Messi wears
67 Brazil's ___ Bernardo do Campo
68 Choreographer Ailey
69 2016 film set in Polynesia
70 Et ___ (footnote abbr.)
72 Document certifiers, for short
74 Countenance
75 Sorting category on iTunes
76 Vacuum tube component
77 Cousin of a spoonbill
81 Alleged psychic exposed by the Amazing Randi
82 Co-authors Margret and H. A.
84 Theatricalize
85 Lhasa ___ (dogs)
87 "Old World Style" pasta sauce brand

by Ed Sessa

92 Glacial deposit
93 Opposition
94 Easy question
95 "I dare you to do better!"
97 Snitched on, with "out"
99 Lucy's place, in a Beatles song

101 "Impossible!"
102 Leash, e.g.
103 Line (up)
104 Ones on the outsides of brackets
105 "Yuck!"
106 Forgeries
108 Pot growers?

111 Kind of vaccine
113 Cardboard container: Abbr.
115 "___ pasa?"
116 Decorative garden item
117 Source of much of Google's income

118 Fictional creature made from heat and slime
119 Unspecified degree
120 ___ milk

63 COUNTERPRODUCTIVE

Note: The circled letters spell a bonus answer related to the puzzle's theme.

ACROSS

1 Sports figures
6 Words said through a car window
11 The Land Shark's show, for short
14 Throw (together)
18 Fervor
19 Reno's county
20 It may come hot or iced
21 ___ Modern
22 This clue's 110-Across, timewise
24 Not definitely going to happen
26 Furry, red TV character
27 Young actress who played two main characters in "The Parent Trap"
28 This clue's 110-Across, at the Olympics
30 Flipped (through)
32 Former executive with the same interior letters as his company
34 As such
35 Complete (for)
36 Opposite of blanc
38 N.Y.C. attraction
40 "I love her ten times more than ___ I did": Shak.
41 Large amount
44 Steak ___
46 End of the sci-fi film titles "First Man . . ." and "Last Days . . ."
49 This clue's 110-Across, as is relevant each November

52 Assessment: Abbr.
53 Mork's boss on "Mork & Mindy"
54 Branching point
55 Leave one's mark?
59 Bro or sis: Abbr.
60 Phillies' div.
61 Staple of Southern cuisine
62 One after whom a Times Square museum is named
63 Prefix with -mester
64 This clue's 110-Across, to the superstitious
69 Martinique, par exemple
70 Words of adulation
72 Mimics
73 Temple athlete
74 Clear, as a table
75 Jordan who directed "Get Out"
76 Feline's warning
77 Home of Oral Roberts University
80 Shakespearean plotter
81 This clue's 110-Across, in chemistry
85 Return fee?
87 Moving companies?
88 Unit of grass
89 Article in a German paper
90 Quash
92 State sch. on the Pacific Coast
93 Co. leader
94 Beethoven dedicatee
97 Pat of "The Karate Kid"
99 Thanksgiving role

102 This clue's 110-Across, in terms of attractiveness
104 2017 U.S. Open winner
107 13th or 15th
109 "My word!"
110 Something to count to understand 22-, 28-, 49-, 64-, 81- and 102-Across
113 "___ It Romantic?"
114 Designer Maya
115 Dramatic battle cry
116 Ornamental crown
117 Rising concerns in modern times?
118 "You rang?"
119 Primetime ___
120 Sen. Thurmond

DOWN

1 "Me too!!!"
2 Warble
3 Snapchat request
4 Uselessly
5 ___ Lanka
6 Has in an old form?
7 Labor agcy.
8 Perform perfunctorily
9 Debt note
10 Certain high school clique
11 One of the stuntmen on "Jackass"
12 Old-fashioned "That's absolutely the last time"
13 The Lonely Mountain, for Smaug
14 Play place
15 Worker
16 Place holders?

17 Kitchen tool
19 "___ have thought . . ."
23 Giddy happiness
25 Recipe amt.
29 As far as one can recall
31 Hero role in "The Force Awakens"
33 Country whose name is also a two-word sentence
36 Badgers
37 Crumbled froyo topping
39 Nickname for a young Darth Vader
41 Be really generous to a waiter
42 Words before "I'm going in"
43 List-ending phrase
44 Weighed, in a way, as a container
45 Orders
47 University in Montreal
48 Seniors' org.
50 ___ Heights
51 Mild cheese
56 Famous password stealer
57 Inundated
58 Trash-filled lot, e.g.
60 Shooting stars?
61 Green lights
62 Mountain ash
65 Been in bed
66 Shipping center
67 French film award
68 Some pears
71 Custardy dessert
76 Family Night entertainment
77 One with a large bill at breakfast?

by Tom McCoy

78 Ones stationed at home
79 Told stories
80 McDonald's slogan introduced in 2003
82 URL ending
83 Push
84 Ride option
85 Hollywood news
86 Businesswoman Huffington
89 Layer of skin
91 Wooden nickels, e.g.
93 Give a ring
95 Blind parts
96 Right-angle shape
98 Fit to be tied
99 2006 film with massive profits in related toy sales
100 One of Mr. Poe's children in a Lemony Snicket book
101 Back in
103 Oleaginous
105 Wrong
106 Blue side, for short
108 Fraud
111 ___ de guerre
112 French connections

ACROSS

1 Per
7 Per ___
11 Feature on the back of some pajamas
15 Conversation interrupter in a car, at times
18 Cured salmon
19 Jazzy Anita
20 Top-shelf
21 Go bad
22 Lists about a port on the Black Sea
24 Guaranteed to succeed
26 Auspice
27 Referring to this clue within this clue, e.g.
28 Neighborhoods surrounded by crime
30 1970s–'90s chess champion
33 Fill-in
35 ___ Store
36 Laura of "ER"
37 Provide cover for, say
39 Fad dance move of 2015
40 Blue-green hue
42 Style of Radio City Music Hall, informally
43 Metal pin stuck in parts of sinks
47 Figure skater Sonja
49 Shout after seeing Godzilla
50 Motorsports vehicle
51 ___ ammoniac
52 Good times
54 Capital of the world's happiest country, per a 2017 U.N. survey
55 QB's cry
56 Unpleasant
58 The dark side
59 One of the principal deities in Hinduism
61 Sliding item on a car
64 Carne ___ (taco option)
67 ___ Dimas, Calif.
68 Flourishes around monsoon events
71 Sample-collecting org.
73 Lush
75 React to a haymaker
76 Slack-jawed
78 Pot note
79 Heaters
80 Major investors in start-up cos.
82 Its filling contained lard until 1997
83 Dangerous vipers
86 Ka-boom!
87 1972 #1 hit with the lyric "No one's ever gonna keep me down again"
89 Regret
90 Ranger's wear
92 Fear among underground workers
95 It goes downhill
97 First name in 1950s comedy
98 Actor John of the "Harold & Kumar" films
99 Nordstrom competitor
100 Shades of tan
102 "Pimp My Ride" network
103 Curry of the N.B.A.
105 Moves, as a plant
109 Coming up in vetoes
112 Got 100 on
114 "I'll get this done"
115 Licorice-flavored extract
116 Crew found inside again and again
120 Spy novelist Deighton
121 Poet ___ St. Vincent Millay
122 Kook
123 "Fawlty Towers" or "The Vicar of Dibley"
124 Need a lift?
125 Looking up
126 And others, for short
127 Gets fresh with

DOWN

1 Nose of a wine
2 Single-___ (like a certain health care system)
3 Does his name ring a bell?
4 Pipe joint
5 "Cool" sort
6 Reason to pull an all-nighter
7 Partner of a crossed "t"
8 Creative sort
9 Something pressed against a conch
10 Game predecessor of Riven
11 Certain spa treatment
12 Baker's container
13 The "I" of "The King and I"
14 ___ dish
15 Bad puns
16 Song with verses by four or more rappers
17 Mounties' hats
18 Understand
23 "Go" preceder
25 Give for a while
29 Hindu exercise system
31 "Do as I say!"
32 Climbing plant in the pea family
34 Broadcaster of many Ken Burns documentaries
38 Something to work through with a therapist
41 Benghazi native
43 Waste
44 Actress Phylicia of "Creed"
45 "Fighting" collegiate team
46 Stella ___ (beer)
48 Another name for Dido
51 Hybrid activewear
53 Santa ___ winds
56 Tailor's measure
57 See 74-Down
60 Take in
62 Blood type of a "universal donor"
63 Ardent
65 "Oh heavens!"
66 Take off an invisibility cloak
69 Lit a fire under
70 Annual event viewed live by hundreds of millions of people, with "the"
72 Big stretches
74 With 57-Down, something filling fills
77 Graceful losers, e.g.
81 Besmirch
83 Magazine places
84 Don Quixote's unseen beloved
85 Sign with an antlered pictogram

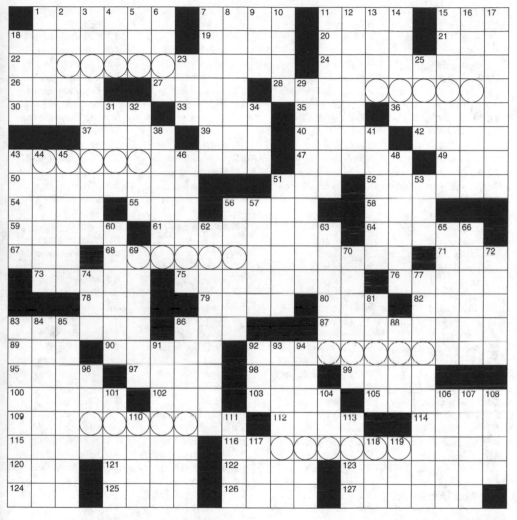

by Jeff Chen

86 Award won by "The Curious Incident of the Dog in the Night-Time"
88 Speedboat follower
91 Continues
92 Hosts, for short

93 Words of empathy
94 "You shouldn't've done that"
96 The Blues Brothers and others
101 Emulate Snidely Whiplash
104 Hack down

106 Chilled
107 Costa Ricans, in slang
108 Modern education acronym
110 Brouhaha
111 Lid irritant
113 "I call that!"

117 Very in
118 Second Amendment org.
119 U.S.O. audience

65 SHELL GAME

ACROSS

1 Browns
7 Four-hit achievement, in baseball lingo
12 Mil. posts
15 System used at Gallaudet Univ.
18 The U.S., in Mexico
20 Milo of "Romeo and Juliet," 1968
21 Hawaii's ___ Day
22 Low
23 "Et tu?" and others
25 Lotion ingredients
26 Suburb of Chicago
28 Joyful internet cry
29 Bubbly mixer
31 Popeye's boy
33 Harassed, in a sense
34 Cartoon seller of Squishees
35 Pyrex glass marking
38 Jackson 5 member
39 Philip who wrote "Portnoy's Complaint"
41 Cain and Abel's younger brother
42 Word before questions or advice
43 Do sales work, informally
44 A part of
45 Band with the 1989 platinum debut album "Junta"
47 Darryl, in the comic "Baby Blues"
49 Accomplishing
51 Poke around
54 The "K" in Kmart
59 Places for plugs
62 Plastic dispenser producer
65 The clue for 128-Down, if this shell game weren't a scam
68 Hardly guzzle
69 Group of pros
71 "Rights of Man" author, 1791
72 Early Cuzco dweller
73 Series of mistakes?
74 Vacation spot
77 Inside dope source
80 Prefix with business
81 Chilled
83 With 13-Down, herbal brew
85 Cartoon seller of Duff Beer
86 The clue for 127-Across, if this shell game weren't a scam
90 Former N.F.L.'ers Detmer and Law
91 All together
93 Shapes of some Halloween cookies
94 Country united in 1990
96 Soft drink options
98 A peeling place?
100 Westernmost of the ABC Islands
103 "Bug"
105 Hosp. worker
107 Prefix with caching
109 2.5, for the set {1, 2, 3, 4}
112 Classic sculpture
114 Novel narrated by a soon-to-be mutineer
115 Material for small buildings?
118 Proctor's warning
119 Students often take them out
121 When some bars close
122 Edict
124 End in ___
125 Style influenced by Cubism
127 Like hand motions during a shell game
129 Professional group with a van
131 Month of l'année
132 Singer Reed
133 Four-time World Series-winning manager
134 In the near future
135 Superfund org.
136 Something to build on
137 Looks fabulous, in slang
138 Pincher

DOWN

1 England and Spain fought one in 1588
2 Smirnoff Ice, e.g.
3 Lacking polish
4 Push
5 Verbal stumbles
6 Walks or runs, for short
7 Work together
8 Fashion inits.
9 Elected
10 Degree of freedom
11 Lightens
12 Like hounds and most bunny rabbits
13 See 83-Across
14 Guru, maybe
15 "Pretty cool, huh?"
16 Johannesburg neighborhood much in the news during apartheid
17 Underground locale
19 Give a ring while on the road?
24 Tizzy
27 Typical Vanidades reader
30 How many TV shows are shown
32 Port. is part of it
36 One caring for a bebé
37 Classical poem
40 Email openers
41 Egghead?
46 Deceitful sort
48 Grp. with lots of pointers
50 Like the verbs "eat" and "drink": Abbr.
52 Bobcat relative
53 Fund-raising org.
55 Fair
56 Warm up for a bout, say
57 Bug
58 Ages and ages
60 With politesse
61 They're symbolized by slashes
62 Minecraft or StarCraft
63 Fantasy novel hero who rides the dragon Saphira
64 Capital 175 miles east of Venice, Italy
66 Lottery winner's cry
67 Record again
70 Dernier ___
72 Philosophy class suffix
75 Marc of fashion
76 Follows a pattern?
78 Much-covered 1955 Bo Diddley hit
79 Juice
82 Verb often said three times in a row
84 It's cut and dried
86 All right
87 Immune system component
88 "Let's do this thing!"
89 Amt. of seasoning
92 Loch on the border of the Highlands
95 Worn-down pencil

by David Steinberg

97 Say quickly
99 One way to run
101 Greyhound offering
102 Most visibly frightened
103 Develop a limp
104 Hybrid music genre of the 2010s
106 Houston-to-Dallas dir.
107 Desert, in a way
108 City west of Binghamton
110 Pulitzer-winning novelist Jennifer
111 Total jerks
113 Group with two top 10 rock operas
116 Runs to
117 They have long necks and round bodies
120 Bear's advice
123 Bearlike creature in sci-fi
124 Oil crisis?
126 Murmur
128 Cook in oil
130 Only three-letter scale note

66

FULL-BODY CAST

ACROSS

1 Take ___ on the wild side
6 Cartoonist Silverstein
10 Before you can say Jack Robinson
18 Academy Award-winning Marisa
19 Hip-hop's ___ Kweli
21 Crisis connections
22 Boo-boos
23 Brings up
25 "Batman" actress, 1967–68
26 A-list topper
28 Nine-time Pro Bowler John
30 Curriculum ___
31 "Traffic" actor, 2000
32 Winter Olympics event
34 ___-de-France
35 Sat ___ (GPS, to a Brit)
36 "Super Mario Bros." actor, 1993
40 Comic book onomatopoeia
43 Irish form of Mary
46 Figure on a foam finger
47 ___ contendere
48 School that lent its name to a collar
50 Like many laundromats
52 Seat of Penobscot County
54 "Bride of Frankenstein" actress, 1935
56 Traditional Filipino dish marinated in vinegar and soy sauce
59 Turn up
60 Bring into harmony
63 Yves's evening
64 Like many write-in candidates: Abbr.
65 "Training Day" actor, 2001
71 Old C.I.A. foe
72 Where people get off
74 Growing art form?
75 "A ___ From St. Nicholas"
77 Roadside establishment much seen in the Southwest
80 "Crouching Tiger, Hidden Dragon" actress, 2000
85 Connive
86 Shaman, e.g.
87 When tripled, a "Seinfeld" catchphrase
88 Eastern European capital
89 Simple top
91 Cell exchanges
93 Deteriorate
94 "Crash" actor, 2004
97 Scottish form of John
99 Operate
101 Deliverance person
102 "Frost/Nixon" actor, 2008
106 Kidney-related
109 Dame modifier
110 Bear claws and such
112 What eight actors took on for this puzzle?
115 Written deeply
117 "Mea ___"
118 Daughter of Oedipus
119 Kama ___
120 Hermione's Patronus, in the Harry Potter books
121 Lure in Vegas
122 Leader wearing the Great Imperial Crown
123 10 cc's and others

DOWN

1 Thing whose size is measured in picometers
2 Floored
3 Pal
4 Country singer Womack
5 What might show participants going neck and neck?
6 Cop
7 Le ___ (French port)
8 "Mr. Blue Sky" band, for short
9 This way
10 "Gotcha"
11 Word implied on Opposite Day
12 Ultimate degree
13 Name of five Norwegian kings
14 Word with torch or bar
15 Ab ___ (from the beginning)
16 Genre for Black Sabbath
17 Lauder of cosmetics
20 Hotel attendant
24 Proust protagonist
27 L.G.B.T. magazine since 1967
29 State as fact
33 Mosque tower
36 Primatologist Goodall
37 Crash, with "out"
38 Pond growth
39 Emotional states
40 N, seen from the side
41 Where I-20, I-75 and I-85 all meet
42 Some advanced researchers, for short
44 Particle named by Faraday
45 Most caloric
49 Catch
51 Face-to-face challenges
52 Pot holder
53 1947, for Jackie Robinson
55 Stripling
56 Depress
57 Ruckus
58 Sphere
61 JFK's former ___ Terminal
62 "Je ___" (French words of affection)
64 Suffix with novel or Nobel
66 Standout hoopsters
67 City planners' designation
68 Undoing
69 Leaves a lot on the table?
70 Nothing
73 Chocolate-coated snack stick
76 Like some winks
78 Branch of Islam
79 Any of the Ninja Turtles
81 "Must've been something ___"
82 The Browns, on a scoreboard
83 Bad spell
84 See 102-Down
86 Vertical landing spots
89 Program saver
90 Like SEALs
92 Cured and dried fish
94 Have as a tenant

by Erik Agard and Laura Braunstein

95 "Dear Evan ___," Best Musical of 2017
96 Like florists' flowers that are already in vases
98 Best-selling Japanese manga series
99 ___ Outfitters (retailer)
100 Where Javert drowned in "Les Misérables"
102 With 84-Down, bit of black attire
103 Real-time tool for meteorologists
104 Isn't level
105 Where one might raise a flap about a reservation?
107 So quiet you can hear ___ drop
108 Isn't up to date
111 Early 2000s outbreak, for short
113 Old résident at Versailles
114 "Star Trek" spinoff, to fans
116 Elevs.

67

OH, ONE LAST THING

ACROSS

1 Neighbor of Sudan
5 Queen in the "Star Wars" movies
12 Basics
16 Things that people like to have ripped?
19 First sentence of a news story
20 Party animal
21 Comedian who was a regular on "The Steve Allen Show"
23 Sources of lean meat
24 Comparatively strong, like some French wine?
26 Grime
28 "Yo!"
29 Went by
30 Fearful
32 1998 De Niro thriller
34 Highway noise barriers
38 One who's in it but doesn't win it
40 Egyptian leader obsessed with his appearance?
43 Certain Lincoln Center soprano?
45 It may pop on a plane
46 Dietary std.
47 China's Chiang ___ -shek
48 Yes or no follower
49 Light on one's feet
51 Submissive
52 Fleet
56 "Totally awesome!"
57 Bit of food . . . or feud?
58 Part of a house
59 Peach ___
61 ___-frutti

62 Buttonhole, e.g.
63 Shooting craps while waiting for one's train?
67 Actress Hatcher
68 All skin and bones
69 "I had a dream, which was not all a dream" poet
70 George Eliot's "___ Marner"
71 Finely decorated
72 Antagonist
74 Much of Mongolia
78 Automaker sold by G.M. in 2017
79 Territory
80 White undercoat
82 Broadbrim, e.g.
83 Inits. for getting around the Loop
84 Protagonist in David Foster Wallace's "Infinite Jest"
85 Comment from a cook who cools the cheese sauce before serving?
89 Woodwind that's O.K. to play?
93 Something that's free of charge
94 Weapon seen on the Kenyan flag
95 Big stinks
96 Done, slangily
97 Units for binge watchers
100 Actor Patel of "Lion"
101 "Don't ___ me"
104 Cupid's catchphrase?
110 Part
111 Attention hog's cry
112 Vigilant
113 "The Dukes of Hazzard" spinoff
114 Intimidate

115 One of eight in "The 12 Days of Christmas"
116 Egg-shaped Hasbro toys introduced in 1971
117 Certain soft drinks, informally

DOWN

1 Score marking
2 Powerful engine, for short
3 Nighttime Cartoon Network programming block
4 Wipe off the map
5 Start of MGM's motto
6 Quaint "I believe"
7 Like Wrigley Field's walls
8 Brave
9 Landon who lost in a landslide
10 Pastoral locale
11 Big name in 1980s–'90s TV talk
12 State capital that's the setting of "Ironweed"
13 Betty ___
14 Mean, lowdown sorts
15 Court conference
16 CNN commentator Navarro
17 The Cougars of the West Coast Conf.
18 Determination in a prenatal exam
22 Holiday meal
25 Came down
27 Long lunch?
31 It's to be expected
32 Leveled
33 Eleven: Fr.
35 Cheesy dish
36 Seminal symbol of mass production

37 Lose
38 Paul who sang "Lonely Boy"
39 King who said "Nothing will come of nothing"
40 Woman's name that means "truth"
41 Disloyalty
42 Loft filler
44 Director of 1991's "Mississippi Masala"
49 Genesis brother
50 Early Beatle
51 Sam who ran the bar on "Cheers"
53 Unconcerned with right and wrong
54 Parts of supermarkets
55 & 57 Very nearly
58 Topic at the Kinsey Institute
60 32-ounce purchase at 7-Eleven
61 Mining supply
63 Free
64 Chasm
65 It decreases a QB's rating: Abbr.
66 Busy hosp. areas
67 Best of the best
70 Knee-highs, e.g.
72 Doesn't know for a fact, say
73 ___ buco
75 Secreted signal
76 El ___
77 Cricket rival of Harrow
79 Material once set afire and put in a catapult
80 Grasp, informally
81 Human, typically, diet-wise

by Andrew J. Ries

84 Announcement upon a grand arrival
85 Entertainment with camels, maybe
86 It sank after W.W. II
87 Go cold turkey
88 Said
90 Goaltender Dominik in the Hockey Hall of Fame
91 Wrinkle-free, say
92 Lincoln's place
96 Wild
98 Old movie dog
99 ___ Valley
100 Give a beating
102 Go forcefully (through)
103 1979 Roman Polanski film
104 Inc. relative
105 Win on "Hollywood Squares"
106 "I shall return," e.g.
107 Des Moines-to-Dubuque dir.
108 Add years
109 Sentence fragments: Abbr.

68

MAKING A FAST BUCK

ACROSS

1 Speedway brand
4 West Indies native
9 Bounds along
14 "Just a ___!"
17 Drain opening
19 Chip away at
20 Symbol of the National Audubon Society
21 Colorado tributary
22 Plot device in "The Shining" that has significance when spelled backward
23 Restaurant chain founded by the Raffel brothers (hence the name)
24 Elevator choice
25 Turns briefly?
26 Some Carnaval performances
28 Called from the cote
30 Telephotos, e.g.
32 Ancient Greek
34 Male that might be in a rut?
35 Stymies
37 Relative of a birch
38 College in Cedar Rapids, Iowa
39 Country singer Crystal
40 Screwy
43 Pitch
46 One of the Wayans brothers
50 Wine: Prefix
51 Christmas ___
52 Prince, e.g.
54 A, in Austria
55 Base supporting a statue
57 Branded baby carriers
61 Symbols on 10 state flags
63 They might be thrown around in a rodeo
65 Digitally endorse
66 Sleigh bell sounds
67 Terminate
68 "___ God" (psalm words)
69 Chemistry exam?
70 Skin art, informally
71 Descartes's conclusion
72 Clear
73 Yule sound?
75 ___ guerre
77 Range grp.
78 & 80 One of TV's Property Brothers
82 "Really!"
83 Spotted
84 Nicholas, e.g.
86 Give a ring?
88 Hallmark.com suggestion
90 Divan
92 "___ welcome!"
93 Cow poke?
94 Avoid a bogey, barely
97 Neighbor of a bishop: Abbr.
98 Souped-up cars
102 Mahershala ___, Oscar winner for "Moonlight"
103 One of the record industry's former Big Four
104 Carpenter's aid
106 Hypotheticals
107 "Just kidding!"
108 Airer of "Christmas in Rockefeller Center"
109 Sanctuary
111 "Hey ___" (1963 #1 hit)
113 Mobile home: Abbr.
114 Actress Audrey of "Amélie"
117 Animal on Scotland's coat of arms
119 Kind of cabinet
122 Written history
123 Who's depicted in this puzzle when the circled letters are connected from A to Z and back to A
124 Games of chance
125 Prison part
126 Sorts, as chicks
127 Downsize?

DOWN

1 Tears to smithereens
2 It's read from a scroll
3 Large column of smoke
4 Terminated
5 Opposite of dep.
6 Heists
7 Description of rustic life
8 Importune
9 It moves a cursor back
10 Body check?
11 Whiz kids
12 Want ad abbr.
13 Having streaks
14 W.W. II ordeal at Leningrad
15 Notably nonunionized workers
16 Mama of song
18 Decorates brilliantly
21 One of a dozen good things?
27 Friend
29 Oodles
31 Vulcan mind ___
33 Beginning to do well?
36 Kind of skirt
40 "Fanfare for the Common Man" composer
41 Hair straighteners
42 Licorice-flavored brew
44 Singer with a #1 hit about 123-Across
45 Feature depicted in the upper left of this puzzle
47 Hatmaker
48 Like van Gogh, in later life
49 Les ___, "WKRP in Cincinnati" news director
51 & 53 123-Across, in song
56 One of many in a Swiss Army knife
58 Letters on some Navy carriers
59 Infantry members, briefly
60 Alternative to JFK
62 1990s tennis great Huber
64 Align
66 First name at Woodstock
74 Political org. since 1854
76 Shout of approval
79 Three ___ Men
81 Didn't hedge one's bets
82 Starting point for an annual flight
83 ___ City (Baghdad suburb)
85 "In your dreams!"
87 Result of a sack on third and long, maybe
89 Bunks in barracks
91 "Brava!" elicitor
93 Punxsutawney prognosticator

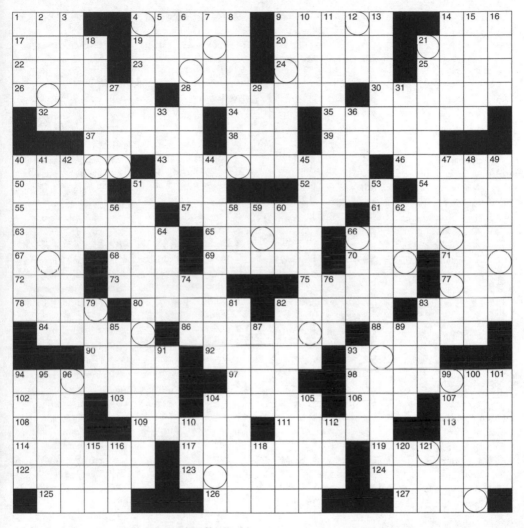

by Mary Lou Guizzo and Jeff Chen

ACROSS

1 Have
4 New Deal org.
7 Motley
13 "Dukes"
18 V.I.P. list
20 Lamborghini rival
21 Arctic people
22 Result of a French powdered drink shortage?
24 1959 Ritchie Valens hit, with "La"
25 Hook's right hand
26 Hägar the Horrible's hound
27 Short rows
29 Nincompoop
30 Secures at sea
32 Fig. checked during re-tire-ment?
33 Legends in the automotive world
35 List of things said by Siri?
38 1920s–'30s Yankees nickname
41 Deceive
42 Sights at charging stations
44 Thingamajig
45 Softhead
48 What an infielder might field a ball on
50 "Reckon so"
52 "Savvy?"
54 ___ Conference
55 Washington, D.C.?
59 Was beaten by
60 Neighbors of Egyptians
61 Attribute to, in a way
62 Three-foot 1980s sitcom character
65 Grammy winner ___ Elliott
66 Cobbler, at times
68 Cowboy Rogers
69 Giant
71 Not just focused
75 Butting heads
76 Struggling sci-fi writer's plea for recognition?
78 Blade runner?
81 Hip-hop's Shakur
82 Attend without a date
83 Country that Menorca is part of
85 If you have it, you might know what this answer is without reading the clue
86 Middle of a simile
88 Quenched
92 "Give me ___"
93 Some 1960s radicals
96 Treat that gives a glowing complexion?
98 Chap
100 Work as a branch manager?
102 Flag
103 Scott of "Happy Days"
104 Nasser's successor as Egypt's leader
107 "What's Opera, Doc?" antagonist
108 Film director ___ C. Kenton
111 Canon competitor
113 Weeklong Irish vacation?
116 Gross
117 Like some turns
118 Chose to take part
119 What if, informally
120 ___ performance
121 Book before Esther: Abbr.
122 Neuron's ends?

DOWN

1 "Wise" sorts
2 "Pow!"
3 Result of a haymaker, maybe
4 1/20 of a ton: Abbr.
5 Pure
6 Couple
7 Torn
8 Dadaist Jean
9 Wimbledon surface
10 Archaeological treasure trove
11 "Nessun dorma," for one
12 Drift
13 Statement made while crossing the fingers, maybe
14 Like the three men of the "Rub-a-dub-dub" nursery rhyme
15 One having trouble with basic arithmetic?
16 Neighbor of the talus
17 Much of a sports recap
19 Good hunting skill
20 Some Guinness Book records
23 Lamp polisher's surprise?
28 "Quién ___?"
31 Batch of Brownies?
32 Harass incessantly
34 Photog's bagful?
35 Feature of Devonshire cream
36 Article in Der Spiegel
37 "March comes in like ___ . . ."
39 Cottonmouth's warning
40 Targets in "Men in Black," informally
43 Stars
46 Childish retort
47 Indiana's state flower
49 Puts forth
51 Historic Mesopotamian city
53 Wand material in the Harry Potter books
56 Thick and green
57 Merchandise: Abbr.
58 Artificial silks
59 Grow feathers
61 Like the French sky
62 Colorful quartz
63 ___ position
64 Some loose dancing?
65 Godfather after being double-crossed?
67 Kyrgyz city
70 Panhandle state: Abbr.
72 Action in FanDuel and DraftKings
73 Close tightly
74 "King Lear" role
76 "The Last Days of Pompeii" heroine
77 ___ bin Laden
78 Legitimate business practices
79 Last Stuart queen
80 Kind of alphabet

by John Lampkin

82 Moo goo ___ pan
84 "Sh," "th" or "ou"
87 1974 C.I.A. spoof
89 Big name in test prep
90 Opposite side
91 Makes a meal of

94 Apple app for viewing reading material
95 Polish, e.g.
97 Green
98 Heeds
99 Eagerly accept
101 County in New Mexico or Colorado

105 Court legend Arthur
106 Eldest member of an organization
107 Falco of "The Sopranos"
109 The Eagles' "___ Eyes"
110 Forever and ever

112 December 31: Abbr.
114 D.C.-based media giant
115 1st, 2nd, 3rd . . . ___

ACROSS

1 Move, as a plant
6 Tiny bit
11 Brit. pounds
14 Morales of "NYPD Blue"
18 Part of the Kingdom of the Netherlands
19 Grammy-nominated song by Alanis Morissette
20 Result of a successful audition
22 Yam, e.g.
23 Found on this page
24 "Sure, that's fine"
25 Instant
27 Like a parental lecture
28 Yellow ___
29 William who invented the steam shovel
30 "Fifty Shades of Grey" woman
31 Boat in "Jaws"
33 Sunni or Shia
35 Part of a dealership
37 In bits
42 Means of achieving things
44 Like many patches
45 Nebraska county or who once lived there
46 Kind of pie
48 Dealer in futures?
49 Exact
51 Fill ___ (be of use)
52 Green topper
54 Lose that loving feeling
56 Sylvia of jazz
57 "You nailed it!"
60 Puffed ___
61 Sneaky
62 Diner offering
66 However, briefly
69 False god
70 Not believable
71 One standing on deck
72 Art type
78 "Ben-Hur" studio of 1925 and 1959
79 Be observant of Lent, say
80 Battery ends
81 Concert pieces
83 # # #
86 Attention-grabbing
87 Try to grab
89 Pinkish bloom
90 Like 0's and 1's in binary numbers
93 Tent alternative
94 Home paper
95 Learn (of)
96 Go (for)
97 Part of a Latin 101 conjugation
100 Beverage that may be served au lait
103 Fissure
105 Card sharp's deception
108 When one might get a pep talk
110 "Red" Holy Roman emperor
111 Farm stores
112 Whole
113 "Taken" star
114 Art
115 When H-Hour happens
116 Quash
117 Screen Bean
118 California's ___ Museum

DOWN

1 ___ Rizzo of film
2 Blow
3 "No. 1" person
4 Acts of deference
5 Agreeably biting
6 Tom's partner
7 Corn syrup brand
8 Repetitive, as in criticism
9 Lush locales?
10 Roman scourge
11 ___-free
12 Assumes
13 Reproving looks
14 Go out
15 "___ you!"
16 Zenith
17 Company with a lot of manual work?
19 Something to pay through?
21 Successor to Holder as attorney general
26 Capital on the Willamette River
27 Workshop power tool
32 Foe in "Rocky"
34 Military strength
36 Said "mea culpa," say
38 Inner tubes, topologically
39 Italian girl's name ending
40 Word with fire or trap
41 Email folder
42 Collect
43 Old records
44 Charge
47 Repeated film role for Skippy
49 Excessively theatrical
50 Some congratulations
53 Nickname
55 They're hard to see through
57 Hustles
58 Shield border, in heraldry
59 Figure often dressed in green
62 "Soldier of Love" singer, 2009
63 Boston's Liberty Tree, for one
64 Adorn, in old literature
65 Stone in Hollywood
66 Smallish London lodgings
67 "Big" star
68 Big, big, big
69 Hooked up with
71 Rub some sticks together, as at camp
72 Country once known as French Sudan
73 Aware of
74 Delete
75 Curfew for a vampire
76 "Maybe . . ."
77 Inspiration for Isaac Newton
79 Tom Wolfe's "___ in Full"
82 Tend to
84 Intercedes
85 Shrubby wasteland
87 Supporting players
88 They vary with circulation
91 Right-hand page

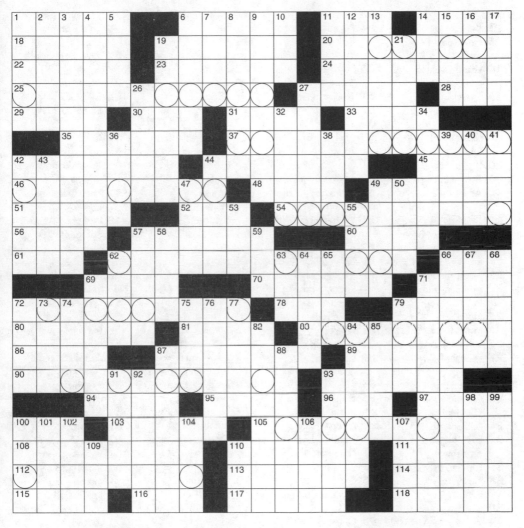

by Matt Ginsberg

HELP WANTED

ACROSS

1 Debate, with "out"
5 How some TV series are sold
10 Use a witching rod
15 Travel with Sinbad, say
19 "Come ___ me, all ye that labor . . ."
20 Port of Puerto Rico
21 Tony-winning Andrew Lloyd Webber musical
22 Children's TV character who refers to himself in the third person
23 Need rural real estate investor to . . .
25 Need retail marketer to . . .
27 Where to begin
28 Peaceful
30 Kind of oil
31 Projector unit
33 Characters in "The Hobbit"
34 Militant grp. in a 1994 peace agreement
35 Chrome alternative
38 Newspaper section, for short
40 See 44-Across
44 What a 40-Across produces in the summer
45 Need cocktail waitress to . . .
49 Photocopier option: Abbr.
50 Constellation between Perseus and Pisces
52 Starting or ending point for a commuter: Abbr.

53 Luxury rental
54 Polo of "Meet the Parents"
55 Bit of sauce
56 Need bakery assistant to . . .
61 Track runner
62 "Get lost!"
64 Vicious
65 Biblical mount that can be seen from three countries
66 Stockpiles
68 Be that as it may
69 Acting monarch
71 What a chair might provide
73 Sudden twist
76 Entered uninvited
79 Maguire of "The Great Gatsby"
80 Need cruise ship band to . . .
82 Prefix with -graph
83 Take orders, say
84 Complain, complain, complain
85 ___ Aviv
86 Something rolling in the dough?
88 Letters of interest
89 Need orchestra conductor to . . .
94 ___ gear
95 Chianti, e.g.
97 Stage of the Tour de France
98 Onetime "Be all you can be" sloganeer
100 Onetime
101 Benjamin of "Law & Order"
103 Diamond protectors
105 Crude house
108 Go over again
110 They can leave scars
114 Need blackjack dealer to . . .

116 Need magician to . . .
118 Member of the 3,000-hit club, informally
119 P. C. Wren's "Beau ___"
120 Classical Greek theater
121 Like certain educational publishing
122 Musical pitch?
123 Board
124 Homage with humor
125 Flow slowly

DOWN

1 O'Hare and Dallas/Fort Worth
2 "What are you, some kind of ___?"
3 Bad eye sight
4 Tabletop cooker
5 Budding comic's opportunity
6 Free, as a bank account
7 Part of a forensic database
8 Obsolescent tape holders
9 Mark off?
10 One side in football
11 Like ones welcomed to the fold?
12 Foxiness
13 The Rams, on scoreboards
14 Erodes
15 It takes two to do this
16 Bit of marine life
17 Man of Allah
18 Less than a full run
24 The "xx" of xx:yy
26 ___ welcome

29 Former first name on the Supreme Court
32 "Warrior" actor Nick
35 Lowercase
36 Cliffside home
37 Need stunt pilot to . . .
39 Calf cries
40 Body opening?
41 Need control tower operator to . . .
42 Parts of Roman homes
43 Part of a forensic database
46 Pumped
47 Coal-mining waste
48 One who walks on the wild side?
51 "Easy there"
54 Part of L.G.B.T., informally
57 Magical start?
58 Actress Salma of "Grown Ups"
59 Wedding or concert, e.g.
60 Overhear
61 Accord
63 Pioneer in Impressionism
65 Indian tourist mecca
67 Promised
70 Source of a gut reaction?
71 Like feudal states, often
72 Freak out
74 Tkt. stub, e.g.
75 Highly emotional, in dated lingo
77 ___ salts
78 Jingle, e.g.
80 Campaign
81 Under attack
84 Easter treat
87 Marks taken off?

by Melanie Miller

89 Muck
90 Listen
91 Suffix with cigar
92 Bull run target
93 It's up in the air
96 Is unsatisfactory
99 Lovers' row
101 Port in western France
102 Page opposite verso
104 D'Artagnan mentor
105 Deep-bodied herring
106 Fill a position
107 Half of a two-volume encyclopedia, say
109 Dullard
111 ___ marker
112 Feel pity (for)
113 Leave undone
115 When doubled, a Ramone
117 Social

ACROSS

1 Engaged
10 Jacques who was "alive and well and living in Paris"
14 Island near the Mariana Trench
18 Pueblo Indian rite
19 Places for light gatherings?
21 Mario who played Enrico Caruso
22 *Pricey wrap
23 *Triple Crown winner who himself sired a Kentucky Derby winner
25 When repeated, an aerobics class cry
26 ___ bar
28 New faces
29 Rejecting higher authority?
33 Dodger manager with two World Series rings
34 Shout from the crow's-nest
37 Seminary subj.
38 Giggle syllable
40 Prefix with state
41 "___ seen enough!"
42 "Skedaddle!"
44 Impressed with
47 Village V.I.P.
51 *Carpenter's tool with a cord
54 "Dogs"
56 Single
57 Black rock
58 White-tailed raptor
60 Dad-blasted
62 Fed. property agency
63 Black ___
65 Half a Beatles title
67 Like the telecast of the 1954 Rose Bowl parade, notably

69 ___ Macmillan, 1950s–'60s British P.M.
72 Plants above the timberline
75 Skin conditioners
76 Ungainly
78 Identified
80 Drink with spices
81 On the ___ (at large)
82 ___ Hall, shortest Harlem Globetrotter
85 Irving protagonist
87 Pit bull biter
90 Dirt pie ingredient
92 ___ shake
94 *Deep Throat's identity
96 Rogen and Green
98 "Show me" type
100 Hunger
101 Budgetary excess
102 N., E., W. and S.
104 Thumbs-up vote
105 Lean-___
107 With understatedness
109 "Two New Sciences" author
112 Hedge clippings, grass cuttings, etc.
115 Ideal setting for a fan
117 Features of green rooms
118 "That's the way the cookie crumbles"
122 *Start a construction project
124 Back then . . . or a hint to the ends of the answers to the starred clues
127 Save up
128 Bone: Prefix
129 Giovanni, in "Don Giovanni"

130 Russo of "30-Down"
131 Morales of "La Bamba"
132 Very cold

DOWN

1 Ones holding hands?
2 French act
3 Comment before "Be that way!"
4 Stamping need
5 Some campaign purchases
6 D.C. ballplayer
7 It's worth 100 smackers
8 Patisserie buy
9 Sunken, as eyes
10 Low voices
11 It may be lined with mailboxes: Abbr.
12 Different rooms in a museum, maybe
13 *Smidgen
14 Cooker with a dial
15 Having no head
16 Luxury Hyundai
17 Gaping things
20 Relative of the Contour Plus
21 Poe poem
24 Like "Annabel Lee" among all Poe poems
27 See 89-Down
30 Wielder of the hammer Mjölnir
31 Lower chamber
32 Some stadium noise
34 Slimming surgery, informally
35 River through Bristol
36 *Tom Seaver, e.g.
39 At 3,000 feet above sea level, the highest provincial capital in Italy

43 ___ cake (dim sum staple)
45 *Dr. Seuss's genre
46 Mysterious sighting
48 *Challenge for a right-handed golfer
49 Newsman David
50 Brings up
52 John McCain, for one
53 Sports org. with the teams Sun and Sky
55 In the mail
59 Wing
61 Household brand name with a lowercase first letter
64 Crib strip
66 Google Wallet alternative
68 Kind of switch
69 They hover over some icons
70 In the know
71 Release to the public, informally
73 Pad thai ingredient
74 Coal locale
77 Actress Diana nicknamed the "Blonde Bombshell"
79 Strong sideless wagon
83 *W.W. II propagandist
84 Suit to ___
86 Directive in some automated messages
88 Holy Land line
89 With 27-Down, firm figure: Abbr.
91 "Stop your nonsense!"
93 Funny-car fuel, informally
95 Danish king who conquered England

by Don Gagliardo and Zhouqin Burnikel

97 Boondocks
99 Catch in the North Atlantic
103 Tough going
106 Al Jolson standard
108 "Aw, c'mon"
109 Songstress Eydie
110 "You're ___ One, Mr. Grinch"
111 Köln coin
113 "Same here"
114 Stars, at the Forum
115 Letter-shaped girder
116 Sounds of scolding
119 Put on board
120 Grieg's "___ Death"
121 Violins and violas: Abbr.
123 U.S.'s largest labor union, in brief
125 Oscar-nominated Joaquin Phoenix film
126 "The Two Towers" denizen

ACROSS

1 Paintball sound
6 City between Turin and Genoa
10 Padlocks lock them
15 Nothing, slangily
19 Spot check?
20 ___ Air
21 Egg producer
22 Drivetrain part
23 Alternative band that sounds like every other alternative band?
25 #1 Billboard artist that's an anagram of 23-Across
27 Check time
28 "Wicked Game" singer Chris
30 Showroom display
31 Documentarian Morris
33 They're new to the family
36 Mystery writer Deighton
38 Deli order
41 Like some drinks and emotions
43 "Nonsense!"
44 Full of frills
45 Invitation for musical plagiarism?
48 #1 Billboard artist that's an anagram of 45-Across
51 Like first editions, often
52 Quirk
54 Cell in a 21-Across
55 Frilly trim
57 Rebels' school
58 Remote possibility?
59 ". . . ___ other name would smell as sweet": Juliet
60 Cellar setup
62 Good deal

63 Carrier letters
66 Greeting to a conductor?
68 #1 Billboard artist that's an anagram of 66-Across
71 Till bill
72 Turn to mush
73 Acrylic container
76 Welcome to the fold?
77 Tide type
79 Enormous
80 Coffeehouse entertainers
82 Excite
85 Oil change, brake test, etc.
86 Performance often in Italian
87 Friendly music genre?
89 #1 Billboard artist that's an anagram of 87-Across
93 Spellbound
94 It's often set at night
96 Kimchi is its national dish
97 See 124-Across
98 Botanist Gray
99 Alternative to an Oscar
102 Pepper ___, Iron Man's love interest
104 "Family Guy" baby
106 Mythical weeper
108 Sea creatures with beaks
112 Part of a hospital playlist?
115 #1 Billboard artist that's an anagram of 112-Across
117 Play thing
118 Emmy-nominated FX comedy
119 "Ohhh, O.K."
120 Ready for use

121 Count (on)
122 Punch in
123 Banks with a lot of money
124 With 97-Across, back some time

DOWN

1 Make a mistake
2 Enrique ___ Nieto, Mexican president elected in 2012
3 Word after leading or cleaning
4 Digression
5 Private sector?
6 Hurt
7 Caution in a movie review, maybe
8 Whips
9 "___ are like beards; men do not have them until they grow up": Voltaire
10 Face wear for Jason in "Friday the 13th" movies
11 Old greeting
12 ___ acetosella (KHO$_2$O$_4$)
13 Human, for one
14 Church council
15 Light blue-green
16 Armpit-related
17 Like military hairstyles
18 Actor Jeong of "The Hangover"
24 Saint with an alphabet named after him
26 Newsroom workers, for short
29 Twenty something?
32 California school attended by Obama, familiarly

34 N.L. East team, to fans
35 New Year's Eve ex-host Carson
37 Org. with a closing bell
38 Triumphant cry
39 Together
40 "Heavens!"
42 Dough used for tortillas, maybe
44 Aristotle's school
46 "Whatever"
47 Head case?
49 "Et tu?"
50 Bunkhouse feature
53 Karaoke need
56 Maa in "Babe," e.g.
57 Leading
58 Turn (into)
61 Jacob's name after he wrestled with the angel
62 Makeshift weapon in a murder mystery
64 Epitome of desolateness
65 Making known
67 ___ coeptis (phrase on the back of a dollar bill)
68 Hooded jacket
69 Nascar sponsor
70 Tries
73 Figure in a Yogi Bear cartoon
74 "The Walking Dead" channel
75 Computer that sounds like a theater when pluralized
78 That: Sp.
79 Noisy talker
81 Virginia's ___ Hill Academy, alma mater of 20+ N.B.A. players

by Joel Fagliano

82 Taj Mahal city
83 Comfort
84 Keeping the beat?
85 ___ wars
88 Persists, as a forest fire
90 Spanish gold
91 Reveal
92 Lose face

95 Hosp. procedure
99 Winter Olympics powerhouse: Abbr.
100 Congressional divider
101 Loaf
103 Something skipped

105 Spot
107 Ornate
109 Bone: Prefix
110 Hit a high point
111 AT&T and Comcast, for short
112 "Science Friday" airer

113 Unseen winning card, in poker lingo
114 Never, in Berlin
116 Limitless quantity

ACROSS

1 Fake blood, e.g.
4 Many establishments on Paris's Boulevard Saint-Germain
9 Enjoy thoroughly
14 Ex-Mrs. Trump
19 Person behind a strike?
20 Cause of a 2014 epidemic
21 Word with light or horse
22 Figure in Jewish folklore
23 One time around
24 "He who hesitates is lost, but . . ."
27 Beat around the bush?
29 Mathematician Fibonacci
30 N.B.A. team once coached by Larry Bird
31 DVR lineup
33 Rich cake
34 Brown who wrote "The Diana Chronicles"
35 Handles
37 Silliness
41 Half-and-half, maybe
42 Park place
46 __ game
49 Kind of arch
50 Frequent subject of fibbing
51 __ Soetoro, stepfather of Barack Obama
52 Longest river entirely within Switzerland
53 Group of Coyotes, for short
54 Name on a toy truck
56 To the point
57 Empty stomach sound
59 __ limit (sign at the edge of town)
60 Sound
62 Crumbly cheeses
64 Arctic lights
66 Regimented resort
68 See 73-Across
69 Locale of the 15-Down Eyjafjallajökull
70 Decked out
71 Like pop-ups
73 Check for 68-Across
74 2006 Pixar film
75 Heavy drinker, in slang
77 Out of the barn, say
79 ESPNU covers it
82 Celestial altar
83 Gladly, old-style
84 Steer closer to the wind
85 It borders the N. Atl.
86 Prison escape path, maybe
88 A sharp equivalent
89 Sing the praises of
91 Unused
92 Give the right
94 Second chances for students
96 Head of an Inn?
97 Caliban in "The Tempest," e.g.
102 Pooh-bah
103 Get into
106 Part of a dominatrix's outfit
108 Babe in the woods
111 "You can't judge a book by its cover, but . . ."
114 "__ no idea"
115 Blazing stars
116 Pairs are seen in it
117 Emulate Isocrates
118 Birth certificate datum
119 Paradises
120 Chemical __
121 Trig functions
122 Boom source

DOWN

1 [Um, this can't be good]
2 All-Star second baseman Infante
3 "Birds of a feather flock together, but . . ."
4 Solo features of six Bach suites
5 Blood type system
6 "Great minds think alike, but . . ."
7 Actress Sommer
8 Clog
9 Till now
10 Left at sea
11 Like some salsa
12 Stackable dessert item
13 2004 musical biopic for which the star won Best Actor
14 Pet in the comic strip "FoxTrot"
15 See 69-Across
16 "Helm __!" (captain's cry)
17 Within view
18 Ratchets (up)
25 Ambient music innovator Brian
26 Put forward
28 "Huh?"
32 It's a trap
34 "Slow and steady wins the race, but . . ."
35 Shanghai nursemaid
36 Winter Olympics sport
38 "Knowledge is power, but . . ."
39 1943 conference site
40 Checked online reviews of, modern-style
43 Here/there connector
44 One on staff?
45 Sphere of civilian activity during war
46 Trifle
47 Cousin of Sven
48 Michael Sheen's character in "Twilight"
55 Mystical Muslims
56 Broadcast
58 Ill-gotten gains
59 Port on the Panama Canal
61 D.C.'s __ Constitution Hall
63 Personal quirk
65 "Born to Die" singer Lana Del __
66 Pretense
67 Galloping
71 Part of SEATO
72 Billet-__
76 Gal __
78 More than once in a while
80 You may have a great one in your family
81 Part of M.F.A.
87 Like some mountain guides

by Lee Taylor

88 Oh-so-bored
90 "Glee" star ___ Michele
91 It may mean "Pet me!"
93 Comedian Daniel and musician Peter
95 Broadsides, informally
97 Rooting interest
98 Compare
99 Not nodding
100 Nov. 11 honoree
101 Community spirit
103 Red in the face?
104 Lummox
105 Inlet
106 Beijing problem
107 Hatcher of "Desperate Housewives"
109 Holiday lead-ins
110 Emoji holder
112 Place for a "me day"
113 Gorged on

DOUBLE DIGITS

ACROSS

1 One raised in church?
6 Beltmaking tool
9 Emailer's need: Abbr.
13 Hand-made percussion
18 Assembly line track
20 Word of parting
21 Ability to borrow
22 On edge
23 Something saved for a rainy day
24 Caribbean capital
25 Nog topper
26 Vessel with a spout
28 Rallying cry during the Polk administration
30 1957 film set almost entirely in one room
33 Unimportant flaw
34 Payment promise
35 Master
38 Lessen the value of, maybe
39 Changes to the bill?
42 Infiltrator
43 Hawk on the street
45 Blotto
47 Fab Four surname
48 Becomes one
49 "Young Frankenstein" assistant
50 Degrees of magnitude?
53 "Kinsey" star, 2004
55 Early manufacturer of home computers
57 Court figure Williams
60 Return date?
63 Ted with a guitar
65 Moving day need
66 0%, in a way
67 Economic org. in D.C.
69 Italian religious figure
70 Game that people rarely agree to play twice
72 Zach's old flame in "A Chorus Line"
74 First name in Objectivism
75 Historical topics
77 Make a point
78 Byproduct in petroleum refining
79 Alejandro G. Iñárritu film with the tagline "How much does life weigh?"
81 Hunts, as a house cat might
83 Glass raiser's word
84 "__ Arrives" (1967 soul album)
87 It "teaches you when to be silent," per Disraeli
88 Wee bit
89 Growing businesses
92 Lively comedies
95 Nomadic conqueror
97 Dealer's customer
98 Trust eroders
99 Kid-lit's Eloise, e.g.
102 Parts of many passwords: Abbr.
104 Imbecile
105 Ornament shape
106 "Oh wow!"
107 2004 rom-com in which a middle schooler is transformed into an adult overnight
110 Contiguous U.S. states, colloquially
114 Org. with conferences
115 At the back
119 Bee, e.g.
120 Cry of dismay
122 Routine-bound
124 Beau Brummell accessories
125 __ Rabbit
126 Car chase sounds
127 Ability
128 Morales of "NYPD Blue"
129 Hieroglyphic symbol
130 L.P.G.A. garment

DOWN

1 "I'm __ it!" (hick's nix)
2 Doozy
3 Use a lance
4 1960s–'70s police drama
5 Make another movie together, say
6 Roadside assistance org.
7 Harder to fool
8 "Inside __ Davis" (Coen brothers film)
9 Adams, Monroe or Grant
10 The Company, in govt. lingo
11 1960s buddy cop sitcom, informally
12 Pop group?
13 Pottery, e.g.
14 Israelite tribe progenitor
15 Slow movements
16 Simple camera's aperture
17 Square figures
19 Pertaining to a sovereign
21 Rock or Pine
27 Broody rock genre
29 Not working, say
31 Film set assistants
32 Stocking fabric
35 Colombia's national airline
36 Re/Max competitor
37 Instantly likable
40 "The Brady Bunch" kid
41 Resource in the board game The Settlers of Catan
42 Tax-exempt bond, for short
44 Has the temerity
46 Rock band from Athens, Ga.
48 Modern rock and news/talk, for two
51 Bit of rain
52 Title IX target
54 Liven (up)
56 Visibly moved
58 Maker of candy wafers
59 Invite to dinner, say
61 Singer with the band Cult Jam
62 Figurative duration of short-lived fame
64 Mel who co-wrote "The Christmas Song"
66 Filibuster feature
68 Birdseed containers
71 Minor predecessor?
73 SeaWorld performer
76 On both sides of
80 Colorado State's team
82 Deeply offended
85 Selling well
86 First name of Dickens's Little Dorrit
89 Clues to a sunken ship's location
90 Diving helmet attachment
91 Hitchcock film with a nameless heroine

by Patrick Berry

93 Rating first used for "Red Dawn"
94 Italian gentlemen
96 Relentless faultfinder
99 Religious outfits
100 "Arabian Nights" predator

101 Serve as a go-between
103 Siesta sounds
106 Bearded ones
108 Drew in books
109 NBC sitcom set at NBC
111 Symbol of England

112 Spa wear
113 Eddie Murphy's big-screen debut
116 West End district
117 Maintain
118 For fear that
121 Sponsor of some PBS programs

123 Word often shortened to its middle letter in texts

ACROSS

1 "We must go"
8 Spiral-horned grazer
12 Santa ___, Calif.
17 View with disapproval
18 Quills
20 Email folder
21 COMPLETE PLAN
24 Brewer's supply
25 Round figures
26 Where Hecuba was queen
27 Certain monthly bill: Abbr.
28 "___ & the Women" (2000 Gere film)
29 Kind of paper
31 Many
34 GRAY FOX
39 It may help you get a grip on things
41 Skips
42 Subduer, of a sort
46 Like dams
47 Certain absentee
49 Lady of la casa
50 BIG DEALS
54 What may unfold in Japanese theater?
55 Place for plates
56 Roly-poly
57 Annoy no end
59 Easter sight
61 Abbr. preceding a year
62 Grp. of women drivers
65 Whole slew
67 Sweeties
69 Like the book "Zhuangzi"
71 "No argument here"
73 "A deadline every minute" sloganeer
75 NEWSPAPER ROUTE
80 Series of lows
82 Saws
83 It signals a lack of support
84 Dish name
85 Door ___
86 Says "You no-good son of a . . . ," say
88 MORE UNITED
92 42-Across, for example
95 School boards
96 Make a selection
99 Letters in a return address?
100 Pause
103 Star trek figures?
104 Harmoniously
106 GO FIGURE
112 Houses named after an old house
113 Not dead, as a football
114 One in business?
115 Malibu ___ ("The Simpsons" parody doll)
116 Top
117 Spoke impulsively

DOWN

1 Borderline
2 Heard
3 Echolocation device
4 Come down wrong, maybe
5 Part of V.M.I.: Abbr.
6 ___-jongg
7 Greek vowel
8 Joshes
9 ___ Chicago Grill
10 Skillful
11 1991 breakup newsmaker
12 A wink or a nod, maybe
13 Ford sold during Ford's presidency
14 Touches
15 Loggers' jamboree
16 1985 instrumental hit named after the main character in "Beverly Hills Cop"
18 Something an "o" lacks
19 ___ Sandoval, 2012 World Series M.V.P.
20 Words to someone who 8-Down
22 Skill sharpener
23 Pop group
29 Part of some showers
30 Sports org. whose first champ was the Pittsburgh Pipers
32 Bears witness
33 Cannon of "Heaven Can Wait"
35 Neuter
36 Certain Kindle download, for short
37 Hampers, say
38 Grammy-winning James
39 Wind or fire, maybe, but not earth
40 "Stupid me"
43 Lightweight protective vest
44 Progressive ___
45 Led . . . or bled
46 Three-pointers: Abbr.
47 Carpentry fastener
48 A waste of good food?
49 Domain of some international law
51 Stressful work?
52 Many figures in the "Doctor Who" universe, for short
53 Something to lead with?
58 Players eligible to suit up
60 In need of coffee, maybe
62 Sprinter's assignment
63 Sci-fi vehicles
64 "Beat it!"
66 Airs from pairs
68 Item in a mechanic's back pocket
69 Nutrition bar introduced in the 1960s
70 Figures after a decimal
72 Ethnic ending
73 One speaking "out"?
74 "Al Aaraaf" writer
76 [Gross!]
77 PC menu heading
78 Confusion
79 Mall bag
81 Monopoly token replaced in 2013
85 Board
86 Recurring element

by Joe DiPietro

87 Sport-___
89 Dough that's been raised overseas?
90 De la Garza of "Law & Order"
91 Pestering, in a way
92 Sorts (out)
93 Steelhead, e.g.
94 Old F.D.A. guideline
97 Identify someone in a lineup, say
98 Conservative I.R.A. asset
101 Get worse
102 Pitch
104 Rights org.
105 Sooner city
107 Cozy footwear, informally
108 Food item dipped in ketchup
109 Largest New Deal agcy.
110 Kind of port
111 No score

Put a Lid on It!

ACROSS

1 Just
5 Many lines of code
8 Legitimate
13 Demolish
17 You can learn something by this
18 Portrait overlooking Tiananmen Square
19 23-Across topper
20 One getting a tax write-off, maybe
21 Filer's concern
23 Fictional archaeologist
25 28-Across topper
26 Indigo plants
27 Kramer's first name on "Seinfeld"
28 Famed frontierswoman
30 Hip-hop name modifier
31 Publishing mogul, for short
32 Toughens, as metal
33 Gain
34 40-Across topper
39 Post-boomer group
40 Subject of "Guerrillero Heroico"
42 Three-time Nobel Prize-winning organization
47 Al Bundy or Phil Dunphy
49 Nixing phrase on movie night
50 Arctic jackets
51 Shoplift, in slang
52 Site of a miracle in Daniel 3
53 They pop up in the morning
54 58-Across topper
55 ___ breve
57 Shipmate
58 Leader of the Free French
64 Quick shot?
67 Jack who ran for vice president in 1996
68 Chits
69 Modern-day hieroglyph
73 South American rodents
76 Bugs, e.g.
78 Contents of a spreadsheet
80 83-Across topper
81 Arctic masses
82 Starts of some one-twos
83 He helped move a piano in "The Music Box"
85 Violinist Leopold
86 Like Mandarin or Cantonese
87 Pinch
88 95-Across topper
91 Loan source for a mom-and-pop store: Abbr.
94 Finish on a canvas?
95 Star of "Sherlock Jr." and "Steamboat Bill Jr."
97 102-Across topper
100 Giving goose bumps, say
101 City about which Gertrude Stein said "There is no there there"
102 Italian pitchman of note
105 Something cooks put stock in
106 Catches a wave
107 More indie, say
108 Absorbed
109 Queen of Jordan
110 Ancient hieroglyph
111 Sends to oblivion
112 Co. that originated Dungeons & Dragons
113 Ballpark amts.

DOWN

1 Otto who worked on the Manhattan Project
2 Powerful bloodlines?
3 Word after in and of
4 Bit of cowboy gear
5 "Been better, been worse"
6 Quality of voices in the distance
7 Swillbelly
8 Poison compounds produced by snakes
9 Confuse
10 Mom on "Family Guy"
11 Journalist Flatow
12 Getting down, so to speak
13 Leeway
14 ___ Christi
15 Actress Kravitz of "Mad Max: Fury Road"
16 Triage locales, for short
19 Like answers on "Who Wants to Be a Millionaire"
20 Some club hires
22 West Point inits.
24 Verizon purchase of 2015
26 Title character in a Sophocles play
29 Desires
30 Perjured oneself
33 "Isn't he great!"
34 Drink that's the subject of several rules in the Code of Hammurabi
35 Still
36 Approached quickly
37 Author Jong
38 "Long ball"
40 Investment instruments, for short
41 Routine
42 Pioneering Arctic explorer John
43 Like the 13 Colonies: Abbr.
44 Barker
45 Pursuer of Capt. Hook
46 Spate
47 Twirlers
48 Invalidating
51 "Out of my way!"
52 ___ bug
54 Continental carrier
56 Velázquez's "___ Meninas"
59 Director Kurosawa
60 Like some tel. nos.
61 Eternities
62 Baltic native
63 Key with four sharps: Abbr.
64 Coors competitor
65 Billy Joel's "___ Extremes"
66 Wes of PBS's "History Detectives"
70 Spanish she-bear
71 One of the Bushes
72 Post-___
74 It parallels a radius
75 Opposite of a poker face
77 Website necessity
78 A long-established history

by Jason Mueller and Jeff Chen

79 Literature Nobelist J. M. Coetzee, by birth
81 Gusto
82 Bo's cousin on "The Dukes of Hazzard"
84 Discordant, to some
85 Museo contents
88 Mashes into a pulp
89 Basketry material
90 Cartoon cries
91 Actor John of "Full House"
92 Bit of wit
93 Angström or Celsius
94 Your, in Siena
95 Darken
96 Solo
97 Hatcher who was a Bond girl
98 Slays, informally
99 Ones going for hikes, for short?
100 As a result
102 CBS show with a 15-year run ending in 2015
103 Nucleus
104 Kerfuffle
105 Cool dude

Note: When this puzzle is completed, 12 squares will be filled with a certain keyboard symbol—which will have a different signification in the Across answers than it does in the Downs.

ACROSS

1 "I Am Not ___" (1975 show business autobiography)
6 "Shoot, shoot, shoot"
12 Cassio's jealous lover in "Othello"
18 Charge
20 Got up again
21 Comes to fruition
22 "Psst! Come hide with me!"
23 Come closer to catching
24 Takes out, as some beer bottles
25 First in a race?
26 Colt, e.g.
27 Ones doing a decent job in the Bible?
29 Magical phrase in an old tale
32 "Shoot!"
34 Takes apart
37 Drink at un café
38 Amt. often measured in ozs.
40 Drink at un café
41 Not as far from
43 LeBron James or Kevin Durant
46 One trillionth: Prefix
47 Welcome site?
48 When some tasks must be done
50 Schwarzenegger film catchphrase
52 Amazon's industry
55 Person of the hour
57 Still
58 Comment after a betrayal
61 Pen
63 Go on foot
64 Link between two names
66 Large goblet
71 Where batters eventually make their way to plates?
74 Catchphrase for one of the Avengers
77 Gap in a manuscript
81 Like some storefronts
83 Farmer, in the spring
84 Repeated bird call?
86 Is unable to
89 Bygone record co.
90 Site of the "crown of palaces"
91 Multicar accidents
93 Travel over seas?
96 N.Y.C. museum, with "the"
97 Honeymooners' site
98 GPS calculation
100 What the ruthless show
101 Author ___-René Lesage
103 What the ring in "The Lord of the Rings" is called
107 Nepalis live in them
109 Hebrew letter before samekh
110 75- and 80-Down, e.g.: Abbr.
112 Tote
113 Google browser
115 Steamy
118 Place
119 Wrinkle preventer, of sorts
120 Beezus's sister, in children's literature
121 Ones making an effort
122 Contraction with two apostrophes
123 Something matzo lacks

DOWN

1 ___ Lanka
2 "Let us spray," e.g.
3 It works for workers, in brief
4 Money, in modern slang
5 Something that may have bad keys
6 Church keys?
7 Leader of a procession
8 ___ War, "The Charge of the Light Brigade" event
9 Swanson on "Parks and Recreation"
10 Ol' red, white and blue's land
11 Material sometimes sold ripped
12 Scourge
13 Recite
14 "What ___!" (cry after some spectacular goalie play)
15 What zero bars means on a cellphone
16 Tools for people picking pockets?
17 @@@
19 Paint type
21 Soda can feature
28 Like a softball interview vis-à-vis a grilling
30 Guessed nos.
31 Assistant number cruncher
33 Art critic, stereotypically
34 Not seemly
35 More nifty
36 "Hakuna ___" ("The Lion King" song)
39 Rings on doors
42 Site of the U.S.'s only royal palace
44 Go on
45 Host
46 Course standard
49 Kettle's accuser
51 Groups that never get started
53 "Lord, is ___?"
54 Wolfish
56 Teachers' grp.
59 C equivalents
60 Royale carmaker of old
62 "Gross"
65 "So you admit it!"
67 Language in Southeast Asia
68 "Cross my heart and hope to die"
69 One seeking the philosopher's stone
70 How one person might resemble another
72 Revolutionary thinker?
73 Feeling the effects of a workout
75 L.A. Institution
76 Bound
77 Wool source
78 Pasta variety
79 Conviction . . . or what's almost required for a conviction
80 The Wahoos of the A.C.C.
82 Romanian currency
85 ___ rate (tax amount per $1,000)

by Tom McCoy

87 iPod model
88 Kind of leg
92 Dictation takers
94 "Git!"
95 Be a gentleman to at the end of a date, say

97 Where many shots are taken
99 Shrewdness
102 "Things are bound to go my way soon"
104 Presidential perk until 1977

105 "That's nothing"
106 Not reacting
108 Muscles worked by pull-ups, briefly
111 Greek portico
112 1940s prez
114 Genetic stuff

116 Stand-___
117 Monopoly token that replaced the iron in 2013

ACROSS

1 Bye at Wimbledon
5 Bonnie who sang "Nick of Time"
10 Needle holder
13 Pop star with the fragrance Miami Glow
16 Scientist Pavlov
17 Move unsteadily
18 Ike's charge during W.W. II
19 What King was king of
21 *Shrink who's always changing his diagnosis?
24 Piece in early Indian chess sets
25 Grasp
26 **What ballet patrons dine on?
28 One side of a childish debate . . . or a phonetic hint to the answers to the four starred clues
30 Take care of
31 Lipton rival
32 30 Rock's location
34 Bend
37 Arias, typically
39 Aerosol sound
40 *Oregon State's mascot played by actress Arthur?
47 Festoon
50 Pick in class
51 Assuming it's even possible
53 Cross, with "off"
54 **A deal on Afro wigs?
60 Commercial lead-in to Balls or Caps
63 "Couldn't be"
64 Not so awesome
65 Court positions
66 In need of a cracker, perhaps
68 Listen to Christmas carolers?
72 Slipshod
73 Overlook
74 Multiple-choice options
75 Justice Kagan
77 Post-op locale
79 Cold War-era territory: Abbr.
80 *How actor Bill feels about houseguests?
86 Hershiser of the 1980s–'90s Dodgers
87 Cannabis ___ (marijuana)
88 Chicago suburb
92 Removes from a can?
95 **Find cake or Jell-O in the back of the fridge?
97 Hunger
98 Drawbridge locale
100 The Spartans of the N.C.A.A.
101 PBS benefactor
102 And other stuff
105 Misconstrue, as words
109 Other side of a childish debate . . . or a phonetic hint to the answers to the four double-starred clues
113 *Fall colors?
117 Talk down?
120 Yawnfest
121 **Question from El Al security?
123 Like lightning rounds
124 Tear-stained, e.g.
125 Investigate, as a cold case
126 Pianist Gilels
127 "Woo-hoo!"
128 Half of a classic Mad magazine feature
129 County of Salem, Mass.
130 High ___

DOWN

1 Small scrap
2 New Balance competitor
3 Employing strategy
4 Pyramid crosses
5 Rubbish
6 Cause of some impulsive behavior, for short
7 It might begin with a "What if . . . ?"
8 Beach walkers
9 Mere vestige
10 They may have you going the wrong way
11 Announcer's cry after a field goal
12 What knows the drill, for short?
13 It has a variety of locks and pins
14 Like buffalo meat vis-à-vis beef and pork
15 Vegas casino with the mascot Lucky the Leprechaun
17 Show piece
19 French cheese
20 Miss
22 ESPN's McEachern a.k.a. the Voice of Poker
23 Edible entry at a county fair
27 Social welfare grp. with a Peace Prize
29 Neighbor of a "~" key
32 30 Rock grp.
33 Pro's position
35 Check
36 Brunch spot
38 "Fire away!"
41 Dress at the altar
42 PC part of interest to audiophiles
43 Author Seton
44 Kick back
45 First name in long jumps
46 Open again, as a keg
48 Sounds of fall?
49 Odette's counterpart in "Swan Lake"
52 QB Tony
55 "Over my dead body!"
56 Prefix with realism
57 London jazz duo?
58 Sudden turns
59 Belgian river to the North Sea
60 Play for a fool
61 Restaurant chain founded by a celebrity chef
62 Febreze target
67 Goof
69 Greeting on el teléfono
70 Supercharges, with "up"
71 Get one's hands on some dough?
76 Alternative to Soave
78 Nominative, e.g.
81 Administrative worker on a ship
82 Smoke
83 Bank asset that's frozen?
84 Google ___
85 Rap shouts
89 Casino activity with numbered balls
90 Dander

by Jeremy Newton

91 Part of a flight plan, for short
92 Pig with pigtails
93 Body of science?
94 Kaplan course for H.S. students
96 Hwy. violation
97 Like bread dough and beer
99 Looney Tunes bird
103 Play the siren to
104 Chatted with, in a way
106 Emotionally distant
107 Arsenal
108 Aligns
110 Where capri pants stop
111 #2s at college
112 Inhumane types
114 Lumber mill equipment
115 Hover craft?
116 Brood
118 Film character who says "I'd just as soon kiss a Wookiee!"
119 Some pipe joints
122 King of old Rome

ACROSS

1 Get by
5 Draw ___ on
10 With 101-Across, screen icon
15 Co. that invented the floppy disk
18 Utah attraction for skiers
19 Certain graduate
20 Headquarters of Royal Dutch Shell, with "The"
21 Shellac finish?
22 Gladly, old-style
23 Tents and the like (2001–08)
26 Wraps
28 See 109-Across
29 Goes after
30 Brought (in)
31 One of two official Philippine languages, along with English
35 Flight figures, for short
36 "Case of the Ex" singer, 2000
37 1964 Charlie Chaplin book (1980–84)
41 Actress Green of "Casino Royale"
43 ___ column
45 All-inclusive, in edspeak
46 Epitome of easiness
47 Northeastern university where Carl Sagan taught
49 Egypt's Port ___
52 Soft wear, informally
54 Long stretch
55 Der ___ (Adenauer)
56 TV show since 10/11/75, eight of whose former stars appear in the circled squares in this puzzle
58 Show-off (1975–80)
62 Stockholders?
64 "Yikes!"
66 Quarter
67 Nashville inst.
68 Muff, e.g. (2005–13)
71 Dessert often topped with cream cheese (1990–93)
76 In the, in Italy
77 TV star who loved oats
79 Shirt style
80 Those girls, in French
81 Berlin standard (1990–96)
86 Spring business?
88 Ambush predators of the sea
89 Pharaoh ___
90 Padre's hermano
91 Slim and trim
93 Thing
95 Trucker's circuit: Abbr.
96 Redhead on kids' TV
99 How "You Make Me Feel" in a Van Morrison song
101 See 10-Across
102 With 120-Across, intro heard every week on 56-Across
107 First American carrier to show movies on flights
109 With 28-Across, letter opener
110 CH$_4$
111 Kitchen pad
114 Dispute
117 "___ thoughts?"
118 Ranger rival
120 See 102-Across
124 Champ's cry
125 Prefix with -centric
126 Taekwondo is its national sport
127 Makes a good impression?
128 El ___
129 Frequent target of ID thieves
130 Destructive 2012 hurricane
131 Latches, say
132 Zapper target

DOWN

1 Not so bright
2 Coat cut
3 15-time guest host of 56-Across
4 One way to get home (2000–06)
5 Cockeyed
6 1974 Best Actress for "Alice Doesn't Live Here Anymore"
7 911 respondent, for short
8 "Wheel of Fortune" buy
9 Gently sponges
10 1953 biblical movie
11 Dorm heads, briefly
12 Ottoman Empire title
13 Bird feeder fill
14 ___-skelter
15 Like the North Pole
16 English county that's home to Reading
17 Snafu
19 Animal without feet
24 Title girl in a 2002 Disney movie
25 "Cheerio"
27 Focus of urban renewal?
32 Some digital camera batteries
33 Soviet labor camp
34 Baseball's Hodges
37 John ___, greaser in "American Graffiti"
38 ___ law
39 Designer of the Florence Cathedral bell tower
40 Class
41 Digital money
42 Alessandro ___, scientist who discovered 110-Across
44 Abbr. of politeness
48 "You ___ worry"
50 Radio host Glass
51 Jeanne ___
53 Class
57 Subsidiary proposition
59 Cool
60 Does a high-wire act, e.g.
61 Centers
63 Cool
65 N.B.A. head coach Steve
69 More open to the outdoors
70 "Get ___!"
72 Find another spot, maybe
73 16-time guest host of 56-Across
74 ___ O'Hara, 2015 Tony winner for "The King and I"
75 German coal city, once
78 Bygone presidential inits.
81 Peer group member?
82 Countermeasures
83 Democratic presidential nominee before Kennedy
84 Shirt style

by David J. Kahn

85 Piece of cake in school
87 "___ we alone?"
92 11 follower
94 Colorful fish
97 "Makes me want seconds!"
98 Vitamin regimen
100 Ship's load
103 Chomps on
104 Loses it, with "out"
105 Italian mount
106 "Actually, I do"
108 Dining partner? (2005–12)
111 Counter orders
112 Lewis who sang the theme for "Avatar"
113 ". . . then again, maybe I'm mistaken"
114 Weeds
115 Old colonnade
116 Go bad
119 Does, e.g.
121 Like the border of Time magazine
122 Ultimate
123 Post-O.R. site

81

BIG NAMES IN E-TAIL

ACROSS

1 Supreme Court justice who once compared the majority's reasoning to "the mystical aphorisms of the fortune cookie"
7 Low part
12 Classify
18 A dozen for Hercules
19 Silk case
20 Words of defiance
22 Admission of a lack of familiarity with Mr. Hockey?
24 Business feature?
25 Ancient Persian
26 Like sailors' talk
27 Celebrity cook Paula
29 Curse (out)
30 Fusses
32 Kyoto concurrence
33 Less serious works by the author of "Brighton Rock"?
36 Take responsibility for
38 Makes fast
40 Roman law
41 One making a roaring start?
45 Only one person can do it
46 Fits comfortably
50 Toque
52 Reason for Brosnan fans to watch 1980s TV?
55 "Home, ___"
56 Beach fronts?
58 A title might be presented in it: Abbr.
59 Being dragged along
60 John Lennon's middle name
61 Brand name whose middle two letters are linked in its logo
62 Cameo stone
63 Some briefs
64 Round house?
65 Trying to sell one's "Au Revoir les Enfants" video?
68 Where safety goggles may be worn
71 Don Juan's mother
73 Plowmen's cries
74 "Rhyme Pays" rapper
75 "Catch-22" pilot
76 Deplete
78 Flaky stuff
79 Foam
80 Challenge for a virologist
82 Explosive side of a former tennis great?
85 Fruitcakes
87 Libation with a floral bouquet
88 Noted second-place finisher
90 Make sense of
91 "Smack!"
92 Maybe not even that
95 Rockies game
96 Comic's copy of "The Importance of Being Earnest"?
100 "Oh no!"
102 Home of Future World
106 Soil: Prefix
107 Upbeat
108 Rocky debris
110 Brazilian berry
111 Applaud
113 Assign blame to the singer of "Blurred Lines"?
117 "Lake Wobegon Days" writer
118 Writing award won multiple times by Alice Munro
119 Where Quiznos and Mapquest are headquartered
120 Erotic
121 "All I ___ Do" (Sheryl Crow hit)
122 Tavern vessels

DOWN

1 Slenderizes
2 Midshipman's counterpart
3 Residence
4 Single copy of "The Bonfire of the Vanities"?
5 N.Y.C. line
6 Questions
7 Farfalle shapes
8 Sore
9 Great Lakes' ___ Canals
10 Disperse
11 Fidgety
12 Net worth component
13 Topsiders?
14 Spain's Costa del ___
15 Go too far
16 Actress O'Connor of "Xena: Warrior Princess"
17 Saturn's largest moon
19 Rum mixers
21 "What we want most, but what, alas! we use worst," per William Penn
23 "Uh-uh"
28 Questioning interjections
31 Like Vatican guards
33 Ripsnorter
34 Pressing work
35 Fidgety
37 Japanese drama
39 Some Thanksgiving decorations
41 Dead-end position
42 Modern-day home of the ancient Ashanti empire
43 Some sites on the National Mall
44 Home of Jar Jar Binks in "Star Wars" films
46 TV's ___ Network (sports presenter)
47 Relaxes and has some fun
48 Chess's ___ ratings
49 Singers do this
51 Nutrition-related
53 Confound
54 Resident of southern Mexico
57 Llama's kin
61 Radio freq.
62 Come-___
63 Nonkosher lunch order
65 Onetime title for Obama and Clinton
66 "They got me!"
67 Preceded, with "to"
69 Former kingdom of Provence
70 Military muckety-mucks
72 Midwesterners, stereotypically
76 Modern TV feature
77 Hundred Acre Wood resident
78 Farrow or Hamm
79 Mother of Ares
80 France's ___ Polytechnique
81 Buy into "Common Sense"?
83 Post office?
84 Hardly fancy

by Dan Schoenholz

86 "L'Amore dei ___ Re" (Montemezzi opera)
89 Sophocles tragedy
92 Sue Grafton's "___ for Innocent"
93 Come in under the radar, say
94 Artist Neiman
96 Raise, with "up"
97 Eyes
98 Poisonous snake
99 Producer of wrinkles, it's said
101 Comprehension
103 First year in Constantine's reign
104 Like some port vessels
105 Levels
108 ___ Fein
109 LAX figs.
112 Jupiter's locale: Abbr.
114 "Got it!"
115 Hankering
116 Riled (up)

82

HALLOWEEN COSTUMES

ACROSS

1 Church leaders
7 Torn asunder
15 In sufficient quantity
20 Collier's transport
21 Fact addition
22 "Truly"
23 Halloween costume for . . . a CNN anchor?
25 Net results?
26 Three times daily, in Rxs
27 Yiddish cries
28 Scand. country
29 Bank abbr.
31 Side dish that's sometimes mashed
32 "Do we have approval?"
35 Misdeed
36 Is a buttinsky
38 7–5, e.g.
39 . . . a former "Dateline" host?
46 No one says his art was pointless
48 Head, for short
49 "Lord, We Ask Thee ___ We Part" (hymn)
50 Turbaned sort
51 Beehive hairstyle, e.g.
52 Brewer Coors
55 Info for an airport run
57 "Cómo ___ usted?"
58 . . . a onetime House speaker?
63 Fender product
64 Winter Olympics event
65 Who said "In waking a tiger, use a long stick"
66 Eastern sch. with a noted film program
67 Tuition, e.g.
68 Longtime Chicago Symphony conductor
71 One of three for J. R. R. Tolkien: Abbr.
73 "Tush!"
75 Aspects
77 ___ fault
78 Goose egg
80 Sports org. with 25-Across
82 Resembles week-old flowers, say
84 Hotel capacity: Abbr.
85 . . . an old Notre Dame basketball coach?
91 Doing
93 Cry of surprise
94 Like the expression "Sakes alive!"
95 Execute perfectly
96 Eponym of a hot dog chain
98 Letters before many a state's name
101 Mil. authority
102 First-aid supply
104 . . . a silent film star?
108 It never goes off
109 Singer Falana and others
110 ___ mission
111 Snares
113 Caviar
115 The George W. Bush years, e.g.
116 Stimpy's TV pal
117 Be unsatisfied with, say
119 Ancient Hebrew liquid measure
120 Insouciant syllables
122 . . . a pop/folk singer with numerous 1970s hits?
128 Gutter locales
129 Majority
130 "Time heals all wounds" and others
131 Forecast that might call for gloves and galoshes
132 Tied
133 Like a pirate's treasure

DOWN

1 One of two at a wedding
2 Wrath
3 You can't predict the weather with this
4 Do really well on a test
5 Spreadsheet input
6 Theater sign
7 Doubtful
8 Cribbage one-pointers
9 One running races for a living?
10 "True"
11 Lace
12 Con man
13 When the French toast?
14 Figure above God's throne, in Isaiah
15 How a phone may be slammed down
16 ___ juice (milk)
17 Doesn't take any chances
18 Actress Kedrova who won an Oscar for "Zorba the Greek"
19 Polite rural reply
24 Impend
30 Position of greatest importance
32 Children, in legalese
33 Like ooze
34 Scored between 90 and 100, say
37 Besides
40 Cool, as soup
41 Hard labor spot
42 Common sitcom rating
43 Equal
44 Coal extractors
45 Vistas
47 Sleep on it
53 Noted remover of locks
54 "Run to ___" (1961 hit)
56 Petty braggart
59 Summer romance, maybe
60 Carpet fuzz
61 Comment made with a handshake
62 "Be that way!"
68 Like Christmas lights
69 Tuba sound
70 Party straggler
72 Religious deg.
74 Tater Tots maker
76 "Where should ___ the check?"
79 Cell part
81 Water, e.g.: Abbr.
83 "Trick" or "treat," e.g.
86 The "V" of R.S.V.P.
87 Slimy stuff
88 Flopped
89 Maxim tear-out
90 Winter Olympics equipment
92 Too, too

by Bill Zais

97 Start of a rationalization
99 Attic function
100 Like some Roman aphorisms
103 Out of action, in baseball lingo
105 Functional

106 Really get to
107 Tic-tac-toe starters?
112 Coke, to Pepsi
113 Hwys.
114 Mouthy?
117 Sauce brand since 1937

118 Conference USA sch.
121 Actor Marvin
123 Book after Exodus: Abbr.
124 Guy whose face might get slapped
125 Mai __

126 Gamer's prefix with pets
127 Retired boomer

83

FRAME JOB

ACROSS

1 "I've heard enough"
8 Consequences of downsizing
15 2014 Emmy-winning miniseries based on a 1996 film
20 Relative of a bug
21 Amu Darya outlet, once
22 Pop-up, sometimes
23 No-hunting zone
25 Mete out
26 Certifications in some college apps
27 Singular
28 Part of the neck?
30 Look shocked
31 What might result from a minor hit
32 Longtime California senator
36 Computer data acronym
40 Part of the biosphere
42 Flowed
43 Mt. Olive offerings
44 Get tough
45 Cursed
49 "Helm's ___!" (nautical cry)
50 Marsh birds
51 World Series of Poker's longtime Vegas home
53 Order from a sports doc
55 Info on a parking ticket
58 Something that doesn't follow the letter of the law?
60 Mars : Roman :: ___ : Norse
61 Father figures
62 Expelled politely
64 L. Frank Baum princess
65 Kind of rock
67 Bar mitzvahs, e.g.
68 City from which Vasco da Gama sailed, to locals
71 Flower girl?
72 It might be full of baloney
74 "Try ___ might . . ."
75 Taipei-to-Seoul dir.
77 It contains a lot of balloons
80 Rap sheet entry
84 Sun Devils' sch.
85 Cooperated with, e.g.
87 Indie rock band Yo La ___
88 The black ball in el juego de billar
89 Kerry's 2004 running mate
91 "Aha!"
93 Capital of Minorca
94 One-to-one, e.g.
95 Homes for Gila woodpeckers
96 Boasts
97 Weightlifting technique
103 Does in
106 What a pitching wedge provides
107 Tip of Italy, once?
108 Catchall abbr.
109 Google SafeSearch target
113 Where Rigel is
115 Brazilian tourist destination
120 Algebraic input
121 Honored academic retiree
122 First name in Disney villains
123 Apply
124 Force under Stalin
125 Spousal agreement

DOWN

1 Goodie bag filler
2 Long
3 Xeric
4 Sleep stages
5 Delta calculation, briefly
6 "Damage" director Louis
7 Big name in printers
8 Primatologist Goodall
9 Tolkien beast
10 Giant image in the sky over Gotham
11 Actor Gulager
12 Andrews or Dover: Abbr.
13 Tertius planeta from the sun
14 Leo with the 1977 #1 hit "You Make Me Feel Like Dancing"
15 Evaluator of flight risks, for short
16 Used up
17 "Chill!"
18 Search blindly
19 Furry frolicker
24 Elementary school science class item
29 Distilled coal product
31 Put-down
32 Fay Vincent's successor as baseball commissioner
33 Suffix with hex-
34 Hothead's response
35 ___ soap
36 Follow the advice "When in Rome . . ."
37 Foolish sort
38 Opaque
39 "Before ___ you go . . ."
41 Like many OPEC nations
44 Survey unit
45 Junior in the Football Hall of Fame
46 Plain to see
47 Voice-controlled device from the world's largest online retailer
48 1998 Jim Carrey comedy-drama, with "The"
50 Minor setback
52 Managed care grps.
54 Mrs. McKinley
56 Dump site monitor, for short
57 Fix, as a pool cue
59 Stick up
63 Lyme disease transmitter
66 Outdoor sports store
67 Libertine
69 Golfer Aoki
70 What Marcie calls Peppermint Patty in "Peanuts"
71 Home theater option
73 "My mistake!"
76 Some collars
78 Macy's, e.g.
79 "Stop kidding yourself"
81 Hair extension?
82 The tiniest bit
83 Crowd sound
86 88-Across + cuatro
90 Circuit for Serena and Venus Williams, in brief
92 Derisive laugh sound
93 Ones putting on acts

by Zhouqin Burnikel

97 Piece of garlic
98 Dr. Seuss environmentalist
99 Paperless I.R.S. option
100 More charming
101 Suffix with hippo-
102 Teased
104 Like black-tie affairs
105 Visible S O S
108 "Buy it. Sell it. Love it" company
109 Nut, basically
110 Like father, like son?
111 Home of the David Geffen School of Medicine, for short
112 "___ she blows!"
114 After deductions
116 Parseghian of Notre Dame
117 Street sign abbr.
118 Casino convenience
119 Staple of a rock band tour

ACROSS

1 Pushovers
8 Horn of Africa native
14 Pushed forward, as a crowd
20 Wellesley grads
21 "Same here!"
22 Paternally related
23 1982 Arnold Schwarzenegger film
25 Vintner Paul who would "sell no wine before its time"
26 Knot on a tree
27 ___ of the earth
28 Like a chestnut
29 ___ Joaquin, Calif.
30 Fell for an April fool, say
31 Verses with six stanzas
33 Bringer of peace between nations
36 ___ qué (why: Sp.)
37 NPR host Shapiro
38 Worked to the bone
39 State bordering Texas
45 Actress Pflug of "M*A*S*H"
46 Dummy
47 Wishing sites
48 Author who inspired the musical "Wicked"
50 Chiwere-speaking tribe
54 Bygone office worker
56 65 or so
57 Rose buds?
60 Spruce up
62 Op-Ed columnist Maureen
63 Spanish airline
64 Met, as a legislature
66 Jason Bourne and others
70 Big name in outdoor and fitness gear
71 2014 land-grab
73 Draft picks?
74 Tarzan's simian sidekick
76 Salad bar bowlful
79 Kung ___ chicken
80 Constellation next to Scorpius
83 Stephen of "Ben-Hur"
84 Alternative media magazine founder
85 Pep
87 Some "Fast and the Furious" maneuvers, slangily
88 Opening of a Hawaiian volcano?
91 Some auto auctions' inventory
94 Unhurriedly
98 One calling the shots, for short?
99 "Well, ___-di-dah!"
100 Land in the Caucasus
102 Deli sandwich filler
107 New ___ (official cap maker of Major League Baseball)
108 Wares: Abbr.
109 Wite-Out manufacturer
110 Caps
111 ___ me tangere (warning against meddling)
112 Costner/Russo golf flick
114 Chocolaty Southern dessert
117 Climate-affecting current
118 How some people break out on Broadway
119 Trig calculation
120 Div. for the Mets
121 It may be filled with bullets
122 Catches some Z's

DOWN

1 Fills to capacity
2 How you can't sing a duet
3 Yellowfin and bluefin
4 Cell that has multiplied?
5 Place to retire
6 Like sushi or ceviche
7 ___ knot, rug feature
8 Some bunk bed sharers, for short
9 Concubine's chamber
10 Half-baked
11 Slanting
12 Caterpillar machine
13 It comes with a charge
14 Iraqi city on the Tigris
15 Like one side of Lake Victoria
16 Ones calling the shots, for short?
17 Chatterbox
18 Ballet headliner
19 Slightly depressed
24 Workers on Times tables, briefly?
29 California wine region
32 Bread substitute?
33 Second-largest dwarf planet
34 Cuisine that includes cracklins and boudin
35 Turn a blind eye to
37 One spinning its wheels?
39 Some I.R.A.s
40 All the rage
41 Pinpoint
42 Greek sorceress
43 Nicholas Gage memoir
44 Anakin's master in "Star Wars"
49 Bridge words
51 Amateur botanists' projects
52 Yellow dog in the funnies
53 Morales of HBO's "The Brink"
55 John in the Songwriters Hall of Fame
57 Writes in C++, say
58 Utensil's end
59 "A Doll's House" playwright
61 Lawyer's clever question, say
62 Showtime crime drama, 2006–13
64 One who has crossed the line?
65 Janis's husband in the funnies
67 Rock, paper or scissors
68 Phishing lures
69 Places for links?
72 Hit AMC series that ended with a Coca-Cola ad
75 Iffy
77 Immediately preceding periods
78 Hokkaido port
79 Magician's word
81 "La ___" (Debussy opus)
82 Dunderhead
85 Intl. group headquartered in Vienna
86 One at the wheel

by Tracy Gray

89 Pellet shooters
90 Got high, in a way
92 Vinland explorer circa A.D. 1000
93 Opponents for Perry Mason, for short
94 Winning blackjack pair

95 Send
96 Romance novelist Banks
97 Going out
101 Dutch town known for tulip tourism
102 Au courant
103 Miners' entries

104 Ruy ___ (chess opening)
105 Skirt style
106 Nutritionists' prescriptions
110 Grp. of teed-off women?
113 Snoop group, in brief

114 POW/ ___ bracelet (popular 1970s wear)
115 Neither red nor blue?: Abbr.
116 Tres menos dos

HAVING ASPIRATIONS

ACROSS

1 Animals at a football game
8 Antithesis of brashness
16 One carrying a spiked club, maybe
20 Case for a lawyer
21 Lay bare
22 Worker hardly making a living wage
23 "So You Think You Can Dance," say?
25 School for James Bond
26 Plenty
27 East German secret police
28 Some letter enclosures, for short
29 A or B, but not O
30 Punk offshoot
31 Kigali native
33 A mean Amin
34 Toni Morrison novel
35 One with monthly payments
37 Shakespeare's Claudius and others
39 Added on, botanically
41 Roller coaster shout from Queen Elizabeth?
45 Geezers
46 Sprinkling on a deviled egg
49 Nuevo ___, state in Mexico
50 Klingon on "Star Trek: T.N.G."
51 It may lead to an unearned run
52 Make out
56 Sad sack
58 AOL competitor
61 Actor Hirsch of "Into the Wild"
62 Without doubt
65 Antique photo
67 ___ Ration (old dog food brand)
68 "Did you mean Doom or Dolittle?"?
70 Tools for cobblers
71 Inverse trig function
73 Succinctly
74 Battlefield cry
75 Literary inits.
76 Actress Streep
78 Coolness, in modern slang
79 Lisa, to Patty and Selma, on "The Simpsons"
80 One-___ (old ball game)
82 Is sick
85 Made an effort
87 Easily
89 Mob Boss Hall of Fame?
93 Like some jeans and apartment buildings
95 Onetime place for Saddam Hussein's image
96 Elite groups
100 Spillane's "___ Jury"
101 Camouflaged
103 Snowbird's destination
105 Wisk competitor
106 Sci-fi/historical fiction writer Stephenson
107 Decorative moldings
110 John ___, "The House of Blue Leaves" playwright
111 "Argo" setting
112 Some salad greens
113 Making a complaint at a restaurant?
116 Iowa State locale
117 Trigger autocorrect, say
118 Beat to the finish
119 Eighty-six
120 Traps in a net
121 You may want to stop reading when you see this

DOWN

1 Hot Wheels maker
2 In
3 "Mad Men" extras
4 Crows' cries
5 "Gee," in Glasgow
6 "Meet the Press" competitor
7 Company that encourages people to lie?
8 Mardi Gras time
9 Locale of the Battle of Tippecanoe
10 Runs the show, briefly
11 Dots in la mer
12 ___ Maar (Picasso's muse)
13 Formal identification
14 Bono bandmate
15 Answer with a salute
16 Precedes at a concert
17 "That milky liquid belongs to me!"?
18 Cousin of a tendril
19 Baseball or Supreme Court lineups
24 Calrissian of "Star Wars" films
31 Put back on the payroll
32 Dudley Do-Right's love
36 Moseys along
38 E.U. member not in NATO: Abbr.
40 Part of a winter stash
42 One with brand loyalty?
43 "Oh . . . my . . . God!"
44 Brian who wrote the score for "Me and Earl and the Dying Girl"
46 Glimpse on the sly
47 Munitions suppliers
48 One in line to rule the ocean?
50 Peter who directed "Picnic at Hanging Rock"
53 Man's name that's Hebrew for "my God"
54 1970 hit with the lyric "I'm down on my knees, / I'm begging you please to come home"
55 Roger who wrote "The Boys of Summer"
57 Stick-in-the-mud types
59 Edit some film
60 Like measuring cups, often
63 Nutritional fig.
64 Cattle calls
66 ___ Trail (Everglades highway)
68 PBS station in the Big Apple
69 Chorus line leader?
72 Japanese porcelain
74 Dis but not dat?
77 "Fargo" assent
81 Negligent
83 Screen abbr.

by Alan Arbesfeld

84 Things found between the poles?
86 Closed tight
87 Show some dumbfoundedness about
88 Declaration on Día de San Valentin
89 Add one's two cents
90 Get cozy
91 Books often not read
92 Built-up
94 "Prove it!"
97 Kind of number
98 Cataleptic state
99 Margaret who founded Planned Parenthood
102 Jefferson's religious belief
104 Mathematician who was the subject of the book "The Man Who Loved Only Numbers"
108 Start of the Bay State's motto
109 Nurses at a bar
111 Calvary inscription
114 Book before Esth.
115 Skater Midori

ACROSS

1 Big gasbag?
6 Sex therapy subject
12 Rap
18 Cat and mouse
20 First name among celebrity chefs
21 Achieve widespread recognition
22 Warrior who follows "the way of the warrior"
23 Charged (with)
24 Part of a mob
25 Threshold of major change
27 Heroic deeds
28 Eritrea's capital
29 Small body of medical research
31 Jack in the box, once?
33 Attempt to debug?
34 Soundly defeat, informally
38 Arthur Conan Doyle title
39 Catchphrase from "Jerry Maguire"
42 Actress Larter of "Heroes"
43 A little light
45 Homer's neighbor on "The Simpsons"
47 ___ facto
48 Winnie-the-Pooh greeting
50 Jet black
51 Like Nahuatl speakers
54 Puffs
56 "31 Days of Oscar" channel
57 Hail or farewell
58 Crocodile tail?
61 Latin lover's word
62 Dance class
63 They sit for six yrs.
65 Was a victim of price gouging
70 ___ Lilly and Company
71 Struggles (through)
73 Dweller along the Wasatch Range
74 "That's lovely!"
75 Rush to beat a deadline
80 Not aweather
81 Penultimate countdown word
82 Messenger ___
83 One of the Golden Girls of 1980s-'90s TV
85 Nonexpert
86 Cubs' home
87 Surrounded by
90 Danced to Xavier Cugat, say
92 "Supposing that's true . . ."
93 Modern spelling?
94 Madame's "mine"
97 Sites for R.N.s and M.D.s
98 Skedaddles
100 Prince's inits.
101 Mark that's hard to hit
104 Red Cross work
106 Where to find some ham
107 "___ in Calico" (jazz classic)
109 It makes flakes
110 Biceps exercise
113 Steamed dish that may be prepared in an olla
115 Rapper né Andre Young
117 British pool stick
122 Fort ___ National Monument
123 They'll make you blush

125 Reindeer relative
126 "That makes sense now"
127 Early Mexicans
128 Up
129 Businesswoman/ philanthropist ___ Heinz Kerry
130 Auto identifiers
131 Launch dates

DOWN

1 Sons of, in Hebrew
2 Drooping
3 Exasperated cry in the morning
4 "A Few Good Men" men
5 First option
6 Rented
7 Last stage of metamorphosis
8 Dogs
9 Rankles
10 Coke Zero, for one
11 "Every dog has his day" and others
12 Zimbabwe's capital
13 It's in the eye of the beholder
14 Formal occasions
15 Be unable to make further progress
16 Part of a Mario Brothers costume
17 Equity valuation stat
18 Prince Edward Isl. setting
19 Talks with one's hands
26 Exact
30 Newfoundland or Labrador
32 Singer Tori
34 Weight room figure

35 Board game popular throughout Africa
36 ___ Games
37 Puffed-grain cereal
40 Language that gave us "bungalow" and "guru"
41 Exact
44 Really enjoy oneself
46 Intimate apparel size bigger than C
49 Jesus on a diamond
52 Site of King Rudolf's imprisonment, in fiction
53 Santa ___
55 Sour candy brand
57 Nile River spanner
59 Typical end of a professor's address?
60 ___ Place (Butch and Sundance companion)
64 Six, in Seville
66 Berry of "Monster's Ball"
67 Beneficial to
68 The best policy, supposedly
69 Exact
72 Winter-related commercial prefix
76 Hoffer or Holder
77 Green garnish
78 Two past Tue.
79 Exact
84 President Garfield's middle name
87 Tire pressure indicator
88 "Let's Get It Started" rapper
89 "Rikki-Tikki-___"
91 Reebok competitor

by Samuel A. Donaldson and Jeff Chen

92 "Positively Entertaining" network
93 Thingamajig
95 It might follow a showstopping performance, in modern lingo
96 Hot
99 Not black-and-white
102 Code of silence
103 Exact
105 Conehead
108 Caffè ___
111 Sports star-turned-model Gabrielle
112 Author Dahl
114 They go around heads around Diamond Head
116 Russian legislature
118 Big name in microloans
119 Subject of the 2002 book "The Perfect Store"
120 Turns bad
121 Exact
124 Draft org.

87

FOUR-LETTER WORDS

ACROSS

1 Key word #1
5 Plants with intoxicating leaves
10 Mosque no-no
15 Key word #2
19 Bon ___
20 Songwriter Carmichael
21 Minor snafu
22 Capital known for 300 years as Christiania
23 Ill-fated seducer in "Tess of the D'Urbervilles"
24 1-Across + 15-Across
26 Erupt
27 What a driverless car drives
29 Pageant V.I.P.s
30 Like some soldiers in the American Revolution
32 Farmyard call
33 You may leave when it's up
34 Endnotes?
35 Portland, Ore.-to-Boise dir.
36 Egg producer
38 The "e" of i.e.
39 ___ Olshansky, first Soviet-born N.F.L. player
41 Villainous
43 1-Across + 122-Across
48 Workers on the board
49 It covers everything quite clearly
50 Decepticon's foe in "Transformers"
54 Sewing case
55 Clio nominees
57 S.U.V. alternative
59 Moolah
60 Benchwarmer
62 Final Four round
64 ___ cards (items used in ESP tests)
65 1-Across + 125-Across
70 15-Across + 122-Across
72 Acronym on the S&P 500
73 Galileo, by birth
75 Take off, as a heavy coat?
76 Venice tourist attraction
78 S.U.V. alternative
80 Golfer Ernie
81 Acted like
85 Goldeneye or harlequin
87 Paul who won a Nobel in Physics
89 1962 Paul Anka hit
91 15-Across + 125-Across
94 Coat fur
97 Ammonium and others
98 Subj. for Bloomberg News
99 Puts in stitches, say
100 Food that's an anagram of 98-Across
101 Washing the dishes, e.g.
103 Plantation device
105 Subj. with many irregularities
106 Shabby
108 Sound in "Eleanor Rigby" and "Yesterday"
110 Disdainful sounds
113 "Little" visitor to Slumberland, in old comics
114 122-Across + 125-Across
117 Holder of small doses
118 Former British crown colony in the Mideast
119 Turbo Tax option
120 As old as the hills
121 Petro-Canada competitor
122 Keyword #3
123 Looking for
124 Go well together
125 Key word #4

DOWN

1 California resort town
2 V, in physics
3 1997 Samuel L. Jackson film
4 Pilaf-like product
5 Pot user?
6 Tic-tac-toe failure
7 "Understand?"
8 Fellow students, generally
9 Brings together
10 "Hook" role
11 Successes in the game Battleship
12 Sister brand of Phisoderm
13 Elation
14 It helps you get ahead
15 Pardner's mount
16 Glimpses
17 Orioles' div.
18 He played Chaplin in "Chaplin"
25 Date
28 QB Bobby who purportedly put a curse on the Detroit Lions
31 Germophobe's need
33 Doesn't pursue
34 Mustard, but not ketchup: Abbr.
36 Stage prize
37 Old TV adjustment: Abbr.
39 Radiologist, e.g.
40 Biological blueprints
42 Makes up (for)
44 Lucius's son, in Harry Potter
45 Fancy marble
46 Fidelity offerings, for short
47 Political insults, so to speak
51 Uncle ___
52 Hershiser who was Sports Illustrated's 1988 Sportsman of the Year
53 Major ally?
56 Islamic mystics
58 Place for a bust
60 Figurine
61 Stemming from
63 Archenemy of Mattel's He-Man
65 General interests?
66 Author Wiesel
67 Tournament organizer since '39
68 "Ha! I was right!"
69 Says "Read you loud and clear . . . over," say
71 Rope in
74 Informer, informally
77 South American tuber
79 Recharge midday
81 Sandpaper and such
82 Creatures that may live inside oysters - hence the name
83 Cable's ___ Classic
84 Springfield exclamations
86 Male lead in Disney's "Frozen"
88 Messy food order at a carnival

by Alex Vratsanos

90 Witty Nash
92 ___ choy
93 Common wedding
reception feature
94 Kind of column
95 "Holy ___!"
96 J. Paul Getty and
others

102 Literally,
"breathless"
103 [You stink!]
104 Ho hi
107 Beast on
Skull Island,
informally
108 Low-lying area

109 Robert who oversaw
the acquisitions of
Pixar, Marvel and
Lucasfilm
110 Ophthalmologist's
concern
111 Burkina ___
(African land)

112 Vending machine
feature
115 Small songbird
116 Burns's "before"

88

WITH DRAWL

ACROSS

1 Butter?
4 Out patient's state
8 Three of a kind, to a poker player
13 Earth, e.g.
19 Marriage agreement?
20 Take a turn
21 American hub
22 Stacked messily
23 Half a sawbuck
24 How you might classify a blade, a gas tank cap or a starter handle?
27 Reason to stay only at Hiltons or Marriotts?
29 "Frozen" reindeer's name
30 Giving evasive answers
31 Roll served at a bar
32 Little one
33 Timeworn words
35 Kind of strength
39 "___ the Housetop" (Christmas song)
42 Extremely, in dated slang
45 Mob that disturbs the peace in new and interesting ways?
49 John of England
50 2013 Spike Jonze dramedy
51 ___ mater (spinal membrane)
52 Affect in a personal way
54 Small, secluded, wooded valley
55 Maker of indoor cars
57 Druggists' implements
59 Hospital worker

61 Attractive blacksmith at a stable?
63 Like Paganini, by birth
65 Food service giant based in Houston
66 CPR expert
67 Corruption
68 Candy brand since 1901
72 Rough
75 Municipal leaders who work the late shift?
78 Director of "Carlito's Way," 1993
81 Panasonic rival
82 Outback runners
83 Songwriter Novello
84 Beseech on bended knee
87 Gaggle : goose :: clowder : ___
88 Trident-shaped letter
89 Bass organs
91 Troy, in the "Iliad"?
95 Cold shower?
96 Word in a New Year's Eve song
97 Never closed, as a resort
98 "We won" gesture
100 Nonprofit network
102 One who gets no credit?
105 Historical chapter
107 "Preparation meeting opportunity," it's said
109 Smallest possible aspirin dose?
113 Normandy's coat of arms, basically?
116 Punk subgenre

117 D-Day invaders
118 Green stuff
119 Wildly enthusiastic
120 Jimmy Fallon's employer
121 Moves quickly, informally
122 Big Easy lunch
123 Hang around
124 "I Ching" concept

DOWN

1 Repeated musical phrases
2 Leave-taking
3 Brothers' keepers
4 Front-wheel-drive coupling, for short
5 French ingredient in French toast
6 Interlock
7 Like many student films
8 Fictional Potawatomi tribesman
9 Butler on a plantation
10 Maker of Healthy Naturals food
11 Supporting
12 Wraps (up)
13 Least bit
14 Honey or pumpkin
15 "Serves you right!"
16 Seismological focus
17 City near Lake Tahoe
18 Pushing the envelope
25 Many a 1950s B-movie
26 Chicago suburb
28 Mother of Zeus
34 First Pierce Brosnan 007 film
36 ___ cup (spillproof container)

37 Northeast octet
38 Dogfight preventers
39 College team named for a tribe
40 Blowtube projectile
41 TV alien's home
43 Occupant of a small house
44 No more than
45 Musician's virtuosity
46 Have another go at
47 Castaway's site
48 Phone button abbr.
53 Treasure from una mina
56 Missouri's original capital
58 Large volume
60 Mike's "Wayne's World" co-star
62 Easily manipulated sort
63 Van ___, "Lane in Autumn" painter
64 Principled
67 Stair's face
69 Bedroom on a train, e.g.
70 Piece of pizza?
71 Actor/activist Davis
73 "___ right?"
74 Unchecked growth
75 Expected amount
76 Kids' outdoor game
77 Chum at sea
78 Does an investigation
79 Maleficent
80 Attempt to pass the bar?
81 Mr. ___ of "The Wind in the Willows"
85 Boston skyscraper, with "the"

by Patrick Berry

86 "___ Darlin'"
(Count Basie
number)
90 Ben of "Zoolander"
92 Place for visual
aids
93 Talking toy since
1965

94 City dweller's yell
99 Suppose
100 Renaissance
painter Uccello
101 Road less
traveled
103 Dance from Cuba
104 Gas station name

105 Dutch export
106 Nestlé candy
brand
108 Dole's 1996
running mate
109 Lava lamp lump
110 Oil field sights
111 Defensive ring

112 Personal assistant
in "Young
Frankenstein"
114 Book jacket
info
115 John of England

89

BANDS TOGETHER

ACROSS

1 Plentiful
6 Pomeranian, e.g.
12 Slow musical movements
19 "God Rest Ye Merry, Gentlemen," e.g.
20 Available, as a London limo
21 A touch of class
22 Elevated sight in the Windy City
24 "Why didn't I think of that?!"
25 Forward, as a letter
26 Quest for the unknown?
28 Aid for a flood-prone house
29 Itinerary abbr.
30 Some are 13-/14-Down
33 It's for the birds
35 Key state geographically or electorally?: Abbr.
36 All the cars going the same way
42 Nominative or accusative
44 "Grand" name in the frozen food aisle
45 "Eww, gross!"
46 Arch type
47 Fatty liquid
49 Brewery kiln
51 Twaddle
55 "Absolutely!"
58 "The King of Queens" co-star Remini
60 Job-related move, for short
61 Certain sorority member, informally
62 They're seen spread on the back of a quarter
65 Title ship in a 1997 Spielberg movie
69 Former baseball boss Bud
71 Times when shops close
72 Kind of pie or doughnut
74 Public spat
76 Medium for cuneiform writing
77 Victoria's home: Abbr.
78 Like child-safe cleaning products
83 Strong and unwavering
86 Cold War capital
87 Investor's concern
88 Recipe amounts
89 Skyrocket
91 ___ Claire, Wis.
94 Org. in "The Martian"
95 Lark for a Halloween hooligan
101 Chemical suffix
102 ___ Mellark, Katniss Everdeen's partner in "The Hunger Games"
103 Bar snacks
104 "Now the truth comes out!"
107 Home Depot competitor
110 Land on the Red Sea
113 A wink or a nod, maybe
115 Gift
117 What many Black Friday shoppers do at midnight
120 Newborns
121 "We've been approved!"
122 Deliverer's assignment
123 Like Crimea, now
124 Sound-related
125 Time and time again

DOWN

1 Capital of Ghana
2 Bill for cable TV
3 Early spring blooms
4 "Livin' La Vida ___"
5 Lover of Sir Lancelot
6 John
7 Symbol of industry
8 "Wheel of Fortune" category
9 Ratchet (up)
10 Nee: Abbr.
11 No-name
12 Bosox division
13 & 14 Figs. in the war on drugs
15 It may be jaunty
16 Not taking sides
17 Peacock's "eyes"
18 Northwest airport named for two cities
21 Big bankruptcy of 2001
23 Open spot in a woods
27 Something bound to sell?
31 Relieve (of)
32 Yelp
34 Show, with "out"
37 No de Cologne?
38 Dermatological sac
39 Sound of disapproval
40 Dating datum
41 Kind of wheel
42 Like the comment "Maybe, maybe not"
43 Order at McSorley's
48 Silently acknowledge
50 Humiliates
51 Carrier inits.
52 Professors' reading
53 Actress Kurylenko of "Quantum of Solace"
54 Fling
56 Travelmate in "On the Road"
57 Clunker
58 China's Chou En-___
59 Goads
62 American ___
63 Chinese: Prefix
64 Pipsqueak
65 They may be taught with a song
66 Undergo ecdysis
67 Who said "Aristotle is my friend—but my greatest friend is truth"
68 Apple Pencil, for one
70 Put away
73 Place to get stuck
75 Films
78 Spectacle
79 Lead role in "Star Wars: The Force Awakens"
80 Solve by logic
81 Golfer Ernie
82 LeShan who wrote "It's Better to Be Over the Hill Than Under It"
84 Typing test fig.
85 Pronto
86 Weigh (down)
89 Baked ___
90 Traveling
92 Candy Crush Saga, for one

by Tracy Gray and Andrea Carla Michaels

93 Czar's decree
95 Singer/actress Lola
96 One of the majors
97 Favored at the 96-Down, say
98 "___ to you!"
99 Area code 801 resident

100 San ___, Argentina
105 Writer Bret
106 TV's ___ twins
108 Start of a Mozart title
109 Classic record label for R&B and soul

111 Book that begins "In the days when the judges ruled, there was a famine in the land"
112 He, in Italian
114 Slip
116 Sport-___

118 ___ Fridays (restaurant chain)
119 Ad follower

90 REBRANDING

ACROSS

1 Chipped beef go-with
6 Plugged in
11 Subjects of frequent updates
15 Tennis's Wawrinka, winner of the 2015 French Open
19 Wet spot
20 Sophomore's choice
21 "Language of the unheard," per Martin Luther King Jr.
22 "Duh, I get it"
23 "Corrected" slogan for a tech company?
26 Matriarch of six of the 12 Tribes of Israel
27 Bounce
28 Regarding
29 Keeper of the flame?
30 Majority of Saudi Arabians
31 Kind of tone
33 "Corrected" slogan for an office supply chain?
37 Anna Karenina's lover
39 Deer hunter's prize
40 Skaters' leaps
41 Who might say "I'm I. M."
42 Rating for many HBO shows
44 Early co-host of "The View"
49 "Corrected" slogan for a fast-food franchise?
52 Feudal superiors
53 "The Boy Next Door" star, to fans
56 Elbow
57 Sources of some rattling
58 Milkmaid's handful
59 Earnings, so to speak
62 Tubs
64 Fall back on, as in desperation
66 "Corrected" slogan for a dessert brand?
71 Gambit
72 Gambit
73 Molly who wrote "Bill of Wrongs"
74 Hogwarts delivery system
75 Dweeb
77 Confine
81 Measure of inflation, for short
82 Calligraphers
83 "Corrected" slogan for a hairstyling product?
87 Shows promise
89 Thom ___ shoes
90 Short note?
91 "When in ___, tell the truth": Mark Twain
93 Second
95 Took, as a test
97 "Corrected" slogan for a frozen breakfast food?
102 Aunt in "Uncle Tom's Cabin"
103 Reflective writing
104 Certification for eco-friendly buildings, for short
105 "Funny bumping into you here"
107 "Unfortunately . . ."
110 Seaside scavenger
111 "Corrected" slogan for a dairy product?
115 Hot rod's rod
116 Took a card
117 President-___
118 "Duck Dynasty" network
119 Action-oriented sorts, supposedly
120 Surfaces, in a way
121 Targets of cons
122 Work with the hands

DOWN

1 "Africa" band, 1982
2 First Ironman locale
3 "From my perspective . . ."
4 Possible black market cause
5 "Naughty!"
6 Buggy people?
7 Drift
8 Driver who won the Indy 500, Daytona 500 and Le Mans
9 European deer
10 Get things wrong
11 "The Terminator" star, to fans
12 Bit of marketing
13 Oktoberfest dance
14 It's a mess
15 Signs of respect
16 Hurricanes' grp.
17 Yoga poses
18 Like three Cy Young games
24 Indirect objects, grammatically speaking
25 "Oh, gross!"
30 Sides in a classic battle
32 "Acoustic guitar" or "terrestrial radio"
34 "Hey, relax!"
35 ___ Pepper
36 Hudgens of "High School Musical"
37 Big lug
38 Shepherd's workplace
39 Pioneering stand-up comedian
43 El Paso setting: Abbr.
45 Admission of 1959
46 Josh
47 Gibes
48 Figures in bedtime stories
50 Nordic wonders
51 Charge
53 "Romeo Must Die" star, 2000
54 Approach evening
55 Missouri River natives
57 It makes a turn at the entrance
58 Globetrot
59 Some jazz
60 Promises
61 Ma uses them
63 Like ibexes
65 Cover's opposite
67 Greeted with respect
68 Like shepherds' charges
69 Holds to be
70 Scrutinized
76 Mint
78 Subject for one studying onomastics
79 Ottawa-based media inits.
80 Flooded with
82 Submarine near the Gulf Coast
83 TV character with the catchphrase "Booyakasha!"
84 Rope from a ship, say
85 "Whoop-de-___"
86 Start of the Lord's Prayer
87 Band with the first video on MTV, with "the"

by Peter Wentz

88 Connectivity issue
91 Having all the add-ons, say
92 Singer of the aria "Ora e per sempre addio"
94 Let, e.g.
96 Barring no one
97 Corporate department
98 Plants
99 Stephenie who wrote "Twilight"
100 Cartoonish shrieks
101 URL ender
102 I.M. sessions
106 "Fiddlesticks!"
108 Photographer/writer Arlene
109 Short timetable?
111 Chemical used to fight malaria
112 Border line?
113 Like
114 Talk up a storm

ACROSS

1 Savor, as a drink
6 Takes down a peg
12 Je t'aime : French :: ___ : Spanish
17 Sell at a discount, say
19 Female toon with a "dollink" Boris
21 Grackles and grebes
23 PP
25 Attic
26 Horror franchise beginning in 2004
27 Lasting for years and years
28 Dirt road hazards
30 Melee
31 Street of film fame
32 You might take it out for a drive
33 Court, for short
35 Pile of stones used to mark a trail
36 DD
39 First antibacterial soap brand
40 "Oh, please, that's enough"
42 Derisive sounds
43 Abbr. in many airport names
44 Jubilant
45 Portrait on Chinese renminbi bills
46 AA
48 Extra bed, maybe
51 Bad thing on a record
53 The Jedi and the Sith, e.g.
54 "Thursday Night Football" airer
55 Alaska tourist attraction
57 Director of 2015's "Chi-Raq"
58 Capital with the Norsk Folkemuseum

60 Travel info source, for short
61 London cathedral
62 Volunteer's response
64 WW
68 Historic German admiral Maximilian von ___
69 Fizzy drink
71 Michael of "Saturday Night Live"
72 Cry to a husky
74 "When I was a ___ . . ."
75 Riot opportunist
76 Locale for cranberries
77 Very much
79 Uniform
81 See 114-Across
82 OO
85 Hodges who managed the Mets to a World Series title
86 Little Rascals boy
88 Tolkien tree creatures
89 Mars features, mistakenly
92 Befuddling
94 Peeps heard by Bo Peep
95 ZZ
97 When repeated, a Yale fight song
98 Playwright Clifford
100 "How ___!"
101 Modern TV feature, for short
102 Hazy memory
103 Grps. with the motto "Every child. One voice."
104 Conquest of 1953
107 Susan of "The Partridge Family"

108 Silas in "The Da Vinci Code," notably
110 NN
113 Dances at the Tropicana Club
114 Santa Claus portrayer in 81-Across
115 Greet from behind the wheel
116 Witherspoon of "Legally Blonde"
117 Shot put and long jump
118 "Auld Lang Syne" and others

DOWN

1 Figured (out)
2 Has an inspiration
3 Agricultural figure in "The Canterbury Tales"
4 Alley ___
5 Pep Boys competitor
6 Whites, informally
7 Strips shortly after getting up in the morning?
8 Rate ___ (be perfect)
9 Spicy fruit beverage often used as a tequila chaser
10 Cornerstone abbr.
11 Singer Crow
12 Identifies in a Facebook photo
13 A Perón
14 Soaring cost?
15 RR
16 Like macho push-ups
18 Explore deeply
20 Calla lily family
22 "Gypsy" composer

24 Techies, stereotypically
29 Gasless car
34 Java order that packs less of a punch
35 What Brits call "red sauce"
37 Major-___
38 Muse for D. H. Lawrence
39 Some lab samples
41 Assets for food critics
43 Put away
44 Annapolis grad.
46 It comes before one
47 Building beam
49 Susan who wrote "The Orchid Thief"
50 Hit with a stun gun
51 "Chill out, will you"
52 FF
53 Wig out
56 Dorm V.I.P.s
57 Durable stocking fabric
59 Like courtroom witnesses
60 Floor
61 X-rated material
63 D.C. athlete
65 Pest control brand
66 Sarcastic "Wonderful"
67 Tori of pop/rock
70 Symbol of Middle America
73 Big name in 35-Down
76 Gaudy wrap
77 Industrious workers
78 Some TVs and smartphones
80 The Impaler
83 Fort Knox valuable
84 To some degree

by Don Gagliardo and Zhouqin Burnikel

85 Beholds
87 It's heard at a hearing
89 West Pointer
90 Opposite of an early adopter
91 Morning run time, maybe
92 Arafat's successor as Palestinian president
93 Budget alternative
94 Next to
95 Peers in a box
96 Meetings arranged through Ashley Madison
99 Helen Mirren, e.g.
100 Like an alarm clock, night after night
103 It may be struck on a runway
105 ___ diagram
106 'Vette choice
109 "N.Y. State of Mind" rapper
111 ___ system (luxury car option, briefly)
112 Romance

ACROSS

1 Patron of the high seas
7 Metric in digital journalism
13 Some marble works
18 Den mother
19 Make less stuffy
20 Opening
21 Reason for an ejection in the M.L.B.
22 Reason for an ejection in the N.B.A.
24 Bank takebacks, for short
25 Snug as a bug in a rug
27 Make mention of
28 *N.F.L. star ejected from 102-Across*
29 "Right on!"
30 Actress/singer Janelle
31 Rudimentary
32 Treats, as a sprain
33 Reason for an ejection in FIFA
37 The Bronx Bombers, on scoreboards
38 Intent
39 Soon
40 Student taking Torts or Property
43 Snowshoe hare predator
44 Brian with the album "Before and After Science"
45 Shorten
48 *N.B.A. star ejected from 105-Across*
51 Sound heard in Georgia?
53 Musician's skill
54 Onetime Sprint competitor
56 Burn a perfume stick in
57 Meursault's love in Camus's "The Stranger"
58 Reason for an ejection in the N.F.L.
61 "Love, when we met, ___ like two planets meeting": Ella Wheeler Wilcox
62 Sepals of a flower
63 Rolls up
64 *M.L.B. star ejected from 87-Across*
65 Belief in one's role as a savior
67 Anatomical lashes
68 Drum held between the knees
69 On fire
70 ___ milk
71 English dialect in which "food shopping" is "makin' groceries"
72 Aries and Taurus
73 Result of a judicial conflict of interest
76 Kabuki sash
77 Bloke
79 Polish up, in a way
80 "Actually, come to think of it . . ."
83 Skill
84 Part of a "fence" in the game Red Rover
87 Seeming opposite of "Ignorance is bliss"
92 Pollyannaish
95 Mends, in a way
96 Some flaws in logic
97 Plays charades, say
98 Tweeter's "Then again . . ."
99 Set down
100 Fruity soda brand
101 A Musketeer
102 Entry fee
105 Stew that's decidedly not very spicy
107 Durkheim who helped found the field of sociology
108 Browned at high heat
109 Hit from behind
110 Array in a cockpit
111 Butterfly-attracting flowers
112 Actress Jean who played Joan of Arc in "Saint Joan"

DOWN

1 Well-formed
2 "Receiving poorly," in CB lingo
3 Retreats
4 Grazing land
5 Organization of Afro-American Unity founder
6 1960s group with a fabric-related name, with "the"
7 Joe can provide it
8 Bell-shaped flower
9 Writer/critic ___ Madison III
10 Hebrew "shalom" to Arabic "salaam," e.g.
11 "Seven Samurai" director
12 Unchanging
13 Pinch
14 Drop from one's Facebook circle
15 Poker-faced
16 Armistice
17 They may hit the ground running
18 Respectable
21 Genius
23 Head turner?
26 It gained independence from France in 1960
30 Principal
31 Discombobulate
34 King of morning TV
35 Poet who invented the terza rima rhyme scheme
36 Bay of Biscay feeder
41 Easter activity
42 "Move on already!"
43 Rodeo ring?
46 Politico Abzug
47 Members of the flock
48 Of base 8
49 One getting onboarded
50 Made into law
51 Bargain hunter's delight
52 Margaret Atwood's "___ and Crake"
55 Standard of living?
57 Country south of Sicily
58 Amazon Prime competitor
59 Ireland, to poets
60 "Rainbow" fish
62 Tax pros, for short
63 They're located between Samoa and Vanuatu
66 Entrance to a cave
67 Revolutionary group
68 Language family that includes Xhosa and Zulu
71 Monastery garb
74 Metonym for local government
75 They're only a few stories

by Natan Last

77 Noted Belle Epoque locale
78 Psyche's beloved
81 Suggests
82 Typical summer intern
84 Forming an upward curve
85 Like oral history

86 FIFA star ejected from 65-Across
88 Choice of cheese
89 ___ Stark, Oona Chaplin's "Game of Thrones" role
90 Russian ethnic group

91 Church title
92 Partitioned, with "off"
93 People of south-central Mexico
94 Director Coppola
100 Author Jonathan Safran ___
101 Land parcel

103 ___ Moines
104 Pique
106 Literary fairy queen

ACROSS

1 Parabolas, essentially
5 Part of a wedding 9-Across
9 See 5-Across
13 Trophy winner
18 He planned for a rainy day
19 Sled dog with a statue in Central Park
20 Jewish month before Nisan
21 Corolla part
22 *Result of a foul on a long basketball shot*
25 Bandleader Shaw
26 Start of Euripides' signature
27 Bargain-basement
29 See 92-Across
30 Took off the board
32 Popular jeans
33 Does, as an animated character
35 A, B or C, in Washington
38 *Albino orca, e.g.*
41 "You're on!" and others
42 Skedaddles
45 Country singer Chesney
46 "It was all ___"
48 Chops down
49 Places for toasters and roasters
51 Word after sock or bunny
54 Subjects of some New Year's resolutions
56 Deli order
57 Reddish
59 When repeated, emergency cry to a fighter pilot
60 Wise-looking
63 Pub orders
64 On base, say
67 *Part of a department store where people sit*
70 Legally confer, as a power
71 Opulent
73 Kind of joke
74 Lilac color
76 High regard
78 Certain intersection
79 Andrew Jackson's Tennessee home, with "the"
83 Family reunion attendee, informally
84 One taking inventory?
87 ___ Pueblo (World Heritage Site)
88 Polite
89 Expensive outing
90 Philadelphia art museum, with "the"
92 With 29-Across, source of a famous smile
93 *Home of the world's only 14-lane suspension bridge*
98 "Atonement" author Ian
100 Old barracks decorations
101 Catches up to
102 Bollywood instruments
105 Man Ray's genre
106 Ham it up
109 Wine orders
112 Good servers
114 *Timekeeper on the Emerald Isle*
117 "Free ___"
118 Text message status
119 Assists in a way one shouldn't
120 One getting the red-carpet treatment
121 Diary passage
122 Avant-garde
123 Father
124 Scottish caps

DOWN

1 Hill and tunnel builder
2 Architect Mies van der ___
3 Complain
4 *What a dairymaid does all day long*
5 Poi plants
6 Chaiken who co-created "The L Word"
7 Printemps follower
8 Source of a deferment in the 1960s draft
9 Syndicate
10 Big fan
11 Yamaha competitor
12 Formerly, once
13 Figurehead?
14 Tim ___, frequent collaborator with Adam Sandler
15 Ancient Greek state with Athens
16 "The Marvelous Mrs. ___" (award-winning Amazon series)
17 "I beg of you"
19 A sharps
23 Aer Lingus destination
24 Performances for Hawaii tourists
28 Plane, e.g.
31 Column in soccer standings
34 Confesses
35 Picket line crosser
36 Hobbes's favorite food in "Calvin and Hobbes"
37 Text message status
39 Leading characters in "Mad Max"
40 Matter in court
43 Pretentious
44 1984 Olympic gymnastics sensation
47 ___ Boston (noted hotel)
49 ___ de leche
50 Somewhat
51 Put an edge on
52 Loopholes
53 "Hey you!"
55 Wanna-___
56 Writer Stieg Larsson, e.g.
58 *Hard way to say the answers to the italicized clues in this puzzle (good luck!)*
60 Willow twig
61 San ___, Calif.
62 Having a frog in one's throat
64 Building direction, briefly
65 What "btw" means
66 Mess (with)
68 Spanish direction
69 Book before Deut.
72 Extend a hand to after a fall, say
75 London's Old ___
77 Beyond that
79 Listens attentively
80 Declare
81 "Jane the Virgin" actress Rodriguez
82 Pizazz
85 Wine: Prefix
86 Was on the verge of collapse
87 *What "light" cigarettes are lower in*
89 Not so hip
90 "The Garden of Earthly Delights" painter

by Lee Taylor

91 Cleverness
93 App release
94 One of the B vitamins
95 Underwater
96 Electrician's concern
97 Like the smell of some bread
99 Where something annoying might be stuck
103 Less welcoming
104 Sample
107 What a headache might feel like
108 Start of a classic Christmas poem
110 James of jazz
111 Ponzi scheme, e.g.
113 Wilbur's home in "Charlotte's Web"
115 Box score inits.
116 Time sheet units: Abbr.

ACROSS

1 Not rumpled, as a bed
5 Slice, for example
9 Veal topper, informally
13 Cookie containers
17 "Yeah, right!"
18 Certain body of believers
21 Part of a Latin 101 conjugation
22 *What kind of tree ___?*
24 High-grade cotton
25 Capital that was home to the world's tallest building before the Burj Khalifa
26 Pears and apples
27 Vladimir Lenin's real last name
29 Nahuatl speaker
30 Answer to 22-Across [Science & Nature]
32 Multipurpose
33 Fixed
34 Polite
36 Moving vehicle
38 "Carmen" and "Elektra"
39 "Jeez!"
40 Mimicking
42 Director Anderson
43 Simulated
46 Answer to 113-Across [Geography]
48 Answer to 13-Down [History]
50 First name on a famous plane
52 Farm females
53 Host for a destructive beetle
55 Abbr. on a label of brandy
58 Class skippers
61 Princess seduced by Zeus
63 Cartesian conclusion
65 Word said before "do"
66 *What 1986 ___ romantic comedy got its title from a song by the Psychedelic Furs?*
68 *Who wrote a 2003 best seller about a ___?*
71 Tres + cinco
72 "Little ol' me?"
73 Fine fabric
75 Asmara is its capital
76 Regard
77 World Cup cry
79 Newspaper units: Abbr.
81 Clammy
82 Answer to 68-Across [Art & Literature]
85 Answer to 66-Across [Entertainment]
89 "Phooey!"
90 Have a bawl
91 Amherst campus, for short
92 Cacophonous
94 Knight's wear, in England
97 Pad
98 Find a new tenant for
99 Calendar units: Abbr.
102 Select, as sides for a game
104 Answer to 39-Down [Sports & Leisure]
106 "To repeat . . ."
108 Lens covers
109 Meerkat in "The Lion King"
111 Living, to Livy
112 Nose out
113 *What ___ comes from a farm bird?*
117 Blacken
118 Song heard at the start of "Saturday Night Fever"
119 Ride provider
120 Some I.R.S. data, for short
121 Not hush-hush
122 Kind
123 What a judge does for much of the day

DOWN

1 Some roadsters
2 Brightly lit
3 Clinton who once ran for president
4 Tour de France stage
5 "Pipe down!"
6 60 minuti
7 Get rid of
8 "When it comes to . . ."
9 Scorer of 12 World Cup goals
10 Spanish ouzo flavoring
11 Nutritional std.
12 Bump on a slope
13 *Where were battleships sunk in an 1894 ___?*
14 Key of Beethoven's "Für Elise"
15 Quimby of children's books
16 Lines on sheet music
18 CBS debut of 2000
19 Comic actor known for his shock humor
20 1966 Donovan hit with a rhyming title
23 "That tastes bleah!"
28 "Holy cow!"
30 Cole Porter's "Well, Did You ___?"
31 Jungle tangle
32 Sweet and kind
35 1962 hit for the Ikettes
36 Part of an itinerary
37 Cost to get a hand
39 *What annual game have the ___ won more than any other team?*
40 Too
41 Condition once called "shell shock," for short
43 Process
44 How chicken teriyaki is usually served
45 Gave reluctantly, with "up"
47 Court plea, in brief
49 Oregon city that was the first permanent U.S. settlement west of the Rockies
51 A, B, C or D, in multiple choice: Abbr.
54 Foal's mother
56 Like Fenway among all major-league ballparks
57 Folds
59 Cinephile's channel
60 "Buzz off!"
62 Natty neckwear
64 Locale for Jacques Cousteau
67 Crankcase device
69 Like a moray
70 Director Burton
74 Follower of the Gospels
78 Wry Bombeck
80 Resilience
83 "It's a waste of time"

by David Kwong

84 Loaves from whole-grain flour
86 Put away, in a way
87 Longtime Steelers coach Chuck
88 Small digit
93 Reeked

94 Gain entry to
95 Kind of scholar
96 Freeman of "Now You See Me"
98 TV Tarzan player
99 Hot stuff
100 Fate
101 Unwelcome looks
103 Be of ___ (aid)

104 Syracuse player, once
105 Sacha Baron Cohen character
107 Original edition of this puzzle's theme
109 Actor Diggs
110 Words of triumph
111 Whack

114 Length of a pool and back
115 Partner of tuck
116 Suffix with elect

EVERYTHING EVENS OUT IN THE END

ACROSS

1 Solo partner
10 Multidecker sandwich
14 Stack at Starbucks
18 Word that follows "standard" and means something nonstandard
19 Abundant
20 Nettie's sister in "The Color Purple"
21 *Likely inexpensive place to get one's hair done*
23 During the time that
24 Baton Rouge sch.
25 Auctioneer's cry
26 Brownish tint
28 Final: Abbr.
29 En ___ (chess move)
33 Jolly time
35 Sports rival of Union College, for short
36 Chemistry unit: Abbr.
37 Wee devil
38 Cry like a baby
40 *Tourist activity in northern Scandinavia*
44 Backpack filler
46 "I dare you!"
48 Make a quick move
49 Chinese dynasty ended by Kublai Khan
50 It's groovy
52 Get to the bottom of
55 Lockup, to Sherlock
57 Villain's hideout
59 *Source of call-ups, in baseball lingo*
61 Prefix with culture
62 Virgil described its eruption in the "Aeneid"
63 "You got it, boss man!"
64 *Posting that blows in the wind*
67 Serenaded
71 Odyssey
72 *Has little excitement for*
77 Florentine : spinach :: lyonnaise : ___
82 Curry go-with
83 To be abroad?
84 *Allen Ginsberg, e.g.*
88 Baby beavers
89 Bird akin to the nene?
90 Arab country expelled from the Arab League in 2011
91 Green, in a way
92 Word cried before and after "all"
94 Governing org. of soccer
96 Reaction of shock
98 Analytics fodder
99 *Bottom-of-page design choice*
103 Spanish muralist José María ___
105 Actor Cariou
106 Place for a bouquet
107 Boston's Mass ___
108 Pb
110 Away from the wind
112 U.F.C. fighting style
113 Get Wired again, say
116 Hotel visit
118 ___-Magnon man
119 Scarecrow portrayer Ray
121 "How lucky was that?" . . . or a hint to the answers to the *italicized* clues
127 Seated yoga pose
128 Well-being
129 Seriously worry
130 What the Joneses may elicit
131 Tater
132 "Crazy Rich Asians" actress whose stage name puns on a bottled water brand

DOWN

1 Bank offerings, for short
2 Fashion line
3 Fashion model Marcille
4 Documents that name executors
5 Tree resin used in fragrances
6 On the same wavelength
7 A.F.L. partner
8 Bullies
9 Grate on
10 Charging station for a smartphone
11 Rapper ___ Yachty
12 Sci-fi saucers
13 Part of N.B.
14 Hula dancer's adornment
15 Subject of many conspiracy theories
16 Knocking out of place
17 End a lawsuit, say
20 Musical ___
22 Speak indistinctly
23 Erase
27 One of South Africa's capitals
29 Oink-filled pen
30 Don who won an Oscar for "Cocoon"
31 Converted splits
32 1400
34 Holiday marking the end of Ramadan
39 Feature of a Welsh accent
41 Winter Olympics host before Salt Lake City
42 Dreadfully slow
43 List in the credits
45 Wearers of striped shirts
47 Calendar column: Abbr.
51 Part of a trunk
53 Worker often found on hands and knees
54 Mini maker
56 Jargons
58 Bled
60 Not to be seen or heard by children
65 Tower construction material
66 Men
68 Infrequently
69 Howe nicknamed "Mr. Hockey"
70 Restrict with a string
72 Challenge for a stain remover
73 Popular Japanese manga series with a schoolgirl heroine
74 Counterpart of local channels
75 Beginning
76 Pranks, in a way, informally
78 Mini, for one
79 "How fancy!"
80 Like a tidied-up room, now
81 Bit of hair
85 Alternative to .net
86 Some Spanish babysitters

by Erik Agard

87 Art studio prop
93 Alternatives to nets
95 HuffPo purchaser in 2011
97 Make easier to eat, as an infant's food
99 Clumsily drop
100 Finished
101 Like a set of measuring cups, typically
102 "Later, luv!"
104 Mother ___
109 Role in "Our Gang" or "Queen Sugar"
111 "To the Lighthouse" novelist
114 ___ milk
115 Swatting sound
117 "Jeez, that's hot!"
120 Man
122 The Sun Devils, for short
123 "No, you shouldn't have"
124 Opus ___
125 Iniquity site
126 Springs for a vacation?

ACROSS

1 Praline ingredients
7 Error at a bridge table
14 Graduated
20 Sci-fi classic made into a 2004 film starring Will Smith
21 "Your money's no good here"
22 Trig function
23 Strauss opera with the "Dance of the Seven Veils"
24 Strains to hear, perhaps
25 Being affected by yeast
26 Vacuum cleaner blockage?
28 Sign at a restricted area of the Playboy Mansion?
30 San Joaquin Valley city
31 All-Star pitcher Severino
32 Some, in Sevilla
33 Not shipwrecked, say
34 Actor James
35 S O S first responders
36 Where G.I.s shop
39 End of some lists
42 Driving through some off-road terrain, say?
46 Moves around aimlessly
48 Ages and ages
49 Fix
50 Artist Joseph Wright's "A View of Catania With Mount ___ in the Distance"
51 "Who ___ kidding?"
52 Cheerios
55 This, e.g.
57 Letter opener?
58 San Francisco Giant, for example?
61 Yahoo alternative
64 Land and such
65 Land, to Livy
67 Like Samuel Beckett's "Endgame"
70 Iranian money
72 Overly serious Irish dancers?
75 Tons
78 Name on a green toy truck
80 Stag
81 Individual's segment of a 4 × 400 relay
82 Fur
83 Sicken with sweetness
85 Uncle Jorge, e.g.
86 Bergman or Borg
88 Write an order to replenish inventory of Levi's?
94 Alpine climber
95 Chummy pair?
96 Sitarist Shankar
97 Smackers
98 D.C. bigwigs
100 Suffix with billion
101 Memory problems
102 Garfield's girlfriend in the comics
105 Throwaway vault at a gymnastics meet?
109 Shower gift for a Gemini baby?
112 Glaciologist's concern
113 Native New Yorkers
115 Beep again
116 Back-and-forth
117 What a record collector might flip over
118 Like Cheerios vis-à-vis Corn Flakes
119 Divisions of the Westminster Dog Show
120 Launched
121 Hairnets

DOWN

1 "Hogwash!"
2 ___ Good Feelings
3 Lemon or lime
4 Chiefly
5 "Easy to clean," in adspeak
6 Not so lenient
7 Kunis of "Bad Moms"
8 Brangelina, at one time
9 Org. of concern to the AARP
10 Lothario
11 Subsequent
12 Out of whack
13 Advanced
14 Ponytail holder
15 Neologism
16 Orgs.
17 Super Bowl ___ (game played February 3, 2019)
18 Last of the Stuarts
19 Rules, briefly
27 Ian : Scottish :: ___ : Portuguese
29 Rapper Rhymes
31 Reclined
34 Walk-in, for one
35 Let off the hook
36 Red Rose
37 TV princess
38 Cyberjunk
39 Key with four sharps: Abbr.
40 Island in the East Indies
41 Chef Waters who wrote "The Art of Simple Food"
43 Jacob's first wife
44 Pocatello sch.
45 Travel bummer
47 Unemotional
53 Shaving aisle brand
54 Texter's bye-bye
55 Cracker brand since 1831
56 Harp-shaped constellation
57 Extended attacks
59 Something to do in a dojo
60 Sits up for food, say
62 Self-confidence, informally
63 Have ___ with
66 Takes advantage (of)
68 People person?
69 Masonry, e.g.
71 Japanese room divider
73 Morlock victims, in sci-fi
74 X-ray ___
75 Top
76 Fertile dirt
77 Twelvesome in "Gone With the Wind"
79 Spot
83 Tesla needs
84 Protective bank
85 48 in a cup: Abbr.
87 Figure out, informally
89 Prioritized in a hospital
90 Tree-lined walk
91 More chilly

by Tony Orbach and Andrea Carla Michaels

92 About 4,200 feet, for the Golden Gate Bridge
93 Caped fighters
99 Eddie Bauer rival
100 Subside
101 Put the pedal to the metal

103 Mystery writer Marsh
104 Did a "rotten" Halloween trick on
105 Barry, Robin or Maurice of the Bee Gees

106 Rent-___
107 French director Clair
108 Kind of stick for incense
109 Plain ___
110 Imposed upon

111 Gen ___ (millennials)
114 Indicator of staccato, in music notation

ACROSS

1 Get along
8 New York's longest parkway, with "the"
15 Eats
19 Exodus figure
20 Well-turned
21 "The Nutcracker" protagonist
22 L×A
24 Actor Gillen of "Game of Thrones"
25 Vodka in a blue bottle
26 Test for college srs.
27 Instrument that represents the duck in "Peter and the Wolf"
28 Lacework technique
30 The Caribbean's ___ Islands
33 Put at stake
35 Police group with an assignment
36 Mystery Writers of America trophy
39 x−y=x−y
42 Certain red algae
45 Middling mark
46 Fishmonger, at times
47 (A− or B+)/7
50 Postwar German sobriquet
54 Abbr. on a phone dial
55 Brest friend
56 Single hair on a carpet, maybe
59 Theresa May, for one
60 "Likewise"
62 Only places to find anteaters in the U.S.
63 Caboose
65 On point
67 √666
71 Dawn goddess
72 Blank section at the start of a cassette
74 Drop acid
75 Tennis's Nadal
77 "Bus Stop" playwright
78 Short cuts
79 "Hey ___"
80 Director Caro
83 Free all-ad publication
86 $$$/X
90 Spanish-speaking Muppet on "Sesame Street"
93 A short while?
94 Brewery named for a New York river
95 3.BB
100 Mullah's decree
101 Like unbaked bread
102 Box score bit
103 Noted dog trainer
106 Founder of Egypt's 19th dynasty
108 WSJ announcements
110 Drop to zero battery
111 Curse word
115 Some giggling dolls
116 X^{Esq}
120 Prognosticators
121 Hobbyist
122 Turned yellow, say
123 Goes off course
124 Actress Portia
125 One way to turn

DOWN

1 Two-stripe NCOs: Abbr.
2 "Sure, I guess"
3 "No sweat"
4 Airport security apparatus
5 Follower of Christ?
6 Like cornflakes, after sitting for a while
7 1,000 large calories
8 K'ung Fu-___ (Chinese name for Confucius)
9 "Now I get it!"
10 Russian blue or Egyptian Mau
11 OxyContin, e.g.
12 Archenemy
13 Martinique, par exemple
14 Dermatologist's concern
15 Fashionable set
16 Angular measurement
17 Relating to radioactive element No. 92
18 Wrist ornament
21 Booking for a wedding
23 Grassy stretches
29 First female singer to have three simultaneous solo top 10 singles
31 Elvis's middle name
32 Guitar inlay material
34 Seller of Famous Bowls
36 Gas brand with an oval logo
37 Pitched low
38 Attempted something
40 Opening to an apology
41 Tapering haircut
43 Nonmoving part of a motor
44 Blobbish "Li'l Abner" creature
48 Painter whose masterwork is said to be the Scrovegni Chapel frescoes
49 Earth Science subj.
51 The ___ Road in America (Nevada's Highway 50)
52 Wynken, Blynken and Nod, e.g.
53 Things that people are warned not to cross
57 Letters sometimes followed by :D
58 Handle online
61 Soldier food, for short
62 Throw in the microwave, slangily
63 R&B group with the 1991 No. 1 hit "I Like the Way"
64 She, in Portuguese
65 Father-and-daughter boxing champs
66 Phnom ___
68 Mystical ball, e.g.
69 Kind of year: Abbr.
70 Former national airline of Brazil
73 Sticks on the tongue?
76 Made an attempt
78 Verve
79 1993 Salt-N-Pepa hit whose title is a nonsense word
81 Didn't doubt
82 Notion
84 Sappho, e.g.
85 Annual athletic awards show
87 For sale in malls
88 Theater reproof

by Adam Fromm

89 Dope
91 Contraction in a Christmas song
92 Like Quakers
95 Actor Gibson of "2 Fast 2 Furious"
96 Doctor
97 Demolition tool
98 Stick on, as a poster
99 Exclamation that might accompany a curtsy
104 Lab-assisted, after "in"
105 Admit
107 Device that comes with 79-Across
109 ___-chef
112 Years in the Roman Empire
113 Abound
114 Fictional Mr.
117 Old-fashioned cry of despair
118 Part of T.G.I.F.: Abbr.
119 W.W. II rationing agcy.

ACROSS

1 Most popular baby girl's name of the 1960s, per the Social Security Administration
5 Squealer
9 Inside info
13 For fear that
17 Juul, e.g., for short
18 Old-time "The Price Is Right" announcer Johnny
19 Bit of greenery
21 Palindromic boy's name
22 Ward of cinema
23 Biography of Ebenezer Scrooge?
25 "Castaway" director Nicolas
26 Bond tightly
28 Colleague of Gorsuch
29 Big name in chicken
31 Biography of Amelia Earhart?
33 "Decorates" on Halloween, say
34 Biography of Archimedes?
36 Beep-booping droid, for short
37 Two-year degrees, briefly
39 Tricked
40 Took out
41 Some endangered ecosystems
42 One-fifth of the Jackson 5
44 Jesus on the diamond
45 Note taker
46 Tip-off for an exam proctor
47 What the "sans" refers to in Comic Sans
48 Diaper : U.S. :: ___ : U.K.
50 Oil magnate Leon who once owned the New York Jets
51 "Girls" home
53 Only mildly sweet
55 Get a Venmo request, say
57 Go through a window?
60 Obvious answer
61 Recreational sailboats
64 Excelled
66 British miler Sebastian
67 Diner sign
69 Shrewd
70 Winged Greek goddess
72 Highest hand value in baccarat
74 Capital of France's Côte d'Or
75 High points
76 Credit score, for short?
77 One side of the G.W. Bridge
78 Clever move
79 ___ monkey
81 Swimsuit material
85 "Step on it!"
86 Have a ___ for
87 Good name, informally
89 Xenophobe's fear, with "the"
90 Pro
91 Verb that's a homophone for a letter
92 Biography of the Venus de Milo?
96 One using a heater, say
99 Sound effects after some one-liners
103 Dramatic award
104 Pair of hearts?
107 Loudly project
109 Adidas competitor
110 & 112 Biography of Elvis?
114 With passion
115 Gate expectations, briefly?
116 Big dos
117 Quad/glute exercise
118 Wear away
119 Dramatic rebuttal
120 Poetic conjunction
121 Lets go of

DOWN

1 Picasso's "___ Demoiselles d'Avignon"
2 Some Antarctic samples
3 They create soft c's and g's
4 Biography of Thomas Crapper?
5 Unvarying charge
6 Its national anthem is "Hatikvah": Abbr.
7 Home to Bourbon St.
8 Showed allegiance, in a way
9 Some H.S. exams
10 "Yikes!"
11 Airport code for O'Hare
12 Elvis Costello hit that starts "I've been on tenterhooks / Ending in dirty looks"
13 Biography of Willie Mays?
14 Cajun dish of shellfish over rice
15 Increases in price
16 Dress (up)
18 Prefix with present
20 Major Argentine export
24 Chihuahua's sound
27 Big features of reality TV
30 Model T competitors
31 John Irving title character
32 Retreats
34 Like the signatures of outgoing people, it's said
35 Altar exchange
38 Author Larsson
39 Fiery look
43 & 44 Biography of Walt Disney?
47 Star turn
49 Hitch together
52 Doesn't go overboard?
54 "You may not have asked me, but . . ."
56 Certain green energy producers
57 Part of a Vandyke, informally
58 The title characters of 1988's "Dirty Rotten Scoundrels," e.g.
59 Iron ___
61 Kind of sheet
62 Tex-Mex offering
63 Stereotypical High Times reader
64 Lovecraftian
65 Pointers
67 Inky stone
68 Between: Fr.
71 Wham!
73 Nonreactive
80 Alaska Airlines hub
82 Suffix with doctor
83 Montreal is part of it: Abbr.
84 State on the Atl. coast

by Sophia Maymudes and Jeff Chen

85 Onetime
88 Like the phase ending after 12
90 Why parodies can't be sued for copyright infringement
92 Classic
93 Corrigenda
94 Daniel Webster, notably
95 Artist with seven posthumous platinum albums
96 ___ distance
97 Detest
98 Grandchild: Sp.
100 Like some flocks
101 Blush, e.g.
102 Seven ___ of Ancient Greece
105 Midwest capital, informally
106 Revenue alternative to subscriptions
107 Bosom buddy
108 Anglerfish's light, e.g.
111 The Science Guy
113 Giant's opposite

ACROSS

1 Metaphor for an aggressive political arena
8 Puts away
15 Source of fries
19 One who didn't even show?
20 Frame part
21 It stayed in Pandora's box
22 *Ballroom dancing event for Beantown residents?
24 Takes a course
25 Relatives of foils
26 Shade of green
27 Dundee dissent
28 Mother-of-pearl
29 Imperfect service
30 Climax
33 *Annoying member of a New York baseball team?
36 Thrills
37 Family moniker
38 Hydrocarbon gas
39 World capital known as Batavia until 1942
42 "Witches' Flight" painter
44 Sparkling white wine
46 Pesticide banned in 1972
47 *Wager in which the winner gets the loser's pants and jersey?
49 They're not hard to swallow
52 ___ Cuervo (tequila brand)
53 Casanova
55 Slapstick actor Jacques
59 "___ over"
60 Contingency phrase
63 Man's name that's the reverse of 60-Down

64 Don hastily
67 *Duo ruling a kingdom on Take Your Daughter to Work Day?
72 It's higher on the Scoville scale than a jalapeño
73 Skin pic?
74 Pallid
75 Certain 35mm camera
76 Major or minor in astronomy?
77 Like chewing gum in Singapore or wearing blue jeans in North Korea (seriously!)
81 Second-largest branch of Islam
82 Attacks à la Don Quixote
85 *Exclamation after a performance of "Every Breath You Take"?
89 Platform for many tablets
92 Building blocks, e.g.
93 Vegetarian gelatin substitute
95 Property recipient
96 "Looks promising!"
98 Covert org.
99 Sailor's cry
100 *Amusement park named after a "Peanuts" boy?
104 College football rival of 110-Across
105 Unembellished
108 Jetson who attends Little Dipper School
109 Broadway show about Capote
110 College football rival of 104-Across
112 Pricey fashion label

114 & 115 Communication system that's a hint to the answer to each starred clue
119 Tireless racer
120 They might hold derbies
121 Fall apart
122 Spots for hammers and anvils
123 Common lease period
124 It may have a lot of intelligence

DOWN

1 Early tower locale
2 Skip the ceremony, in a way
3 Strong point
4 Mechanical
5 Shakespearean sorcerer
6 Janis ___, singer of the 1975 hit "At Seventeen"
7 Earth-shattering invention?
8 Unpleasantly wet
9 Like child's play
10 Artist Jean
11 Defeats soundly
12 Greek goddesses of the seasons
13 Signature scent since 1968
14 Total mess
15 Sword holder
16 Took stock?
17 Good news for a stockholder
18 Early name for Utah
20 Forensic material
23 Does some grilling
28 What a stiffed server receives
31 ___'acte
32 Noted exile
34 Falls for someone who's already married?

35 Testing stage
36 Bread box?
39 Sport that emphasizes pinning and throwing
40 Terse bar order
41 Traps
42 Former G.M. make
43 First N.L. player to hit 500 home runs
44 Laila of the ring
45 Big maker of lawn care products
48 Like-minded voters
50 Receptionist on "The Office"
51 "Hold it!"
54 Mañana preceder
56 Inundated with
57 Five-star
58 Furious
60 Man's name that's the reverse of 63-Across
61 End of a French film
62 Snobbish
65 L.B.J.'s veep
66 "Star Wars: The Last Jedi" heroine
68 Idiot, in British slang
69 "___ Kett" (old comic strip)
70 Something taken in by sailors
71 Infant's early word
78 ___ Nautilus
79 Ring letters
80 Make a wrong move
81 Change one's mind about changing
83 Source of many an imported boot, appropriately
84 Site of a 1796 Napoleon victory
86 "___-voom!"
87 Patron saint of Norway

by Trenton Charlson

88 One fighting an uphill battle?
89 Altar offering
90 "C'est magnifique!"
91 Official with a pistol
94 Pygmalion's beloved
97 Stews (over)

98 One of 32 for Ireland
99 Reformed demon on "Buffy the Vampire Slayer"
101 Edith Wharton's "___ Frome"
102 Composed

103 Having less vermouth, as a martini
105 Shul scholar
106 Dancing partner for Fred
107 Fire extinguisher
111 Puts on a show, for short

113 Plows (into)
115 Vietnamese noodle soup
116 Poet's "before"
117 Kind of screen, in brief
118 Maven

Note: Drop one letter from each set of shaded letters in the grid to name a major-league baseball team. The letters thus removed, in order from top to bottom, will spell an appropriate answer at 76-Down.

ACROSS

1 Top 10-rated sitcom each season from 1972 to 1976
6 Chilling
11 Payment vouchers
16 Dugout propeller
19 Mexico City daily
20 Dish of cooked buckwheat
21 Site of a 2019 Trump/Kim meeting
22 ___ hug
23 Moved stealthily, colloquially
24 Not a nice look
25 Pronounces breathily
27 Hearty pasta topping
29 Absolute truth
31 A singer can carry one
32 Some plumbing joints
33 Ask too-personal questions
34 Tailor's tool
35 Uses as a perch
37 Mold into something new
39 Historic San Francisco thoroughfare
41 ___ y Plata (Montana's motto)
42 Aid in tapestry-making
43 Itinerant sorts
44 Outfits in the operating room
48 Stockholm stock unit
50 "Look at me ___ I did it!"
54 Precisely
55 Saint in a children's rhyme
56 ___ Maria (coffee liqueur)
57 Sister in a children's story
59 Small pain
60 Upright building support
61 Travel group
64 Big name in 1950s politics
65 "Flowers" and "Sticky Fingers" for the Stones
66 Some Sunday broadcasting
69 Cakes and ___ (simple material pleasures)
70 Buncha
72 Hockey venues
73 Wonka portrayer
74 Rock band with the 1994 4x platinum album "The Downward Spiral," for short
75 Many Jazz fans
77 Elusive sort
78 Smooth-talking
79 ___ Reader (quarterly magazine)
80 Prefix with scope
81 Bestow
84 "The Wonder Years" star
86 Goldman's partner in banking
88 Symbol of poverty
89 Unwieldy boat
90 Visited out of deference (to)
94 Bright light in inclement conditions
98 Doesn't bring up again, say
99 "Sad to say . . ."
100 Go off
101 Dodgers broadcaster Hershiser
102 K–12
103 Casting choice
105 Colorless mode at a copy shop
107 Strong servings with dessert
109 Bit of dental work
111 Where the Firestone tire company was founded
112 "___ Beso" (Paul Anka hit)
113 Sharp
114 Bull ___
115 Tilted, in Stilton
116 Barbecue bone
117 Awful-smelling
118 Went back, as a tide
119 Like the Chelsea neighborhood in Manhattan

DOWN

1 Physician Franz who coined the term "animal magnetism"
2 Variant of a gene
3 Unsurprising people to show up
4 "Inside voices, please"
5 ___ Lodge
6 "All right, why not"
7 With 90-Down, first woman to lead a major party in Congress
8 "Mm-hmm"
9 Narrator of "Evita"
10 Tremendous auditory pleasure, in slang
11 Drink after drink?
12 Trunk fastener
13 Not remotely
14 Traveler's holder of bathroom supplies
15 "Kind ___" (term of politeness)
16 Thickheaded
17 Playground comeback
18 Nevada senator Jacky
26 Sworn (to)
28 Fitting
30 Make a decision
34 New Mexico county or its seat
36 Hit sign
38 Wall St. professional
39 Hotel rollouts
40 "Look what I found!"
42 Schubert compositions
44 Burning the midnight oil
45 Dessert with a sugary syrup
46 Drake, for one
47 Something seen with a tiny flashlight
48 What cowboys are, in poker lingo
49 High praise
51 Home of Spelman College
52 Business transaction
53 Property recipient, legally
56 Related to pitches
58 Intensify, with "up"
60 Hall-of-Famer Musial
61 Like some porch chairs
62 Popular radio format
63 Farmer's concern
67 Turn sharply
68 John le Carré specialty
71 "No turning back now"
76 [See note]
78 List for charitable givers, for short
79 Sunscreen ingredient

by Andrew J. Ries

82 Something removed when changing a tire
83 Pompous sort
84 Domino, familiarly
85 8/
87 Throw in
88 Former Indianapolis sports venue
90 See 7-Down
91 Pulsating
92 Analyzed
93 "Xanadu" band, briefly
94 Loose around the edges
95 Peak in Genesis
96 They have thick skins
97 Good supply
98 Outcast
100 Make blank
104 Legendary humanoid
105 Shapeless mass
106 Hacienda room
108 Mil. program discontinued in 1976
110 Head, in slang

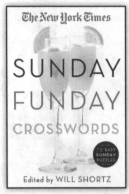
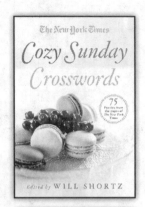

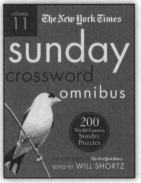

1

L	A	R	D	S		S	W	A	G		F	R	O	G	S		N	A	S	A
A	F	O	O	T		A	I	D	E		I	O	N	I	A		O	P	E	C
P	R	O	J	E	C	T	G	U	T	E	N	B	E	R	G		H	O	A	R
S	O	S	O	R	R	Y			T	V	S		A	L	E		E	S	S	O
E	S	T		E	A	R	A	C	H	E		E	R	S		A	L	T	O	N
		D	O	G		P	R	E	S	E	N	T	C	O	M	P	A	N	Y	
U	R	G	E	S		U	P	O	N		Y	O	H	O	H	O		T	A	M
P	E	R	F	E	C	T	S	C	O	R	E	S		U	N	R	E	E	L	S
S	H	E	A	T	H	E			D	I	F		S	T	O	O	L			
H	E	A	T		E	R	I	C		D	U	M	A			U	L	T	R	A
O	A	S		P	R	O	D	U	C	E	L	A	B	E	L	S		H	E	R
T	R	Y	T	O		E	R	O	S		G	E	N	E		S	E	A	R	
		W	O	L	F	S		H	O	P		A	N	A	T	O	L	E		
M	A	H	A	L	I	A		C	O	N	T	R	A	C	T	T	E	R	M	S
A	R	E		T	E	N	S	O	R		C	O	L	T		T	R	Y	S	T
D	I	S	C	O	U	N	T	S	T	O	R	E	S		E	E	N			
E	S	S	A	Y		E	R	A		D	U	G	O	U	T	S		P	S	A
A	T	I	T		A	D	A		P	O	I			T	A	T	T	L	E	S
B	I	A	S		C	O	N	V	E	R	S	E	A	L	L	S	T	A	R	S
E	D	N	A		T	U	G	O	N		E	R	I	E		T	O	N	G	A
T	E	S	T		S	T	E	W	S		R	E	L	Y		O	P	T	E	D

2

M	A	Z	D	A	S		H	E	R	O	D		H	M	O		S	E	A	S
O	N	E	A	C	T		A	D	O	B	E		E	E	L		U	C	L	A
A	N	S	W	E	R	I	N	G	M	A	C	H	I	N	E		R	O	A	R
N	U	T	S		E	G	G	Y		M	A	U	N	A		S	E	L	M	A
A	L	S	O	R	A	N	S		A	F	R	I	C	A	N	L	I	O	N	
		N	E	M	O		I	R	E		L	E	E	W	A	Y				
P	A	T		A	E	R	A	T	O	R				S	W	I	N	G	B	Y
S	Q	U	I	R	R	E	L	E	D	A	W	A	Y		L	O	O	I	E	
A	U	L	D			E	M	S		E	V	E	S			T	O	T	O	
T	A	I	L	I	N	G			C	R	O	A	K	E	D		D	E	W	
		P	E	R	S	U	A	S	I	V	E	W	R	I	T	I	N	G		
P	C	B		S	A	L	I	N	A	S			T	A	P	E	R	E	D	
U	H	U	H		F	R	O	G		A	H	A			H	I	L	O		
G	A	L	A	S		S	W	O	R	D	A	N	D	S	H	I	E	L	D	
S	I	B	L	I	N	G		E	D	U	C	A	T	E		F	A	O		
		F	L	O	R	A	L		A	S	L		M	R	E	D				
A	V	O	C	A	D	O	R	O	L	L		D	I	A	L	E	C	T	S	
S	O	L	O	S		A	T	E	I	T		W	E	A	N		B	O	O	P
A	C	L	U		K	N	O	W	S	A	T	H	I	N	G	O	R	T	W	O
H	A	I	R		L	E	I		P	L	I	E	S		E	D	I	T	E	D
I	B	E	T		M	R	S		S	K	E	E	T		R	E	S	A	L	E

3

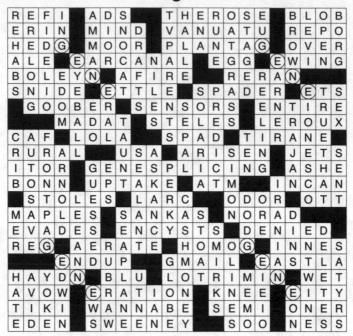

4

5

TRANS · AGED · ODDS · ALBUS
BALOO · ROLE · PERM · TEENA
SHERYLCROW · SCOUTFINCH
PAVE · IHOP · LOTR · SELL
· LEARN · GEO · TAP · AMUSE
· SIGOURNEYWEAVER ·
· APOLUNE · PAP · DIALECT
FRANKIE · TOTEM · LIESLOW
RUM · END · ATSEA · ILE · ANA
ABET · EASY · RUNS · PRAY
TALIB · YOLO · DING · TOILS
· AMES · TOREROS · MELC
ABSOLUT · RAGON · DUELERS
YOUROCK · STOIC · OSMOSIS
ENE · WHOSWE · DRUNKS · TAN
SAMS · ASTI · ARSE · GALS
· ATMS · AFGHANS · TSAR
BARRE · ARTMUSEUM · TYLER
RITADOVE · ASP · LADYBIRD
IDITAROD · IKE · ATALANTA
MANILOW · LYN · EMERGES

6

KING · HOGAN · PROTIP · ELF
ASEA · AGORA · RAVINE · CEO
THELORDOFTHERINGS · HER
· GAPED · CASED · REPORT
WHEATON · SHUTS · DATA
HANDY · OWETO · TITANIC
ASTO · CITIZENKANE · MOP
LSAT · ANTS · ELKS · TAME
ELI · REPOS · FLAKY · DUMBO
DELOUSE · DIECI · SETSON
· PLANETOFTHEAPES ·
OUSTER · LENTO · LORISES
SPEED · SMASH · UNDUE · APU
LEWD · STIR · MEET · SLIP
ONE · MARYPOPPINS · TAPE
· DRACULA · ELLEN · NAMER
· LUGE · NAIAD · ADORING
AGEING · NINNY · SPORT
BIG · ALEAGUEOFTHEIROWN
EVA · RENNET · FLAIR · ERIE
TED · DROOLS · FUNDS · KONG

```
DRAT    DATIVE  SLIMUP
RECUT  CINEMAX  SPANISH
INTRO  AMILATE  LANDTAX
QUINCEJELLY  QUINCE
   POTUS   CUSP  EXAMS
 GERMAN  AYEAYESIR  MAW
DAFOE  ABAFT  THO  LORI
ELF  DOBBYTHEHOUSEELF
WASABIPEA  OVID  TIBET
 GETIT  HADES  REPAY
 SEIZE  POWER  SEIZE
 ACITY  MOTES  SOMNI
AMISS  TAUT  GODISGOOD
DUETOTHEFACTTHAT  DUE
INNS  MRS  KAZOO  NOICE
ORC  DIETMENUS  FRENCH
SAYSO  ARCS  SIEVE
 LOSTIN  TRANSLATION
BUSYBEE  AKRONOH  DETOO
ITALIAN  BIOLOGY  ARTOO
GENYER  BATONS  MYOB
```

```
DESPAIR  DRJ  SEPT  ORME
ENCARTA  YOO  TRIO  NEIL
EGOTRIP  SKY  RINGCYCLE
REPRESSYOURLUCK  HMONG
 LEIA  HEN  IOC  ISE  VEY
 ORIEL  SDAK  SEALE
EMIT  RELATETOTHEPARTY
VIDA  STALK  HUH  DOUGIE
EXACT  STAIN  TEAL  RILE
 TOP  ITEM  UNITARDS
AIR  RESENTPACKING  LAH
THELORAX  SARA  GIS
PACE  FLED  LIMOS  FELIX
AVENGE  CEO  MERIT  CONE
RESTOCKSANDBONDS  OWNS
 SORTA  TYRA  ICAHN
IMP  GOT  HOY  STA  EDAM
NOOSE  RETURNTHETABLES
SNOWSKIER  UIE  SIDEONE
UGLI  INLA  NNE  ARTSALE
MOST  RASP  SOL  ROOTFOR
```

9

10

11

A	B	B	A		I	C	U		S	C	A	D	S		A	P	C	A	L	C
D	E	E	D		F	O	P		O	A	K	E	N		H	O	O	R	A	H
A	L	L	H	A	I	L	H	A	L	L	A	L	E		A	R	M	A	N	I
G	L	I	D	E		L	I	B	E	L		G	A	G		K	A	N	Y	E
E	Y	E		I	T	A	L	O		R	A	K	E	D		C	A	F		
		B	O	O	B	L	U	R	R	E	D	B	L	U	E	B	I	R	D	
D	E	P	A	U	L		T	E	A	P	O	Y		B	R	A	N	D	O	
I	M	A	N		I	C	E		I	M	O		E	L	I	T	I	S	M	
S	O	N	E	R	V	O	U	S	N	O	S	E	R	V	I	C	E			
U	T	E		D	E	N	C	H		N	E	M	E	A	N		A	X	E	S
S	E	R	R	A		C	H	A	N		D	E	N	S		H	U	E	V	O
E	S	A	U		W	A	R	R	E	D		N	O	I	R	E		D	E	W
			S	T	E	V	E	D	O	R	E	D	I	V	A	S	T	O	R	E
S	A	L	T	I	N	E		P	A	T		R	E	D		O	U	S	T	
A	G	E	I	S	T		A	G	E	N	T	S			I	D	O	T	O	O
D	U	T	C	H	T	O	W	N	T	O	U	C	H	D	O	W	N			
T	I	M			O	R	E	O	S			R	A	I	S	E		S	P	F
A	L	E	U	T		R	E	C		S	T	O	N	Y		E	M	C	E	E
L	E	T	T	E	R		B	C	H	O	R	D	K	E	Y	B	O	A	R	D
E	R	R	A	T	A		I	H	O	P	E		I	R	E		O	N	C	E
S	A	Y	H	E	Y		T	I	P	S	Y		E	S	P		S	T	Y	X

12

P	A	P	A	S		C	O	M	B	A	T			S	L	I	M	J	I	M
T	B	I	L	L		B	L	U	E	C	A	P		P	E	N	T	O	D	E
A	C	Q	U	I	R	E	A	C	H	O	I	R		I	N	C	E	N	S	E
S	T	U	M	P	E	R		H	E	R		F	C	C		A	T	B	A	T
	V	E	N	O	M				A	N	O	I	S	E	A	N	N	O	Y	S
		I	N	S	I	P	I	D		S	R	I		I	T	A	N			
L	S	U			V	I	M		P	U	M	M	E	L	S		J	A	W	
A	P	P	A	L	L	A	P	A	U	L		I	D	S		P	O	N	Y	
R	E	D	B	E	A	N	S		N	A	S	S	A	U		D	E	V	I	L
S	W	O	R	E	T	O		A	U	N	T	E	M		C	E	R	I	S	E
			A	R	I	V	A	L	S	A	R	R	I	V	A	L	S			
A	F	G	H	A	N		T	E	E	H	E	E		O	U	T	O	F	I	T
C	R	O	A	T		D	E	E	D	E	E		M	I	L	A	N	E	S	E
D	E	E	M		P	E	A		A	T	T	A	C	K	S	A	T	A	X	
C	D	S		T	O	Y	L	A	N	D		E	N	E			T	O	T	
	P	A	S	O		I	R	E		C	A	N	D	I	E	S				
A	V	O	W	E	L	A	V	O	W	A	L			K	L	E	I	N		
B	A	S	A	L		D	E	M		B	O	S		L	E	A	R	N	E	D
O	N	T	R	I	A	L		A	P	A	T	C	H	Y	A	P	A	C	H	E
R	C	A	D	O	M	E		S	A	T	H	O	M	E		S	P	A	I	N
T	E	L	S	T	A	R		P	E	S	T	O	S		E	E	N	S	Y

13

```
K O D A K   R U B S   C O B     L I C I T
A L I E N   E R A T   E N O   F U T U R E
Y E S N O   A G R E E D T O   L I S T E N
      T E L L L E F T F R O M R I G H T
S Q U A L I D       T I P   O P I O I D S
O U R S   V E A L   S C O L D   T N U T
B I B   T E A R E D   F E I N T   G N U
  D I S H   L A G U N A   S N O W D E N
B   A P E S   B O D I C E S   W O O D   W
L     A M E S   L E X E M E S   H O G   H
A   G R A N A D A     I N A D A Z E   I
C   E T S   C O N C H E S   T O N I   T
K   T A S K   A D V E R S E   A D E S   E
  B O N E S A W   S N A I L S   E S P N
A R F   S U S A N   S O L O E D   O O F
W I F I   C Y A N S   N A L A   I N T O
S O A N D S O   K O N   A V E N G E R
  S P O T T H E D I F F E R E N C E
B A H A M A   I D I T A R O D   D O B B Y
A D O R E R   L L C   D A N A   E M O T E
M O T T S   L Y E   E T S Y   D E B U T
```

14

```
T U B A S   E N O K I   N A G   G O S H
O C E A N   L E W I S   C O I L   U N T O
G O A H E A D W I T H O U T M E   S E L L
A N N   E M O T E   S T I L E T T O E D
S N O O Z E R S   S C H E M E   H A N O I
    M E S A   T H E A Y E S H A V E I T
A S E A   D R O O L   S A M
I W A N T T O B E A L O N E   L E T S B E
R E T I R E   I S T   P E L L   S I C O N
S A L   A X E   B U R L A P   L I D S
  T U R N A B O U T I S F A I R P L A Y
G E N E   S A P P H O   T A R   T O T
M R C U B   Y A D A   P S A   D O S I D O
A S H P A N   H O W N O W B R O W N C O W
    R E S   A P A C E   E A R N
C O G I T O E R G O S U M   S P A R
A R E N A   N O S O A P   S T A R D U S T
S C R U B B E D U P   E I E I O   M I A
T H A R   A G E I S J U S T A N U M B E R
R I L E   R A N T   A N A I S   S E E T O
O D D S   B L T   R A I N Y   E G R E T
```

15

A	T	L	A	S		A	P	E	R	C	U			B	A	B	A	W	A	W	A
L	E	A	P	T		R	O	M	E	O	S			E	A	R	T	H	D	A	Y
T	A	U	P	E		S	P	I	L	L	E	D	T	H	E	B	E	A	N	S	
E	R	R		A	B	E			Y	U	R	I		S	W	A	R	M			
R	U	E		L	A	N	A	I		M	I	S	C			T	E	S	L	A	
S	P	L	I	T	H	A	L	F	A	N	D	H	A	L	F			C	O	G	
			S	H	A	L	L	O	T				R	E	I	M	P	O	S	E	
S	A	P	P	Y			L	A	C	K	E	D	A	F	I	L	T	E	R		
E	B	A	Y		P	I	E	D		H	A	L		S	T	R	U	T	S		
R	B	I		T	H	A	N		L	A	G	E	R		H	A	M				
F	A	R	F	R	O	M	Y	O	U	R	A	V	E	R	A	G	E	J	O	E
		A	Y	N		A	W	M	A	N		D	O	V	E		U	R	L	
	H	E	R	O	E	S		L	E	D		I	S	E	E		B	A	L	M
R	A	N	O	U	T	O	F	S	T	E	A	M			S	O	N	Y	S	
I	N	D	E	T	A	I	L			M	O	R	O	C	C	O				
M	O	I		G	R	O	U	N	D	S	F	O	R	F	I	R	I	N	G	
S	I	N	G	S		G	O	E	R		F	I	D	O	S		T	E	A	
	A	R	E	S	T		M	A	A	M			E	S	S		H	U	M	
G	O	T	I	N	T	O	H	O	T	W	A	T	E	R		O	R	A	T	E
R	A	I	N	D	A	T	E		E	E	Y	O	R	E		R	A	C	E	R
P	R	E	S	S	B	O	X		R	R	A	T	E	D		S	T	A	R	S

16

N	P	R		A	P	I	A	R	Y		P	I	S	C	E	S		A	P	P
O	R	E		L	E	S	L	I	E		A	R	M	A	D	A		C	A	L
M	I	C	R	O	C	H	I	P	S		P	L	U	R	A	L		P	L	O
A	D	O	U	T		S	E	N	S	E		R	O	M		E	L	A	N	
D	E	N	G		A	S	T	R	O	K	E	O	F	B	A	D	L	U	C	K
			R	A	N	T	S		U	T	N	E		M	I	D	G	E	S	
A	S	S	A	N	G	E		P	L	E	A	T		E	V	E				
C	A	P	T	A	I	N	H	O	O	K		I	T	S		A	R	F	E	D
E	K	E		L	E	T	U	P	S		G	R	E	E	D		W	E	A	R
S	E	E	D	Y		L	E	I	L	A			T	E	N	A	N	T	S	
		D	I	S	T	R	A	C	T	E	D	D	R	I	V	I	N	G		
B	O	B	S	T	A	Y		E	A	S	Y	A		E	D	S	E	L		
A	L	A	S		R	A	B	I	D		D	E	N	T	A	L		H	W	Y
A	E	G	I	S		N	A	S		W	E	D	G	E	I	S	S	U	E	S
	D	O	E		T	A	G	O	N			P	R	E	C	I	S	E		
D	O	T	E	L	L		S	A	L	K		G	E	E	N	A				
I	R	O	N	D	E	F	I	C	I	E	N	C	I	E	S		R	P	M	S
T	N	U	T		G	A	G		S	N	A	R	F		E	J	E	C	T	
H	E	P		W	A	L	N	U	T		N	O	T	U	P	T	O	P	A	R
E	R	E		E	N	C	A	S	E		A	N	E	M	I	A		S	T	U
R	Y	E		S	T	O	L	E	N		S	E	D	A	N	S		I	S	M

17

S	W	E	E	T			O	A	R		E	X	P	O			P	O	N	E
H	A	S	B	R	O		F	E	E		X	M	A	N		M	O	T	E	S
A	S	S	E	E	N	O	N	T	V		M	A	K	E	S	A	L	I	S	T
H	A	I	R	S	A	L	O	N	S		A	S	U		A	S	K	S	T	O
S	T	E	T		R	I	T	A		P	R	E	L	I	M	S				
			B	A	N	E		P	A	I	S	A	N		A	F	I	R	E	
P	R	A	I	R	I	E		R	E	I	N		T	A	C	O	B	A	R	
T	U	N	N	E	L		F	E	E	D	E	R		H	E	R	E	I	G	O
A	N	N	U	M		S	L	U	R		R	E	N	E	G	E		Z	E	D
S	T	E	R	E	O	T	Y	P	I	C		T	A	K	E		A	D	E	
			E	N	L	A	I		N	A	G		T	N	U	T	S			
A	L	A		D	I	N	G		R	A	D	I	O	S	H	A	C	K	S	
M	I	C		B	A	D	G	E	S		Y	E	O	W		E	L	R	O	Y
I	R	E	S	I	G	N		T	U	N	E	I	N		V	I	S	I	O	N
G	A	L	I	L	E	E		P	E	T	S		C	U	R	A	B	L	E	
A	S	A	D	O		S	C	R	E	W	Y		P	O	L	S				
		X	L	S	H	I	R	T		D	O	U	G		F	A	H	D		
A	R	A	B	I	A		I	C	U		R	O	L	L	A	C	I	G	A	R
T	O	T	E	M	P	O	L	E	S		A	C	I	D	T	O	N	G	U	E
O	B	I	T	S		S	I	R	E		M	K	T		E	M	A	I	L	S
M	E	T	A		U	S	S	R		P	S	Y		E	L	E	S	S		

18

21

22

23

```
A B L E . . . W I L D E . T E T . H A D J
W O O D S . F I V E R S . O R A T O R I O
O R C H E S T R A T E S . D I N E T T E S
L E O . R E L E N T S . L O C K S M I T H
. . M O A N E R S . S P A . . A S I F . .
G R O U P I E S . G E R I A T R I C I A N
M A T T E L . . W E R E . L O D E . C L U
A M I D . E I G H T . E B B S . . P I E T
I B O O K . C U E S . M O U S E T R A P S
L O N . A R E N A . F I R M . S A I L H O
. . . S L E D . T I R E D . C A L M . . .
L I F T E D . T I T O . E E R I E . P E T
I D E A L O G U E S . B A L I . S C H M O
L E V Y . . A L S O . R U M B A . L A C E
T S E . I N R I . P A I X . . R O A R E R
S T R A T O S P H E R E . D U L C I M E R
. . I L L S . . I N B . L I N E A R A . .
M I S T L E T O E . O R I G I N S . C O O
I S H E D E A D . P R O F I T E E R I N G
A L L R O U N D . R E L E T S . Y A S I R
S A Y S . M G S . O D O R S . . . E T T E
```

24

```
A P S E . M I S S A L S . F I B . C R E D
D E U X . O N T A R I O . U R E T H A N E
I N I T . O C E L O T S . T O R R A N C E
O U T R U N . E T N A . B I N G E R R O R
S P E A K S F L Y . F O I L . . . I R E .
. . . V E E R . G I M L E T . S H O E S .
H O P I . T A Y . U R A L . A W A I T S .
Q U I R K . N E A T E R . M E T E . . . .
S I E G E . K A R T . S L U M B E R P A Y
. . R I G . R E C . A M I E S . R R R . .
I C O N . N A M E D R O P P E R . L O T S
M U G . S O F I A . U S E . . J O B . . .
P R I M C O L O R S . A L P E . U T I C A
. . A O N E . E G G S O N . T U T O R . .
. P O R T E R . P E R E . E D U . S Y N C
T O N Y S . S E R I E S . O N C E . . . .
D E E . . . G E N A . E A R L Y A M E N .
P H O N E M A R S . S A R I . E L T O R O
A L C A P O N E . M I N O R C A . E R I N
S E A L I O N S . R E D D E E R . R A C E
S R T A . R E S . T R I E S O N . S L A T
```

25

Puzzle 25:

	F	I	F	E		S	W	A	T	S		M	A	K	E	S		C	A	B
E	R	R	O	R		K	E	Y	U	P		I	R	A	T	E		O	X	O
G	E	O	R	G	I	A	N	E	R	A		K	E	S	H	A		B	I	G
B	E	N	T	O	N		T	S	K		N	A	T	H	A	N	H	A	L	E
E	B	A	Y		M	U	S	H		W	A	D	E	I	N		E	L	L	Y
R	I	G		P	I	S	T	A	C	H	I	O	S		A	O	R	T	A	S
T	E	E		O	D	E	A		H	A	L			F	L	U	B			
			P	T	A		G	R	A	T	E		K	I	L	T		J	E	W
W	A	S	S	A	I	L		E	N	I	D		O	R	E	S		A	S	H
E	Y	E	S	T	R	A	I	N		F	I	G	M	E	N	T		R	C	A
R	E	C	T	O		C	H	E	R		T	U	B	A		A	S	F	O	R
E	A	R		C	D	T	O	W	E	R		S	U	R	F	N	T	U	R	F
O	Y	E		H	E	A	P		C	O	L	T		M	O	D	E	L	T	S
N	E	T		I	T	I	S		A	D	I	O	S		R	I	M			
			S	P	E	D		N	E	E		O	V	E	N			S	L	R
A	C	C	E	S	S		A	S	T	O	U	N	D	I	N	G		C	U	E
D	O	U	R		T	O	P	T	E	N		I	A	M	S		T	H	R	U
D	A	D	B	L	A	S	T	E	D		B	C	C		I	C	E	M	E	N
O	C	D		I	B	S	E	N		C	R	E	A	M	C	H	E	E	S	E
N	H	L		A	L	I	S	T		H	E	N	N	A		A	N	A	I	S
S	K	Y		M	E	E	T	S		I	D	E	S	T		D	A	R	N	

26

Puzzle 26:

S	T	H	E	L	E	N	A		A	C	T	S	O	N		S	P	A	M	S
T	E	A	T	I	M	E	S		L	O	V	A	T	O		A	R	T	O	O
I	N	T	H	O	U	G	H	T	A	S	M	U	C	H		G	O	D	N	O
F	U	T	O	N	S		B	O	N	M	O	T			L	A	B	A	T	T
F	R	I	S	T		S	I	N	S	O	M	E	S	M	A	L	L	W	A	Y
S	E	P		A	V	O	N			S	E	A	N		E	N	G			
			E	M	I	T		W	E	E	P		G	R	A	M	M			
	R	A	B	I	D		S	I	N	G	O	F	O	M	I	S	S	I	O	N
P	A	R	E	N		C	A	T	D	O	O	R			G	E	N	R	E	
S	T	I	N	G	I	N	T	H	E	S	H	O	W	E	R		C	A	L	I
H	A	Z	E		F	E	Y				R	A	N		T	W	A	S		
A	T	O	Z		S	T	R	I	N	G	O	P	E	R	A	T	I	O	N	S
W	A	N	E	S			C	O	Y	N	E	S	S		H	O	R	D	E	
S	T	A	R	I	N	G	Q	U	A	R	T	E	T		K	E	N	D	O	
			S	T	O	L	I		H	O	O	K		H	I	P	S			
	A	M	C		L	E	N	A			P	E	D	I		C	O	G		
S	T	A	R	T	I	N	G	D	A	G	G	E	R	S		A	S	A	N	A
A	E	R	O	B	E		D	R	E	A	M	Y		A	N	I	M	A	S	
B	A	L	O	O		S	T	A	R	T	L	I	N	G	L	I	N	E	U	P
E	S	I	G	N		O	H	M	A	M	A		N	O	I	S	E	T	T	E
R	E	N	E	E		Y	E	S	Y	E	S		E	A	S	T	W	O	O	D

27

```
L O S T D O G ■ B E C K ■ ■ P R E E M P T
A R M O I R E ■ A L O E ■ ■ S H A N T I E S
T E A R G A S ■ L I N T ■ ■ E A S T A S I A
■ ■ ■ S I C ■ E L E C T ■ N E P A L ■ ■
D O R O T H Y G A L E ■ A D D I N ■ E B B
U N O S ■ ■ O E D I P A L ■ R E G A L I A
B I B ■ A S K S ■ ■ T H E D A R L I N G S
Y O Y O D I E T E R ■ A S U ■ ■ E M O T E
A N N U A L ■ S T E T S ■ R A T S ■ R O D
■ ■ T P K S ■ H A I ■ B A J A ■ R T E ■
■ L I T T L E O R P H A N A N N I E ■ ■
■ B E E ■ I O N S ■ S A Y ■ R K O S ■ ■
B A A ■ P E E R ■ G Y R O S ■ I M E L D A
A B D U L ■ ■ O P E ■ P U T O N A N A C T
N I C K A N D N O R A ■ O V I D ■ S E A
N E A R Y O U ■ R E D T A P E ■ S I L L
S S R ■ M S N B C ■ J O N A R B U C K L E
■ ■ M A C A O ■ M O U N T ■ A I R ■ ■
G O T O T O W N ■ E U R O ■ L I N E O U T
T E A S E R A D ■ T R E Y ■ U T T E R E D
O D Y S S E Y ■ ■ E N D S ■ X S A N D Y S
```

28

```
C I S C O ■ E S U R A N C E ■ T H E R A M
U S T E N ■ S H A W N E E S ■ M A D A M E
B A R E S ■ Q U E R Y W A S H I N G T O N
I D I ■ P E S T ■ ■ O S S E O ■ G A P E D
S O V I E T ■ S P I N ■ E X T S ■ R A B E
T R E N C H Q U O T E ■ ■ L E D ■ C A R
S A N G ■ ■ U P T O ■ B A B Y Q U A K E S
■ ■ R O L O ■ H O P E S O ■ S E A ■ ■
M A R A C A I B O ■ L I L L E ■ T A P I R
A P A T H Y ■ R O H A N ■ O R G ■ ■ I S E
H E R E S L O O K I N G A T Y O U Q U I D
A R E ■ ■ A V A ■ P E S C I ■ T R U S T Y
L Y R E S ■ A D E P T ■ C E S T L A V I E
■ ■ T A U ■ A Y E S I R ■ H I S N ■ ■
Q U I C K B O X E R ■ D U M A ■ T A P A
U S S ■ S E N ■ ■ P E A C H Y Q U E E N
A H A S ■ R I F E ■ L O L L ■ E A M O N N
H E I N E ■ O U T T A ■ A E O N ■ L A O
O R D E R I N T H E Q U A R T ■ T W I N Y
G I S E L E ■ O N E U N D E R ■ A P A C E
S N O R E D ■ N O S E C O N E ■ S A N E R
```

```
C Z A R . . S A I D Y E S . A P R I O R I
P O S E D . A R M H O L E . R O U N D E R
R O S I E . M I S S U S A . A L L U D E S
. M E G A T S . . D E F . G O E S . . . .
. . E N R O U T E T O . A P O . D E G A S
B A N . M O N A M I . K R O N A . . R I P
A L O N E . G R A N N I E S . C A M E R A
B I N G . . I H E A R T . I S E E I T . .
A C T O R S . P L A Y S . P E D U N C L E
R E V . B U R R I T O . D O L T . U E Y S
. . M I N I O N S . M O N K E Y S . . . .
D O P E . K P M G . F I N E S S E . T B A
E N H A N C E D . F A C T S . T H U M B S
L E A N T O . A R E N D T . . . R I G A .
E A R T H S . T E A G R E E N . A N N U M
T C M . T R E A T . O L D E S T . U N I .
E T A T S . E S L . E P L U R I B U S . .
. . R U D E . T W A . . . F R E N Z Y . .
G E M I N I S . A I R F L O W . S W E A R
I T S O N M E . L I N E A R A . T E R R Y
T A N S I E S . K U S H N E R . D O N E .
```

```
F A R F R O M . P C B S . P U N I T I V E
A L A B A M A . O H O H . A V E M A R I A
K I D I N A CY S T O R E . PA E X P R E S S
E V A . I N S I P I D . M C A T . G N A T
S E R F . . N I C E D A Y . . G E E S .
. S U I T S . E E L E D . P L O T . . .
. . C R E A M . LO C A L R I S S I A N
A L L HS O N D E C K . I M B E A T . A D O
T I E I N . R O A N . E S S I E . M A T
T V M A . B A C K L O T . A S A . W P A
H E M . Y A N K E E D O O D L E DY O T S
E W E . E R A . S T R A I T S . A M I E
B I S . A S S T S . O C H O . B R A V A
A T E . H O A G I E . H U R R I C A N E SY
T H E A M A Z I N G RI . S E R U M . . .
. P A P I . G O G E T . S E P I A .
. G M E N . D I S H R A G . . S C A R
P A I R . W E A N . T O B A C C O . C U E
E L A S T I C BS . A F I S H C A L L E D WA
C O M O E S T A . D I C E . E R E A D E R
S P I N S H O T . S T A T . D E S C E N D
```

31

32

```
PEST  TAPE  PAREE  BPLUS
TACH  EVEN  OCALA  ABASE
STARESANDSTRIPS   PACER
DEPORT  NAIF  SAYST  USA
 NEWMOM  STASIS  HICCUP
CIGS  FATHERINONESCAPE
ANO  STAR  DMX   ELMER
PTA  MICAH   REAL  DADS
NOTEAMOMENTTOSPAR  CIO
   ALE  SEAOOZE  CATHER
CHURL   DRT    GRAZE
HYPNOS  PRESUME  WEI
OPS  JETEPROPELLEDPLAN
WEAR  XING   DELTA  EMO
 NUDIE   AID  NAST  GEM
HADLESSHORSEMANE  KITE
ELDEST  URBANA  OAFISH
AGO  ASAMI  PETS  SALLYS
VOWEL  LEASTBUTNOTLAST
ERNST  ORNOT  RYAN  ETTA
NESTS  PIANO  EXES  REST
```

```
JUTS  FAROFF   RUTH  JOY
ATOM  COOKIE  SYRIA  AMI
WATERCLOSETFIELDS  NEE
SHOAL   FIRE  SITWELL
  REMISS  SIRS  LOOPED
 PHYSICALTHERAPYBOATS
BAD  STATUE  DANO  EDU
ENDS  REMAP  DWI  ELAN
ADVANCEDPLACEMENTNEWS
DADDYO   RAP  LSU  YEA
  EMMA  VILLA  LANA
AHA  EMS  ALA  NINEPM
POLITICALLYCORRECTLAB
PELT  TOM  SONIA  ZOLA
 NAM  TOWN  WAFTED  RAS
PUBLICSCHOOLILOVEYOU
ISAIAH  OATS  RENATA
LATCHES  MRIS   EMOJI
ABE  ANTEMERIDIEMRADIO
FLA  MEATY  ICANSO  HINT
SEM  MYNA  SKYCAM  ANNA
```

35

```
A B E A M   ■   I T S T I M E   ■   P H O B O S
B O X T O P   ■   N A T A L I E   ■   L O N E L Y
B A T T L E S H I P R I S K   ■   A W A R D S
A T R A   ■   R A E   ■   A S A   ■   S I T I N   ■
■   A C Q U I R E T I C K E T T O R I D E
M A C H U   ■   L I B   ■   I L O   ■   E R E
O S H E A   ■   S T R O   ■   A D H O C   ■   O M A N
T H E S I S   ■   S O R R Y D I P L O M A C Y
R O E   ■   L I D   ■   D I E   ■   S U N O C O   ■
I R S   ■   B A M A   ■   O A T S   ■   E C O   ■
N E E   ■   M E M O R Y T R O U B L E   ■   R B S
■   N I L   ■   I T O O   ■   W E R E   ■   Y A M
■   B L I N I S   ■   G U S   ■   A S S   ■   A G O
C R A N I U M T W I S T E R   ■   S I N N E R
H A V E   ■   S I G H S   ■   Y V E S   ■   E A G L E
I V E   ■   T I O   ■   A C U   ■   G R O S S
C O N N E C T F O U R C H E C K E R S   ■
■   D O L L Y   ■   R O O   ■   I R A   ■   A L M A
F I E F I E   ■   T A B O O O P E R A T I O N
E R R A T A   ■   A T A S K E T   ■   O P E N T O
Z E S T E R   ■   B A N T E R S   ■   E D G E S
```

36

```
N B A J A M   ■   P S A S   ■   S W A M   ■   B A T
S A T I R E   ■   R U N T   ■   I A G O   ■   S O L E
F R E N C H C O N N E C T I O N   ■   E A T S
W R A P S   ■   O N R E P E A T   ■   O P E R A S
■   E L I   ■   O C T A   ■   O R S O   ■   H Y D R A
E L O N   ■   B O O Y A H   ■   D R E A M   ■
P E N G U I N   ■   S E A N B E A N   ■   E R A
A D E   ■   S T U D F I N D E R   ■   H O M E E C
■   B E S T I E   ■   R U B B E R M A T C H
A W E D   ■   B E R Y L   ■   N A S T I E S
P E T   ■   P A S T A   ■   T R I S H   ■   R N S
F A S T C A R   ■   M A S O N   ■   B O G S   ■
A C T I O N I T E M S   ■   F L I P O N   ■
C H E E S E   ■   O P E N F L A M E S   ■   M E T
E E R   ■   T R I N I D A D   ■   M O N D A V I
■   N A N A S   ■   P A C T E N   ■   A K I N
A Z U R E   ■   M I M E   ■   H E N S   ■   T E L
M I N E R S   ■   T O O T S I E S   ■   P A I G E
A P I N   ■   O R G A N I C C H E M I S T R Y
S P O T   ■   R O U T   ■   C A L E   ■   O N E S I E
S O N   ■   T O Y S   ■   K N E E   ■   B A T O N S
```

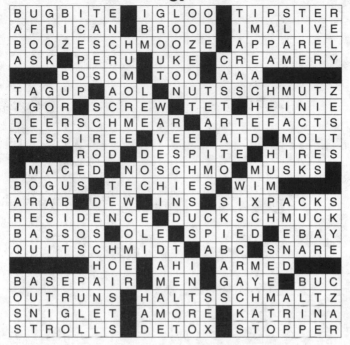

B	U	G	B	I	T	E		I	G	L	O	O		T	I	P	S	T	E	R
A	F	R	I	C	A	N		B	R	O	O	D		I	M	A	L	I	V	E
B	O	O	Z	E	S	C	H	M	O	O	Z	E		A	P	P	A	R	E	L
A	S	K		P	E	R	U		U	K	E		C	R	E	A	M	E	R	Y
		B	O	S	O	M		T	O	O		A	A	A						
T	A	G	U	P		A	O	L		N	U	T	S	S	C	H	M	U	T	Z
I	G	O	R		S	C	R	E	W		T	E	T		H	E	I	N	I	E
D	E	E	R	S	C	H	M	E	A	R		A	R	T	E	F	A	C	T	S
Y	E	S	S	I	R	E	E		V	E	E		A	I	D		M	O	L	T
		R	O	D		D	E	S	P	I	T	E		H	I	R	E	S		
	M	A	C	E	D		N	O	S	C	H	M	O		M	U	S	K	S	
B	O	G	U	S		T	E	C	H	I	E	S		W	I	M				
A	R	A	B		D	E	W		I	N	S		S	I	X	P	A	C	K	S
R	E	S	I	D	E	N	C	E		D	U	C	K	S	C	H	M	U	C	K
B	A	S	S	O	S		O	L	E		S	P	I	E	D		E	B	A	Y
Q	U	I	T	S	C	H	M	I	D	T		A	B	C		S	N	A	R	E
			H	O	E		A	H	I		A	R	M	E	D					
B	A	S	E	P	A	I	R		M	E	N		G	A	Y	E		B	U	C
O	U	T	R	U	N	S		H	A	L	T	S	S	C	H	M	A	L	T	Z
S	N	I	G	L	E	T		A	M	O	R	E		K	A	T	R	I	N	A
S	T	R	O	L	L	S		D	E	T	O	X		S	T	O	P	P	E	R

	C	O	A	S	T		A	T	A	T	I	M	E		C	H	I	T	A	
M	A	N	T	L	E		T	R	I	S	T	A	N		H	O	T	E	L	S
A	G	E	F	O	R	D	R	I	N	K	I	N	G	L	E	G	A	L	L	Y
Y	E	T		B	R	E	A	S	T		S	C	R	I	E	S		E	T	D
A	S	I	A		O	M	I	T		H	A	M	S		E	X	O	N		
N	U	M	B	E	R	O	N	E	A	L	B	U	M	B	Y	A	D	E	L	E
S	P	E	L	L				P	O	E				D	I	D	D	Y		
			A	R	A	B	S		P	C	T		T	E	N	L	B			
G	U	N	S	I	N	A	M	I	L	I	T	A	R	Y	S	A	L	U	T	E
O	N	E	T	O	O	M	A	N	Y			E	L	I	E	W	I	E	S	E	L
O	C	C			B	L	T			O	P	T				T	R	I		
F	A	C	S	I	M	I	L	E	S		M	A	L	E	F	I	C	E	N	T
S	P	O	T	S	O	N	A	L	L	S	I	D	E	S	O	F	A	D	I	E
			R	I	T	A	S		I	N	N		S	T	E	N	S			
S	H	O	U	T				W	C	S					O	E	S	T	E	
W	I	N	N	I	N	G	B	L	A	C	K	J	A	C	K	T	O	T	A	L
I	S	A	K		E	U	R	O				E	L	L	E		F	A	V	A
L	P	S		H	A	V	A	N	A		S	T	I	E	R	S		R	E	P
L	E	T	T	E	R	S	I	N	T	H	E	S	E	A	N	S	W	E	R	S
S	E	A	G	A	L		N	O	N	A	G	O	N		E	T	H	A	N	E
	D	R	I	L	Y		S	L	O	G	A	N	S		L	S	A	T	S	

C	O	M	P	A	S	S	■	C	O	S	T	A	R	■	O	M	E	G	A
A	D	M	I	R	A	L	■	R	E	T	I	N	A	L	C	A	N	O	N
N	E	V	E	R	G	E	N	E	R	A	L	I	Z	E	■	A	D	D	O	N
■	■	R	E	S	E	E	D	■	■	■	M	E	I	N	■	E	R	G	O
S	P	E	C	S	■	P	O	O	F	R	E	A	D	C	A	R	F	U	L	Y
C	O	V	E	T	■	■	S	E	E	N	■	A	N	Y	O	N	E	S
A	G	E	D	■	S	P	A	■	T	E	T	R	A	■	C	A	R	■
N	O	S	E	N	T	E	N	C	E	F	R	A	G	M	E	N	T	S	■
■	■	A	O	R	T	A	L	■	■	U	T	A	H	■	V	O	I	D
S	B	A	R	R	O	■	A	M	P	S	■	P	O	T	■	U	S	A
P	A	S	S	I	V	E	S	M	U	S	T	B	E	S	H	U	N	N	E	D
R	D	S	■	E	S	O	■	S	A	S	E	■	A	N	O	D	E	S
Y	E	A	H	■	A	U	D	I	■	L	O	S	T	I	T	■	■
■	D	O	N	T	U	S	E	C	O	N	T	R	A	C	T	I	O	N	S
■	L	E	O	■	A	M	I	N	O	■	E	T	H	■	C	H	A	T
P	O	W	E	R	U	P	■	A	C	R	E	■	P	E	N	N	E
A	V	O	I	D	R	E	D	U	N	D	A	N	C	Y	■	A	B	O	U	T
C	E	R	N	■	S	N	O	B	■	T	O	O	K	T	O	■
M	R	M	O	M	■	A	V	O	I	D	R	E	D	U	N	D	A	N	C	Y
A	G	E	N	T	L	E	A	K	I	E	R	■	T	E	R	R	I	E	R
N	O	D	E	S	■	S	T	E	E	D	S	■	H	E	Y	D	A	Y	S

G	O	F	A	S	T	■	H	O	M	E	R	■	A	B	A	S	H	E	D
O	M	E	G	A	S	■	F	I	N	A	L	E	■	S	O	T	H	E	R	E
B	A	S	E	B	A	L	L	T	E	R	M	S	■	S	T	R	O	B	E	S
I	N	T	E	L	■	A	I	M	S	■	H	E	E	H	A	W	■
■	■	S	E	A	B	E	E	■	F	R	O	S	T	■	E	B	B	S
V	F	W	■	B	O	S	■	C	I	A	O	S	■	B	O	R	R	O	W
E	L	E	A	N	O	R	■	H	A	N	D	T	O	O	L	S	■	I	R	A
R	E	A	R	E	R	■	A	R	K	S	■	L	I	C	■	D	A	Y
G	E	T	S	A	T	■	D	R	I	■	G	R	E	N	A	D	A	■
E	T	H	E	R	■	C	A	R	O	M	■	L	E	A	D	R	O	L	E
S	E	E	N	■	F	A	M	O	U	S	P	O	E	T	S	■	T	T	Y	L
■	D	R	I	V	E	R	O	D	■	N	O	R	S	E	■	T	E	H	E	E
■	W	O	O	L	E	N	S	■	S	I	E	■	N	A	D	I	R	S
G	T	O	■	I	L	E	■	A	L	I	E	■	I	D	O	N	O	T
O	R	R	■	C	A	R	D	S	U	I	T	S	■	S	P	A	N	G	L	E
S	U	D	S	E	S	■	O	T	R	O	S	■	B	O	A	■	S	L	R
H	E	S	A	■	T	R	A	I	N	■	T	E	N	T	H	S	■
■	■	L	I	N	E	A	R	■	I	A	G	O	■	O	P	A	L	S
A	L	L	O	W	I	N	■	M	E	A	N	S	O	F	T	R	A	V	E	L
D	I	A	M	O	N	D	■	A	L	C	O	T	T	■	U	N	D	O	N	E
E	S	S	E	N	E	S	■	P	L	A	N	E	■	B	Y	E	N	O	W

41

42

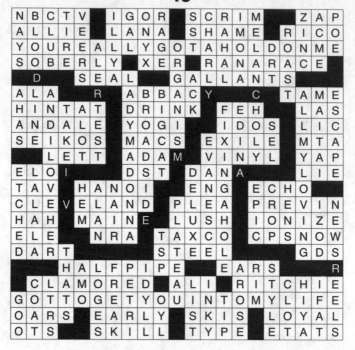

43

Puzzle 43 Grid:

N	B	C	T	V	■	I	G	O	R	■	S	C	R	I	M	■	■	Z	A	P
A	L	L	I	E	■	L	A	N	A	■	S	H	A	M	E	■	R	I	C	O
Y	O	U	R	E	A	L	L	Y	G	O	T	A	H	O	L	D	O	N	M	E
S	O	B	E	R	L	Y	■	X	E	R	■	R	A	N	A	R	A	C	E	■
■	D	■	■	S	E	A	L	■	■	G	A	L	L	A	N	T	S	■	■	■
A	L	A	■	R	■	A	B	B	A	C	Y	■	C	■	■	T	A	M	E	■
H	I	N	T	A	T	■	D	R	I	N	K	■	F	E	H	■	L	A	S	■
A	N	D	A	L	E	■	Y	O	G	I	■	I	D	O	S	■	L	I	C	■
S	E	I	K	O	S	■	M	A	C	S	■	E	X	I	L	E	■	M	T	A
■	■	L	E	T	T	■	A	D	A	M	■	V	I	N	Y	L	■	Y	A	P
E	L	O	I	■	■	D	S	T	■	D	A	N	A	■	■	L	I	E	■	■
T	A	V	■	H	A	N	O	I	■	■	E	N	G	■	E	C	H	O	■	■
C	L	E	V	E	L	A	N	D	■	P	L	E	A	■	P	R	E	V	I	N
H	A	H	■	M	A	I	N	E	■	L	U	S	H	■	I	O	N	I	Z	E
E	L	E	■	■	N	R	A	■	T	A	X	C	O	■	C	P	S	N	O	W
D	A	R	T	■	■	■	S	T	E	E	L	■	■	■	■	G	D	S	■	■
■	■	■	H	A	L	F	P	I	P	E	■	■	E	A	R	S	■	■	R	■
■	C	L	A	M	O	R	E	D	■	■	A	L	I	■	R	I	T	C	H	I	E
G	O	T	T	O	G	E	T	Y	O	U	I	N	T	O	M	Y	L	I	F	E
O	A	R	S	■	E	A	R	L	Y	■	S	K	I	S	■	L	O	Y	A	L
O	T	S	■	S	K	I	L	L	■	T	Y	P	E	■	E	T	A	T	S	■

44

Puzzle 44 Grid:

A	S	S	U	A	G	E	S	■	B	E	T	C	H	A	■	A	M	A	N	A
C	H	I	P	M	U	N	K	■	F	A	I	L	A	T	■	S	O	L	E	D
T	O	X	I	C	I	T	Y	■	F	R	E	E	Z	E	A	C	R	O	W	D
S	E	C	■	■	D	E	E	T	■	D	D	A	Y	■	F	E	N	N	E	L
■	■	H	O	V	E	R	■	E	R	R	O	R	■	F	I	N	A	G	L	E
O	N	A	P	A	R	■	S	P	O	O	F	■	N	E	E	D	Y	■	■	■
K	A	R	E	N	■	C	H	E	A	P	F	R	I	L	L	S	■	S	A	W
I	R	A	N	■	B	A	L	E	D	■	A	C	I	D	■	B	E	L	A	■
E	C	C	E	H	O	M	O	■	S	P	A	C	E	X	■	O	R	A	L	S
■	■	T	R	I	R	E	M	E	■	R	B	I	■	A	R	A	R	A	T	■
B	A	E	■	F	E	L	O	N	I	O	U	S	M	O	N	K	■	C	H	E
A	F	R	A	I	D	■	T	O	M	■	M	A	D	D	A	S	H	■	■	■
W	I	S	P	S	■	K	R	O	N	O	S	■	T	E	E	N	W	O	L	F
D	R	I	P	■	B	E	A	M	■	A	B	U	T	S	■	A	F	A	R	■
Y	E	N	■	M	I	F	F	B	U	S	T	E	R	S	■	S	N	A	K	E
■	■	R	E	L	I	T	■	N	A	I	V	E	■	O	R	K	N	E	Y	■
D	O	N	E	F	O	R	■	R	E	N	E	E	■	F	R	O	Y	O	■	■
I	N	A	F	I	X	■	N	E	A	R	■	L	A	R	A	■	■	F	B	I
S	E	C	U	R	I	T	Y	F	R	E	T	■	L	A	N	D	O	F	O	Z
C	U	R	E	S	■	I	S	I	T	M	E	■	A	N	G	E	L	E	N	O
S	P	E	L	T	■	M	E	T	H	O	D	■	S	K	E	W	E	R	E	D

O	L	A	V	S			P	J	S		N	E	B	S		P	O	S	H	
N	A	D	I	R	S		H	A	I		E	R	L	E		A	P	I	A	N
L	I	V	E	I	T	D	O	W	N		W	R	E	N		Y	E	S	N	O
A	N	A	T		Y	I	N	A	N	D	Y	A	N	G		D	R	A	K	E
N	I	N		L	M	A	O		F	R	O	N	D		B	I	A	L	Y	S
D	E	T	R	A	I	N		W	E	I	R	D		E	A	R	N			
		A	O	N	E		R	E	I	N	K		K	N	I	T	T	I	N	G
S	E	G	U	E		F	R	A	N	K		B	E	T	O			F	O	E
O	L	E	G		D	O	R	R		S	O	L	A	R		A	D	A	M	N
W	I	S	H	F	U	L		S	H	A	R	O	N	A		C	U	T	E	X
		C	O	C	K	T	A	I	L	L	O	U	N	G	E	S				
I	N	F	U	N		T	O	W	E	L	E	D		C	O	S	T	N	E	R
W	A	L	T	Z		A	S	A	D	A		K	N	E	W		M	O	A	N
I	V	E		P	L	A	Y		R	A	N	A	S		F	O	N	T	S	
N	E	D	R	O	R	E	M		C	O	R	O	T		A	L	P	S		
		E	P	O	S		C	R	U	E	T		I	L	O	S	T	I	T	
S	T	I	V	E	S		P	H	O	N	Y		S	P	A	R		A	N	I
A	I	D	A	N		S	E	E	A	D	O	C	T	O	R		E	R	T	E
I	T	E	M	S		A	T	W	T		U	N	E	D	U	C	A	T	E	D
D	R	A	P	E		L	E	O	I		I	B	N		M	I	S	E	R	Y
	E	L	S	A		E	R	N	A		N	C	O		V	E	R	N	E	

A	C	M	E			H	A	S	O	N			I	B	M		C	N	N
M	O	O	N	S		E	L	O	P	E		O	N	E	A		R	Y	E
F	L	U	S	H		A	I	L	E	S		O	U	T	A	N	D	O	U	T
M	E	N	U	O	P	T	I	O	N	S		N	T	H		D	E	W	
	T	R	E	E	S			L	I	T	T	L	E	P	R	I	N	C	E
N	U	K	E		N	E	A		Y	E	A		A	P	I	A		J	A	X
O	S	E		P	A	Z		D	R	Y	I	N	K		E	S	T	
H	O	N	O	L	U	L	U		A	B	A	A		N	E	E		W	T	O
O	N	Y	X	E	S		L	A	H	R		M	L	K		H	E	L	L
W	E	A	L	T	H		D	O	U	G	I	E		P	R	O	L	E	S
		I	M	E		P	R	O	B	O	N	O		E	A	R			
M	A	P	P	E	R		B	I	T	E	A	T		T	I	N	P	A	N
A	G	E	S		A	J	A		C	P	O	S		E	T	E	R	N	E
D	O	A		F	C	C		N	I	K	E		W	H	A	T	D	I	D	O
E	U	R		A	R	C	T	A	N		A	E	C		M	E	N	
O	T	B		N	O	O	R		G	I	T		N	I	H		C	A	S	S
F	I	R	S	T	C	R	U	S	A	D	E		S	E	W	E	D	
	A	A	A		D	S	O		C	A	N	I	T	R	Y	S	O	M	E
P	A	N	T	S	U	I	T	S		A	S	A	M	I		L	A	N	E	D
A	I	D		I	P	O	S		R	E	S	I	N		E	R	N	I	E
W	R	Y		A	N	N		D	R	A	N	G		E	A	R	N

47

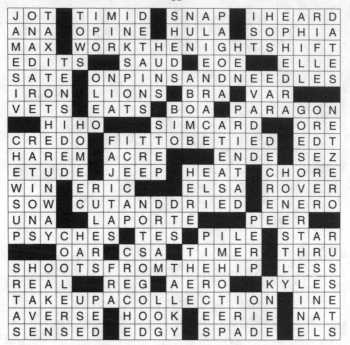

J	O	T	■	T	I	M	I	D	■	S	N	A	P	■	I	H	E	A	R	D
A	N	A	■	O	P	I	N	E	■	H	U	L	A	■	S	O	P	H	I	A
M	A	X	■	W	O	R	K	T	H	E	N	I	G	H	T	S	H	I	F	T
E	D	I	T	S	■	■	S	A	U	D	■	E	O	E	■	■	E	L	L	E
S	A	T	E	■	O	N	P	I	N	S	A	N	D	N	E	E	D	L	E	S
I	R	O	N	■	L	I	O	N	S	■	B	R	A	■	V	A	R	■	■	■
V	E	T	S	■	E	A	T	S	■	B	O	A	■	P	A	R	A	G	O	N
■	■	■	H	I	H	O	■	■	■	S	I	M	C	A	R	D	■	O	R	E
C	R	E	D	O	■	F	I	T	T	O	B	E	T	I	E	D	■	E	D	T
H	A	R	E	M	■	A	C	R	E	■	■	E	N	D	E	■	S	E	Z	■
E	T	U	D	E	■	J	E	E	P	■	H	E	A	T	■	C	H	O	R	E
W	I	N	■	E	R	I	C	■	■	E	L	S	A	■	R	O	V	E	R	■
S	O	W	■	C	U	T	A	N	D	D	R	I	E	D	■	E	N	E	R	O
U	N	A	■	L	A	P	O	R	T	E	■	■	P	E	E	R	■	■	■	■
P	S	Y	C	H	E	S	■	T	E	S	■	P	I	L	E	■	S	T	A	R
■	■	■	O	A	R	■	C	S	A	■	T	I	M	E	R	■	T	H	R	U
S	H	O	O	T	S	F	R	O	M	T	H	E	H	I	P	■	L	E	S	S
R	E	A	L	■	■	R	E	G	■	A	E	R	O	■	■	K	Y	L	E	S
T	A	K	E	U	P	A	C	O	L	L	E	C	T	I	O	N	■	I	N	E
A	V	E	R	S	E	■	H	O	O	K	■	E	E	R	I	E	■	N	A	T
S	E	N	S	E	D	■	E	D	G	Y	■	S	P	A	D	E	■	E	L	S

48

A	V	A	S	T	■	B	A	H	■	C	U	R	B	■	N	A	M	E
D	I	S	C	O	S	■	I	B	I	S	■	O	R	E	O	■	U	R	A	L
D	E	P	A	R	T	■	G	A	L	L	E	O	N	S	O	F	M	I	L	K
■	■	■	I	N	C	A	S	■	B	L	O	C	K	■	O	R	D	E	A	L	S
W	A	R	S	H	I	P	S	A	T	T	H	E	A	L	T	A	R	■	■	■
O	R	E	■	■	R	Y	E	■	O	H	O	■	P	E	Z	■	O	M	A	N
O	D	D	S	■	S	C	A	L	P	S	■	G	P	S	■	S	U	A	V	E
L	O	T	U	S	■	A	R	E	■	R	E	A	■	S	U	N	D	A	E
■	R	O	C	K	E	M	S	O	C	K	E	M	R	O	W	B	O	A	T	S
■	■	K	I	A	■	N	O	A	H	■	E	L	I	■	M	A	O
G	O	B	S	■	S	E	M	I	T	R	A	W	L	E	R	■	D	E	R	N
R	N	A	■	T	W	O	■	T	A	S	E	■	L	E	I	■	■	■
A	I	N	T	S	E	E	N	N	O	T	H	I	N	G	Y	A	C	H	T
C	O	N	A	I	R	■	T	E	N	■	S	I	R	■	R	E	A	R	S
I	N	E	P	T	■	R	H	O	■	R	O	S	C	O	E	■	S	N	I	P
E	Y	R	E	■	C	A	L	■	F	O	R	■	H	U	G	■	G	P	A
■	■	■	D	I	R	T	Y	D	O	U	B	L	E	C	R	U	I	S	E	R
P	O	L	E	C	A	T	■	A	G	G	I	E	■	H	E	N	R	I	■
A	P	P	L	E	F	R	E	I	G	H	T	E	R	■	S	W	A	T	H	S
S	A	G	A	■	T	A	R	S	■	S	A	K	E	■	S	E	Q	U	E	L
S	L	A	Y	■	S	P	R	Y	■	L	S	D	■	D	I	P	P	Y

49

50

51

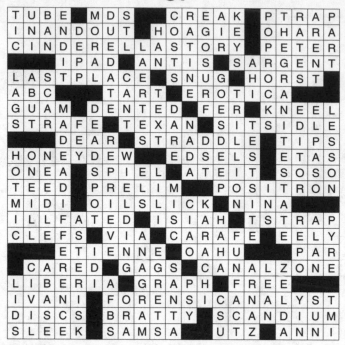

T	U	B	E		M	D	S			C	R	E	A	K		P	T	R	A	P
I	N	A	N	D	O	U	T		H	O	A	G	I	E		O	H	A	R	A
C	I	N	D	E	R	E	L	L	A	S	T	O	R	Y		P	E	T	E	R
		I	P	A	D		A	N	T	I	S		S	A	R	G	E	N	T	
L	A	S	T	P	L	A	C	E		S	N	U	G		H	O	R	S	T	
A	B	C			T	A	R	T		E	R	O	T	I	C	A				
G	U	A	M		D	E	N	T	E	D		F	E	R		K	N	E	E	L
S	T	R	A	F	E		T	E	X	A	N		S	I	T	S	I	D	L	E
		D	E	A	R		S	T	R	A	D	D	L	E		T	I	P	S	
H	O	N	E	Y	D	E	W		E	D	S	E	L	S		E	T	A	S	
O	N	E	A		S	P	I	E	L		A	T	E	I	T		S	O	S	O
T	E	E	D		P	R	E	L	I	M		P	O	S	I	T	R	O	N	
M	I	D	I		O	I	L	S	L	I	C	K		N	I	N	A			
I	L	L	F	A	T	E	D		I	S	I	A	H		T	S	T	R	A	P
C	L	E	F	S		V	I	A		C	A	R	A	F	E		E	E	L	Y
		E	T	I	E	N	N	E		O	A	H	U				P	A	R	
	C	A	R	E	D		G	A	G	S		C	A	N	A	L	Z	O	N	E
L	I	B	E	R	I	A		G	R	A	P	H		F	R	E	E			
I	V	A	N	I		F	O	R	E	N	S	I	C	A	N	A	L	Y	S	T
D	I	S	C	S		B	R	A	T	T	Y		S	C	A	N	D	I	U	M
S	L	E	E	K		S	A	M	S	A			U	T	Z		A	N	N	I

52

D	I	S	O	R	D	E	R		A	R	R	O	W		S	P	A	R	E
U	L	T	R	A	C	O	O	L		L	E	I	L	A		W	A	L	E	S
B	O	A	R	D	I	N	G	O	F	F	I	C	E	R		A	R	E	N	T
		G	E	O		S	U	R	E	R			M	A	R	Q	U	E	E	
S	T	E	R	N	O		I	N	T	E	R	N	E	T	R	O	U	T	E	R
T	O	N	Y		A	T	S	E	A		A	R	C	H	I	V	E			
A	R	A		S	H	A	H			S	A	O			S	T	R	A	W	
I	M	M	A	N	U	E	L	K	A	N	T			O	K	S	U	R	E	
D	E	E	R	E			Y	A	L	E	A	L	U	M	N	I		L	I	E
		G	A	O	L		H	E	W		E	M	I	T		S	E	E	D	
G	O	O	D	W	I	L	L	A	M	B	A	S	S	A	D	O	R	S		
B	E	N	T		N	O	B	U		O	R	R		S	P	U	D			
L	E	E		N	I	N	J	A	L	O	A	N	S		M	O	I	S	T	
I	N	A	P	E	T			I	N	S	T	A	G	R	A	M	M	E	R	
P	A	L	A	U		T	N	T		U	T	E	S		P	G	A			
		W	R	E	C	K	E	R		B	A	T	O	N		A	R	O	D	
C	O	R	P	O	R	A	T	E	E	L	I	T	E		O	S	M	O	S	E
O	V	E	R	P	A	R		E	L	O	P	E		C	A	V				
M	A	R	I	A		A	N	I	M	A	L	M	A	G	N	E	T	I	S	M
B	R	U	N	T		T	O	P	U	P		S	N	O	T	N	O	S	E	D
S	Y	N	T	H		S	H	A	M	S			S	T	H	E	L	E	N	S

53

```
B E S A F E   J U L I A     N A S C A R
A S H R A M   A N O I N T   C O M P O T E
S T A T I C C Y C L I N G   O N E O N T A
H E R   L E E Z A       I O S   R A I D
  S K Y T E L   S I L O F R E Q U E N C Y
    S A O   I C E D I N   S L U G S
S L I M   A A R   Y L E M   L A L A S
H E P   P C C Y C L O N E S   R I C C I
Y A H W E H   P O I   O T T E R S   I N N
A V O I R   S T A S H   H A L E   C O L A
W E N T P R O   S T A H L   B L A R N E Y
A S S T   A L O T   M O A N A   L U C A S
Y O O   S T O K E R   T B A   L A D O G A
  N U B I A   D R A W S S I N A I   M U Y
    P A R T V   S N I P   V O X   M M E S
    R E A I R   U N U S E D   G A I
S I L E N T S U P P O R T   O B O I S T
T R I X   I M A     R I F L E   S E E
R E N A U L T   S A I G O N F I S H I N G
E N E M I E S   S C R U B S   S A M O S A
W E S S E X   T E N E T   S T O N E D
```

54

```
S E A W A R S   F E A T   D A L I   A S H
I M R I G H T   A M M O   E L E G A N C E
L O B S T E R M I D O R   B E V E R O O M
O T O H   S U T R A   T I T   A T T I R E
S E R B   U T A U S T I N   P R I O N S
    O P S   S H E L T E R   T O T E M
P I A N O   S I E   L L A N O S   E S A
U N D E R O O F   B L A C K B O A R D E R
L A D   T O N I E R   T E E T H E
S T E R   M I D E A S T   S E N E C A
A I R E S   C O N C E R I E S   M A X E D
R E S C U E   E Q U A L T O   L I S A
    A L T P O P   E N M E S H   L A P
C O M P U T E R A T O R   S P O I L E R T
R N A   A S T R A L   E T H   L O D E S
Y A Y M E   T H E P I P S   P L O
  S P A D E S   N A N O T U B E   S P A M
C L O V E S   O T S   S A T Y R   E L L A
R O L E R S A L   B A T T E R M I N A L S
O P E N L A T E   A R I E   D I L U T E S
W E S   E Y E S   R A T S   S T E P O N E
```

O	P	E	N	E	R	A		G	A	T	E	W	A	Y		A	R	S	O	N
P	O	S	E	D	A	S		O	N	S	T	A	G	E		N	E	W	D	O
C	A	T	C	H	M	E	I	F	Y	O	U	C	A	N		C	L	A	I	R
I	C	E	T		J	A	M	A		T	I	K	I		S	H	A	M	U	S
T	H	R	A	C	E		B	R	I	S		O	N	E	M	O	T	I	M	E

ROTOR SIC SPARE
PAIR MOAN ATTIRE MIX
MAANDPAKETTLE TDBANK
ESME OLES OLDE EDGE
ATE ILL OOPS MICHAELS
LETSKEEPTHISINHOUSE
WITHMAYO RONI REP EWE
AVIA SEAL BOER ENOL
RENTAL EVERYTHINGSOK
MSG DOUBLE ALTA AGED
MOANA ZIN OBEYS
HITORMISS SKIM ISHALL
INADAY EERO LADS ENYA
CELEB OHTOBEINENGLAND
KRILL SITUATE BEELINE
STALE STEERED TRESSED

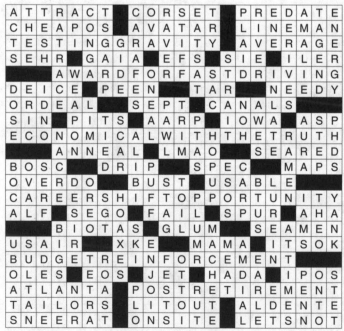

ATTRACT CORSET PREDATE
CHEAPOS AVATAR LINEMAN
TESTINGGRAVITY AVERAGE
SEHR GAIA EFS SIE ILER
AWARDFORFASTDRIVING
DEICE PEEN TAR NEEDY
ORDEAL SEPT CANALS
SIN PITS AARP IOWA ASP
ECONOMICALWITHTHETRUTH
ANNEAL LMAO SEARED
BOSC DRIP SPEC MAPS
OVERDO BUST USABLE
CAREERSHIFTOPPORTUNITY
ALF SEGO FAIL SPUR AHA
BIOTAS GLUM SEAMEN
USAIR XKE MAMA ITSOK
BUDGETREINFORCEMENT
OLES EOS JET HADA IPOS
ATLANTA POSTRETIREMENT
TAILORS LITOUT ALDENTE
SNEERAT ONSITE LETSNOT

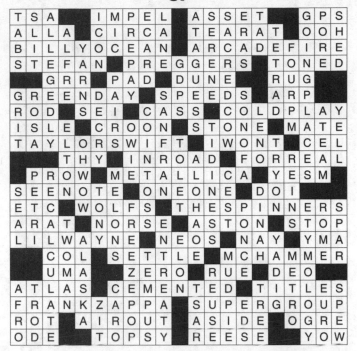

Puzzle 57 grid:

T	S	A			I	M	P	E	L		A	S	S	E	T			G	P	S
A	L	L	A		C	I	R	C	A		T	E	A	R	A	T		O	O	H
B	I	L	L	Y	O	C	E	A	N		A	R	C	A	D	E	F	I	R	E
S	T	E	F	A	N		P	R	E	G	G	E	R	S		T	O	N	E	D
		G	R	R		P	A	D		D	U	N	E			R	U	G		
G	R	E	E	N	D	A	Y		S	P	E	E	D	S		A	R	P		
R	O	D		S	E	I		C	A	S	S		C	O	L	D	P	L	A	Y
I	S	L	E		C	R	O	O	N		S	T	O	N	E		M	A	T	E
T	A	Y	L	O	R	S	W	I	F	T		I	W	O	N	T		C	E	L
			T	H	Y		I	N	R	O	A	D		F	O	R	R	E	A	L
	P	R	O	W		M	E	T	A	L	L	I	C	A		Y	E	S	M	
S	E	E	N	O	T	E		O	N	E	O	N	E		D	O	I			
E	T	C		W	O	L	F	S		T	H	E	S	P	I	N	N	E	R	S
A	R	A	T		N	O	R	S	E		A	S	T	O	N		S	T	O	P
L	I	L	W	A	Y	N	E		N	E	O	S		N	A	Y		Y	M	A
		C	O	L		S	E	T	T	L	E		M	C	H	A	M	M	E	R
	U	M	A			Z	E	R	O		R	U	E		D	E	O			
A	T	L	A	S		C	E	M	E	N	T	E	D		T	I	T	L	E	S
F	R	A	N	K	Z	A	P	P	A		S	U	P	E	R	G	R	O	U	P
R	O	T		A	I	R	O	U	T		A	S	I	D	E		O	G	R	E
O	D	E			T	O	P	S	Y		R	E	E	S	E			Y	O	W

58

Puzzle 58 grid:

M	B	A		C	A	W		J	A	C	K		N	O	S	E	J	O	B
P	O	W	E	R	N	A	P		O	H	H	I		A	S	A	R	U	L	E
G	R	A	V	E	T	R	A	I	N	E	E	S		B	U	S	R	I	D	E
	E	Y	E	D		S	D	S		M	E	S	A	S		S	E	C	S	
S	I	G	N		E	A	R	L	S		Z	E	D		R	E	D	E	A	L
I	N	A	S		T	W	E	E	T	B	I	R	D	I	E	S		P	L	Y
T	O	M	T	I	T		S	T	O	A	T		E	A	T		P	A	T	E
	N	E	E	D	E	R		S	N	L		A	D	M	I	R	E	R		
		V	A	S	E		E	E	G	S		B	L	E	A	T	E	D		
R	A	C	E	R		D	O	G	T	R	E	A	T	I	E	S		I	R	E
A	T	O	N	E	S		C	O	O		T	M	I		S	O	M	E	A	N
S	T	U		S	T	U	D	R	O	O	M	I	E	S		N	E	S	T	S
H	A	N	G	A	R	S		E	L	M	O			I	P	A	D			
		T	U	Y	E	R	E	S		A	V	E		N	O	T	I	P	S	
A	M	F	M		A	D	A		S	H	I	N	E		T	E	A	A	C	T
B	O	A		S	M	A	R	T	P	A	N	T	I	E	S		S	L	O	B
A	N	I	M	U	S		L	O	L		G	I	D	D	Y		T	A	R	S
	T	R	I	M		K	E	Y	U	P		R	E	I		H	O	T	S	
M	A	I	N	M	A	N		G	R	O	C	E	R	S	T	O	R	I	E	S
O	N	E	T	O	G	O		U	G	L	I		S	O	U	R	M	A	S	H
E	A	S	Y	N	O	W		N	E	O	N			N	B	A		L	E	E

59

O	K	S	■	P	A	N	D	A	S	■	P	O	D	I	U	M	■	M	A	A
S	A	T	■	O	P	I	A	T	E	■	E	V	E	N	S	O	■	A	D	S
C	H	R	I	S	T	T	H	E	R	E	D	E	E	M	E	R	■	D	O	S
A	L	I	C	E	■	■	A	G	A	I	N	■	A	R	T	W	A	R	E	■
R	I	V	E	R	T	H	A	M	E	S	■	T	U	T	■	I	A	M	B	S
■	L	E	I	■	V	E	G	■	S	T	R	I	P	E	■	C	R	E	S	S
■	■	T	O	M	L	I	N	■	L	I	M	B	■	A	I	N	T	■	■	■
A	T	M	■	M	A	L	L	O	F	A	M	E	R	I	C	A	■	U	R	L
G	R	E	T	A	■	N	E	V	E	■	■	R	A	T	E	■	S	A	O	■
E	A	T	I	N	T	O	■	E	T	N	A	■	I	T	O	■	I	S	T	O
W	I	L	L	I	E	■	C	L	U	B	M	E	D	■	U	B	O	A	T	S
O	N	I	T	■	T	W	A	■	S	C	A	B	■	S	T	A	T	U	R	E
R	E	F	■	■	R	I	P	A	■	Z	E	A	L	■	N	A	D	A	L	■
N	E	E	■	L	I	T	T	L	E	M	E	R	M	A	I	D	■	S	P	Y
■	■	S	H	E	S	■	C	A	M	I	■	T	B	T	E	S	T	■	■	■
M	O	T	I	F	■	T	H	R	O	A	T	■	L	E	D	■	R	E	C	■
O	R	A	N	T	■	H	A	M	■	T	I	M	E	S	S	Q	U	A	R	E
R	E	D	T	A	P	E	■	B	W	A	N	A	■	■	■	D	E	S	E	X
E	L	I	■	J	E	F	F	E	R	S	O	N	M	E	M	O	R	I	A	L
L	S	U	■	A	R	E	O	L	A	■	R	E	V	E	R	B	■	E	T	A
S	E	M	■	R	U	D	E	L	Y	■	E	S	P	O	S	A	■	R	E	X

60

■	P	O	D	I	A	■	G	I	F	S	■	V	P	S	■	G	U	M	S
C	H	A	R	A	D	E	■	O	M	A	R	■	A	L	A	K	A	Z	A	M
H	A	K	U	N	A	M	A	T	A	T	A	■	L	A	N	E	L	I	N	E
A	S	T	I	■	■	P	S	Y	C	H	■	M	O	I	■	R	E	G	A	L
N	E	R	D	■	D	E	K	E	■	E	C	A	R	D	S	■	A	G	T	■
G	R	E	S	C	O	R	E	■	P	R	O	V	E	■	E	C	O	L	E	■
E	S	E	■	S	H	O	W	M	E	T	H	E	M	O	N	E	Y	■	■	■
■	■	■	S	P	A	R	■	O	R	I	O	N	■	R	E	D	S	T	A	R
■	■	B	O	O	■	P	L	U	M	S	■	W	I	S	E	■	A	L	E	■
■	D	O	L	T	■	A	R	I	S	E	■	B	A	N	C	■	A	X	O	N
C	R	U	I	S	E	L	I	N	E	■	L	E	D	G	E	R	L	I	N	E
H	A	N	D	■	A	L	M	A	■	M	E	M	E	S	■	E	P	E	E	■
A	C	C	■	E	T	N	A	■	V	A	P	I	D	■	F	E	D	■	■	■
R	O	Y	A	L	W	E	■	T	O	K	E	N	■	H	A	L	S	■	■	■
■	■	■	C	H	E	W	I	E	W	E	R	E	H	O	M	E	■	F	A	A
■	B	A	S	I	L	■	S	E	E	M	S	■	A	M	E	X	C	A	R	D
G	O	V	■	■	L	T	S	U	L	U	■	G	R	I	N	■	A	C	T	V
O	N	E	A	S	■	Y	U	P	■	C	R	E	P	E	■	■	L	E	H	I
F	O	R	D	L	I	N	E	■	W	H	Y	S	O	S	E	R	I	O	U	S
O	B	S	E	R	V	E	R	■	W	O	E	S	■	■	T	H	E	C	U	R	E
R	O	E	S	■	■	E	R	S	■	I	F	S	O	■	■	S	C	O	T	S

61

Puzzle 61 grid:

M	S	N		S	U	C	R	O	S	E			B	I	G	T	A	L	K
O	H	O		U	P	A	H	E	A	D		M	E	D	I	A	B	I	A	S
W	A	Y	N	E	S	W	O	R	L	D		A	L	L	A	B	O	A	R	D
S	H	O	O		E	S	S		T	I	N	G	L	Y		A	U	R	A	S
		U	S	F	L			S	E	E	Y	A		A	R	N		
G	O	D	H	E	L	P	U	S		D	R	A	G	A	N	D	D	R	O	P
I	C	I	E	R		I	H	O	P		F	R	I	S	K	S		A	G	E
L	T	D	S		E	L	F	M	A	N		S	O	P	H		T	I	R	E
D	E	N		I	L	L		E	R	O	S				S	O	O	N	E	R
A	T	T	A	C	K	A	D	S		E	L	S	A		P	W	N	S	
		T	H	E	R	O	A	D	N	O	T	T	A	K	E	N		
	J	A	W	A			N	Y	E	T		U	P	H	O	L	S	T	E	R
L	A	B	A	T	T		P	R	O	B		W	C	S		H	U	E
A	F	A	R		H	A	S	P		Y	A	H	W	E	H		B	E	L	T
W	A	C		R	E	H	E	A	T		F	U	E	L		T	U	B	E	R
D	R	I	V	E	I	N	A	R	U	N		B	E	L	O	W	Z	E	R	O
		A	C	R		N	O	N	O	S			L	A	Z	E	
O	U	T	I	E		S	P	L	A	S	H		O	C	D		E	G	O	T
B	R	E	N	D	A	L	E	E		P	A	T	H	F	I	N	D	E	R	S
I	A	M	L	E	G	E	N	D		I	D	A	H	O	E	S		E	E	K
	L	A	Y	D	O	W	N		N	E	R	I	S	S	A		S	O	S

62

Puzzle 62 grid:

G	I	F	F	O	R	D		A	C	L	U		A	N	I	M	I	S	T	S
I	N	E	R	R	O	R		W	R	E	N		D	I	N	E	D	O	U	T
S	Q	U	A	N	D	E	R	L	U	S	T		A	L	A	N	A	L	D	A
		M	A	S	S	E				O	R	I	E	N	T		V	O	N
I	M	S	E	T		S	Q	U	E	A	L	E	R	D	E	A	L	E	R
T	O	Q	U	E	S		R	A	N	D	D		E	L	L	A	
S	O	U	P		H	A	S	B	R	O		R	E	L	Y		N	S	F	W
M	R	I		T	A	M	P	A		O	A	T		P	I	Q	U	E
E	E	R		S	Q	U	I	N	T	E	R	S	T	A	L	E		U	M	A
		M	T	A		S	T	E	A	D	I	E	S		E	A	S	I	E	R
A	M	H	E	R	S	T		P	I	G		I	M	P	A	S	S	E
L	O	O	N	I	E		M	A	I	L	E	D	I	N		O	O	H
V	A	L		S	Q	U	I	R	R	E	L	Y	B	I	R	D		L	E	A
I	N	E	R	T		R	E	T		N	I	T	E	S		I	M	P
N	A	S	A		M	I	N	I		F	L	O	S	S	Y		T	S	O	S
		G	R	O	G		S	T	O	O	D		S	C	O	T	T	O
	S	Q	U	A	R	E	S	T	H	E	B	E	E	F		A	P	S	E	S
B	T	U		T	A	L	E	S	E			W	A	S	N	T		
E	R	E	C	T	I	L	E		S	Q	U	A	W	K	A	T	H	O	N	S
T	A	U	T	E	N	E	D		K	U	R	D		E	L	B	A	R	T	O
S	P	E	N	D	E	R	S		Y	E	N	S		S	K	E	T	C	H	Y

63

S	T	A	T	S			H	O	P	I	N		S	N	L		S	L	A	P
A	R	D	O	R		W	A	S	H	O	E		T	E	A		T	A	T	E
M	I	D	N	I	G	H	T	H	O	U	R		E	V	I	T	A	B	L	E
E	L	M	O		L	O	H	A	N		D	I	V	E	R	S	G	O	A	L
	L	E	A	F	E	D			E	I	S	N	E	R		P	E	R	S	E
		V	I	E		N	O	I	R		M	O	M	A			E	E	R	
O	C	E	A	N		T	A	R	T	A	R	E		O	N	M	A	R	S	
V	O	T	I	N	G	A	G	E	I	N	A	M	E	R	I	C	A			
E	V	A	L		O	R	S	O	N		N	O	D	E		G	R	A	D	E
R	E	L		N	L	E			O	K	R	A		R	I	P	L	E	Y	
T	R	I		B	A	D	L	U	C	K	S	Y	M	B	O	L		I	L	E
I	M	A	F	A	N		A	P	E	S			O	W	L		B	U	S	
P	E	E	L	E		H	I	S	S		T	U	L	S	A		I	A	G	O
			A	R	G	O	N	S	A	T	O	M	I	C	N	U	M	B	E	R
	R	A	N	S	O	M		T	R	O	U	P	E	S		B	L	A	D	E
D	E	R		V	E	T	O		U	C	S	D		C	E	O				
E	L	I	S	E		M	O	R	I	T	A		C	A	R	V	E	R		
R	E	A	L	L	O	O	K	E	R		N	A	D	A	L		I	D	E	S
M	A	N	A	L	I	V	E		A	N	S	W	E	R	L	E	N	G	T	H
I	S	N	T		L	I	N		T	O	A	R	M	S		T	I	A	R	A
S	E	A	S		Y	E	S		E	M	M	Y	S			S	T	R	O	M

64

	A	P	I	E	C	E		D	I	E	M		F	L	A	P		G	P	S
G	R	A	V	L	A	X		O	D	A	Y		A	O	N	E		R	O	T
R	O	Y	A	L	T	A	S	T	E	R	S		C	A	N	T	L	O	S	E
O	M	E	N			M	E	T	A		T	H	E	F	A	R	E	A	S	T
K	A	R	P	O	V		T	E	M	P		A	P	P		I	N	N	E	S
			A	B	E	T		D	A	B		T	E	A	L		D	E	C	O
D	R	I	V	E	T	R	A	I	N	S		H	E	N	I	E		R	U	N
R	A	L	L	Y	C	A	R			S	A	L		B	L	A	S	T	S	
O	S	L	O		H	U	T		I	C	K	Y		Y	I	N				
S	H	I	V	A		M	O	O	N	R	O	O	F		A	S	A	D	A	
S	A	N		B	R	A	I	N	S	U	R	G	E	O	N	S		E	P	A
	D	I	P	S	O		S	E	E	S	T	A	R	S		A	G	A	P	E
		I	O	U		G	A	T	S		V	C	S		O	R	E	O		
A	D	D	E	R	S		B	A	M		I	A	M	W	O	M	A	N		
R	U	E		B	E	R	E	T		M	I	N	D	R	E	A	D	E	R	S
S	L	E	D		D	E	S	I		C	H	O		S	A	K	S			
E	C	R	U	S		M	T	V		S	E	T	H		R	E	P	O	T	S
N	I	X	O	N	T	A	P	E	S		A	C	E	D			O	N	I	T
A	N	I	S	E	O	I	L		T	H	R	O	W	I	N	G	R	I	C	E
L	E	N		E	D	N	A		Y	O	Y	O		B	R	I	T	C	O	M
S	A	G		R	O	S	Y		E	T	A	L		S	A	S	S	E	S	

65

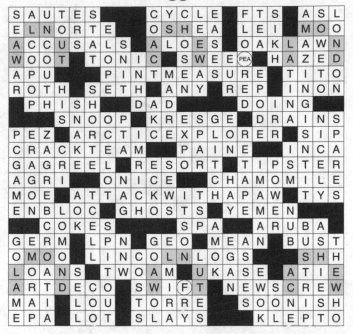

S	A	U	T	E	S			C	Y	C	L	E		F	T	S		A	S	L
E	L	N	O	R	T	E		O	S	H	E	A		L	E	I		M	O	O
A	C	C	U	S	A	L	S		A	L	O	E	S		O	A	K	L	A	W	N
W	O	O	T		T	O	N	I	C		S	W	E	E	(PEA)		H	A	Z	E	D
A	P	U			P	I	N	T	M	E	A	S	U	R	E		T	I	T	O
R	O	T	H		S	E	T	H		A	N	Y		R	E	P		I	N	O	N
	P	H	I	S	H		D	A	D			D	O	I	N	G	
	S	N	O	O	P		K	R	E	S	G	E		D	R	A	I	N	S
P	E	Z		A	R	C	T	I	C	E	X	P	L	O	R	E	R		S	I	P
C	R	A	C	K	T	E	A	M		P	A	I	N	E		I	N	C	A
G	A	G	R	E	E	L		R	E	S	O	R	T		T	I	P	S	T	E	R
A	G	R	I		O	N	I	C	E		C	H	A	M	O	M	I	L	E
M	O	E		A	T	T	A	C	K	W	I	T	H	A	P	A	W		T	Y	S
E	N	B	L	O	C		G	H	O	S	T	S		Y	E	M	E	N
	C	O	K	E	S			S	P	A		A	R	U	B	A
G	E	R	M		L	P	N		G	E	O		M	E	A	N		B	U	S	T
O	M	O	O		L	I	N	C	O	L	N	L	O	G	S			S	H	H
L	O	A	N	S		T	W	O	A	M		U	K	A	S	E		A	T	I	E
A	R	T	D	E	C	O		S	W	I	F	(T)		N	E	W	S	C	R	E	W
M	A	I		L	O	U		T	O	R	R	E		S	O	O	N	I	S	H
E	P	A		L	O	T		S	L	A	Y	S			K	L	E	P	T	O

66

A	W	A	L	K		S	H	E	I			I	N	N	O	T	I	M	E
T	O	M	E	I		T	A	L	I	B		H	O	T	L	I	N	E	S
O	W	I	E	S		E	V	O	K	E	S	(EAR)	T	H	A	K	I	T	T
M	E	G	A	S	T	A	R		E	L	W	A	Y		V	I	T	A	E
	D	O	N	C	(HEAD)	L	E		S	L	A	L	O	M		I	L	E
		N	A	V		J	O	H	N	(LEG)	U	I	Z	A	M	O
Z	A	P		M	O	I	R	A		O	N	E		N	O	L	O
E	T	O	N		C	O	I	N	O	P		B	A	N	G	O	R
E	L	S	A	L	A	N	(CHEST)	E	R		P	O	R	K	A	D	O	B	O
	A	T	B	A	T		A	T	T	U	N	E		S	O	I	R
I	N	D		D	E	N	Z	E	L	W	A	(SHIN)	G	T	O	N		K	G	B
S	T	O	P		B	O	N	S	A	I		V	I	S	I	T
T	A	C	O	S	T	A	N	D		M	I	C	H	E	L	L	(EYE)	O	H
	S	C	H	E	M	E		H	E	A	L	E	R		Y	A	D	A
	K	I	E	V		T	E	E		T	E	X	T	S		R	O	T
	R	Y	A	N	P	H	I	L	(LIP)	P	E		I	A	N
U	S	E		S	A	V	I	O	R		O	(LIVER)	P	L	A	T	T
R	E	N	A	L		N	O	T	R	E		P	A	S	T	R	I	E	S
B	I	T	P	A	R	T	S		E	T	C	H	E	D		C	U	L	P	A
A	N	T	I	G	O	N	E		S	U	T	R	A		O	T	T	E	R
N	E	O	N	S	I	G	N		T	S	A	R		D	O	S	E	S

67

68

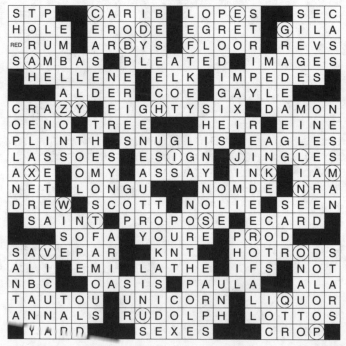

```
OWN   CCC     RAGTAG   FISTS
WHOSWHO   FERRARI   INUIT
LASTTANGINPARIS   BAMBA
SMEE   SNERT   SPATS   TWIT
   BATTENS   PSI   ACURAS
CELLRECITAL   THEBABE
LIETO   TESLAS   ITEM   SAP
ONEHOP   IGUESS   GETME
TED   POLGROUNDS   FELLTO
   SUDANESE   BLAMEON
ALF   MISSY   SOLER   ROY
GOLIATH   OBSESSED
ATODDS   INEEDAHUGO   FAN
TUPAC   GOSTAG   ESPANA
ESP   ASAN   SLAKED   AHINT
   YIPPIES   URANIUMOREO
OLDBOY   LOP   PENNANT
BAIO   SADAT   ELMER   ERLE
EPSON   SEVENDAYSINMAYO
YUCKY   HAIRPIN   OPTEDIN
SPOSE   ENCORE   NEH   ENS
```

```
REPOT   SKOSH   STG   ESAI
ARUBA   THANKU   CALLBACK
TUBER   HEREIN   OKAYBYME
SPLITSECOND   STERN   SEA
OTIS   ANA   ORCA   SECT
   CARLOT   TORNTOSHREDS
AVENUES   SEWEDON   OTOE
MINCEMEAT   SEER   SPOTON
ANEED   SOD   DRIFTAPART
SYMS   SOTRUE   OATS
SLY   SCRAMBLEDEGGS   THO
   BAAL   FLIMSY   SWAB
MIXEDMEDIA   MGM   ATONE
ANODES   AMPS   HASHMARKS
LOUD   SWIPEAT   TEAROSE
INTERMINGLED   LEANTO
   DEED   HEAR   OPT   AMAT
THE   CLEFT   FASTSHUFFLE
HALFTIME   OTTOII   SILOS
UNBROKEN   NEESON   CRAFT
DDAY   END   ORSON   GETTY
```

```
HASH  ONDVD  DOWSE  SAIL
UNTO  PONCE  EVITA  ELMO
BUYTHEFARM  FILLTHEGAP
STEPONE  SERENE  SESAME
    LUMEN  RUNES  IRA
SAFARI  OBITS   SNOWCAP
MELT  CALLTHESHOTS  LTR
ARIES  STA  LIMO  TERI
LIP  TAKETHECAKE  TRAIN
LETMEBE  SAVAGE  ARARAT
  HOARDS  YET  REGENT
AGENDA  WRENCH  CRASHED
TOBEY  ROCKTHEBOAT  EPI
WAIT  CARP   TEL  YEAST
APR  FACETHEMUSIC  RIOT
REDWINE  ETAPE  USARMY
   OLD  BRATT  TARPS
SHANTY  REREAD  TRAUMAS
HITTHEDECK  DOTHETRICK
AROD  GESTE  ODEON  ELHI
DEMO  GETON  ROAST  SEEP
```

```
AFFIANCED  BREL   GUAM
RAINDANCE  ATRIA  LANZA
MINKSTOLE  SEATTLESLEW
STEP   TAPAS  STRANGERS
  ATHEISTIC  LASORDA
LANDHO  REL  HEE  TRI
IVE  OUT  TAKENBY  ELDER
POWERSAW  WIENIES  LONE
ONYX  ERNE  DRATTED  GSA
  OPS  OBLADI   INCOLOR
HAROLD  ALPINES  TONERS
AWKWARD  PEGGED  NOG
LAM  TOOTALL  GARP  FLEA
OREO  PROTEIN  MARKFELT
SETHS  SKEPTIC  YEN  FAT
  PTS  YEA  TOS  SUBTLY
  GALILEO  YARDWASTE
HOMECOURT  SOFAS  ALAS
BREAKGROUND  INTHEPAST
AMASS  OSTEO  SERENADER
RENE   ESAI  HEARTLESS
```

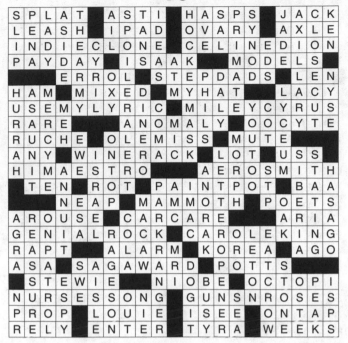

S	P	L	A	T		A	S	T	I		H	A	S	P	S		J	A	C	K
L	E	A	S	H		I	P	A	D		O	V	A	R	Y		A	X	L	E
I	N	D	I	E	C	L	O	N	E		C	E	L	I	N	E	D	I	O	N
P	A	Y	D	A	Y		I	S	A	A	K		M	O	D	E	L	S	
			E	R	R	O	L		S	T	E	P	D	A	D	S		L	E	N
H	A	M		M	I	X	E	D		M	Y	H	A	T		L	A	C	Y
U	S	E	M	Y	L	Y	R	I	C		M	I	L	E	Y	C	Y	R	U	S
R	A	R	E		A	N	O	M	A	L	Y		O	O	C	Y	T	E
R	U	C	H	E		O	L	E	M	I	S	S		M	U	T	E	
A	N	Y		W	I	N	E	R	A	C	K		L	O	T		U	S	S
H	I	M	A	E	S	T	R	O			A	E	R	O	S	M	I	T	H
	T	E	N		R	O	T		P	A	I	N	T	P	O	T		B	A	A
		N	E	A	P		M	A	M	M	O	T	H		P	O	E	T	S
A	R	O	U	S	E		C	A	R	C	A	R	E			A	R	I	A
G	E	N	I	A	L	R	O	C	K		C	A	R	O	L	E	K	I	N	G
R	A	P	T		A	L	A	R	M		K	O	R	E	A		A	G	O
A	S	A		S	A	G	A	W	A	R	D		P	O	T	T	S	
	S	T	E	W	I	E		N	I	O	B	E		O	C	T	O	P	I
N	U	R	S	E	S	S	O	N	G		G	U	N	S	N	R	O	S	E	S
P	R	O	P		L	O	U	I	E		I	S	E	E		O	N	T	A	P
R	E	L	Y		E	N	T	E	R		T	Y	R	A		W	E	E	K	S

G	O	O		C	A	F	E	S		S	A	V	O	R		I	V	A	N	A
U	M	P		E	B	O	L	A		O	P	E	R	A		G	O	L	E	M
L	A	P		L	O	O	K	B	E	F	O	R	E	Y	O	U	L	E	A	P
P	R	O	W	L		L	E	O	N	A	R	D	O		P	A	C	E	R	S
		S	H	O	W	S		T	O	R	T	E		T	I	N	A	
A	L	I	A	S	E	S						I	N	A	N	I	T	Y
M	U	T	T		B	E	N	C	H		B	L	A	M	E		O	G	E	E
A	G	E			L	O	L	O		A	A	R	E				N	H	L
H	E	S	S		A	D	R	E	M		G	R	O	W	L		C	O	R	P
			A	U	D	I	O		F	E	T	A	S		A	U	R	O	R	A	E
F	A	T	F	A	R	M			F	I	T			I	C	E	L	A	N	D
A	T	T	I	R	E	D		A	R	C	E	D		T	R	Y	O	N
C	A	R	S		D	I	P	S	O		L	O	O	S	E		N	C	A	A
A	R	A			F	A	I	N		L	U	F	F				E	U	R
D	U	C	T		B	F	L	A	T		E	X	T	O	L		M	I	N	T
E	N	T	I	T	L	E						R	E	T	E	S	T	S
		B	O	A	R		S	L	A	V	E		N	A	B	O	B	
A	C	C	E	S	S		S	T	I	L	E	T	T	O		O	W	L	E	T
C	L	O	T	H	E	S	M	A	K	E	T	H	E	M	A	N		I	V	E
N	O	V	A	E		P	O	K	E	R		O	R	A	T	E		S	F	X
E	D	E	N	S		A	G	E	N	T		S	I	N	C	S		S	S	T

75

```
ALTAR █ AWL █ ACCT █ █ CLAPS
GUIDERAIL █ CIAO █ CREDIT
ILLATEASE █ TARP █ HAVANA
NUTMEG █ EWER █ 54 40 ORFIGHT
█ 12 ANGRYMEN █ NIT █ IOU
ACE █ MAR █ NOSEJOBS █ MOLE
VEND █ LIT █ STARR █ FUSES
INGA █ PHDS █ NEESON
ATARI █ SERENA █ APRIL 15
NUGENT █ BOXES █ SKIM █ IMF
CRISTO █ 52 PICKUP █ CASSIE
AYN █ ERAS █ SCORE █ ETHANE
█ 21 GRAMS █ MOUSES █ SALUD
█ ARETHA █ TACT █ MITE
FARMS █ ROMPS █ HUN █ USER
LIES █ CITYGIRL █ NOS █ ASS
ORB █ GOD █ 13 GOINGON 30
THELOWER 48 █ NCAA █ DORSAL
SOCIAL █ OHNO █ INAGROOVE
ASCOTS █ BRER █ SCREECHES
MEANS █ ESAI █ EYE █ SKORT
```

76

```
ITSTIME █ KUDU █ CLARA
FROWNAT █ SPINES █ OUTBOX
FINISHAHEADOFSCHEDULE
YEAST █ ORBS █ TROY █ TEL
█ DRT █ MANILA █ LOADSOF
█ AGEBEFOREBEAUTY
█ PINETAR █ OMITS █ TASER
FEMALE █ TRUANT █ SENORA
GRANDOPENINGSALES █ FAN
SINK █ ROTUND █ EATAT
█ LILY █ ESTD █ LPGA █ SCAD
█ DEARS █ TAOIST █ TRUE
UPI █ WAYBEHINDTHETIMES
MOOING █ ADAGES █ NOVOTE
PETRI █ PRIZE █ MUTTERS
█ ONEAFTERANOTHER
STUNGUN █ SLATES █ OPT
IRS █ REST █ MAGI █ ASONE
FORMFOLLOWINGFUNCTION
TUDORS █ INPLAY █ SILENTI
STACY █ PEAK █ BLURTED
```

```
FAIR  IFS   VALID  RAZE
ROTE  MAO   FEDORA DONOR
IRSAUDIT    INDIANAJONES
STETSON  ANILS  COSMO
CALAMITYJANE  LIL
HEF  ANNEALS  WIN  BERET
     GENX  CHEGUEVARA
REDCROSS  TVDAD  SEENIT
ANORAKS  BOOST  FURNACE
EGGOS  KEPI  ALLA  TAR
   CHARLESDEGAULLE
PIC  KEMP  IOUS  EMOJI
AGOUTIS  BUNNY  DATASET
BOWLER  BERGS  LEFTJABS
STANLAUREL  AUER
TONAL  NIP  PORKPIE  SBA
   TKO  BUSTERKEATON
   TOQUE  EERIE  OAKLAND
CHEFBOYARDEE  CONSOMME
SURFS  EDGIER  ATE  NOOR
IBIS  DOOMS  TSR  ESTS
```

```
SPOCK  OHCRUD  BIANCA
RUSHAT  REROSE  PANSOUT
INHERE  GAINON  UNCASES
   ADAM  ARM  FIGLEAVES
   "OPENSESAME"  NERTS
UNMAKES  EAU  NTWT  VIN
NEARERTO  NBASTAR  PICO
MAT  ASAP  "ILLBEBACK"
ETAIL  HONOREE  ATREST
"ETTUBRUTE"  WRITE
TRAIPSE  AKA  CHALICE
   IHOPS  "HULKSMASH"
LACUNA  TOLEASE  SOWER
"NEVERMORE"  CANT  EMI
AGRA  PILEUPS  PARASAIL
MET  ISLE  ETA  NOMERCY
ALAIN  "MYPRECIOUS"
   HIMALAYAS  NUN  SCHS
HANDBAG  CHROME  EROTIC
SITUATE  HANGER  RAMONA
TRYERS  TWASNT  YEAST
```

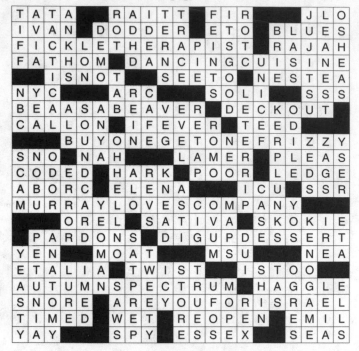

```
S C A L I A   ■   B A S S O   ■   A S S O R T ■
L A B O R S ■   C O C O O N   ■ S H O V E I T
I D O N T K N O W H O W E   ■ S I L E N T I
M E D E ■ S A L T Y ■   D E E N   ■ R E A M
S T E W S ■ H A I ■ L I G H T G R E E N E
■   O W N ■ S E C U R E S ■ L E X ■
M G M L I O N ■ S O L O ■   N E S T L E S
C H E F S H A T ■ B U N S O F S T E E L E
J A M E S ■ B R A S ■ I T A L ■ I N T O W
O N O ■   K O O L ■ O N Y X ■ B V D S ■
B A R ■ S H O P P I N G M A L L E ■ L A B
■   I N E Z ■ H A W S ■ I C E T ■   O R R
D R A I N ■ M I C A ■ H E A D ■ E B O L A
V O L C A N I C A S H E ■ N U T C A S E S
R O S E T E A ■   H A R E ■ P R O C E S S
■   P O W ■ I F A T A L L ■ E L K ■
J O K E R S W I L D E ■ E E K ■ E P C O T
A G R O ■ R O S Y ■   S C R E E ■ A C A I
C L A P F O R ■ L A Y I T O N T H I C K E
K E I L L O R ■ O H E N R Y ■ D E N V E R
■ S T E A M Y ■ W A N N A ■ S T E I N S
```

```
V I C A R S ■ I N P I E C E S ■ A M P L Y
O R E C A R ■ F O O T N O T E ■ N O L I E
W E R E W O L F B L I T Z E R ■ G O A L S
■   T I D ■ O Y S ■ S W E ■ A P R ■ Y A M
I S I T A G O ■   S I N ■ P R I E S ■
S E T ■ T O M B S T O N E P H I L L I P S
S E U R A T ■ L A V ■ E R E ■ M Y S T I C
U P D O ■ A D O L P H ■ E T A ■ E S T A
E Y E O F N E W T G I N G R I C H ■ A M P
■   S L A L O M ■ M A O ■ N Y U ■ F E E
S O L T I ■ I N I T ■ P O O H ■ M I E N S
T O A ■ N I L ■ N H L ■ D R O O P S ■
R M S ■ G R A V E D I G G E R P H E L P S
U P T O ■ O H O ■ Q U A I N T ■ N A I L
N A T H A N ■ U S S ■ C M D ■ I O D I N E
G H O S T B U S T E R K E A T O N ■ D U D
■   L O L A S ■ O N A ■ E N T R A P S
R O E ■ E R A ■ R E N ■ R U E ■ H I N ■
T R A L A ■ B L A C K C A T S T E V E N S
E A V E S ■ L E G A L A G E ■ A D A G E S
S L E E T ■ E V E N E D U P ■ I L L G O T
```

83

S	P	A	R	E	M	E	■	J	O	B	C	U	T	S	■	F	A	R	G	O
W	I	R	E	T	A	P	■	A	R	A	L	S	E	A	■	A	L	E	R	T
A	N	I	M	A	L	S	A	N	C	T	U	A	R	Y	■	A	L	L	O	T
G	E	D	S	■	L	O	N	E	■	■	F	R	E	T	■	G	A	P	E	■
■	■	■	D	E	N	T	■	B	A	R	B	A	R	A	B	O	X	E	R	■
A	S	C	I	I	■	F	A	U	N	A	■	■	R	A	N	■	■	■	■	■
D	I	L	L	S	■	H	A	R	D	E	N	■	S	W	O	R	E	A	T	■
A	L	E	E	■	S	O	R	A	S	■	T	H	E	R	I	O	■	M	R	I
P	L	A	T	E	N	U	M	B	E	R	■	M	A	I	L	F	R	A	U	D
T	Y	R	■	P	A	S	■	L	E	D	O	U	T	■	■	O	Z	M	A	■
■	G	A	R	A	G	E	■	R	I	T	E	S	■	L	I	S	B	O	A	■
R	O	S	E	■	H	O	A	G	I	E	■	■	A	S	I	■	N	N	E	■
C	O	M	I	C	B	O	O	K	■	P	R	I	O	R	A	R	R	E	S	T
A	S	U	■	H	E	L	P	E	D	■	T	E	N	G	O	■	O	C	H	O
■	E	D	W	A	R	D	S	■	O	H	I	S	E	E	■	M	A	H	O	N
■	■	■	T	I	E	■	■	C	A	C	T	I	■	■	C	R	O	W	S	■
C	L	E	A	N	A	N	D	J	E	R	K	■	O	F	F	S	■	■	■	■
L	O	F	T	■	L	I	R	A	■	■	E	T	A	L	■	S	M	U	T	■
O	R	I	O	N	■	C	O	P	A	C	A	B	A	N	A	B	E	A	C	H
V	A	L	U	E	■	E	M	E	R	I	T	A	■	C	R	U	E	L	L	A
E	X	E	R	T	■	R	E	D	A	R	M	Y	■	Y	E	S	D	E	A	R

84

P	A	T	S	I	E	S	■	S	O	M	A	L	I	■	S	U	R	G	E	D
A	L	U	M	N	A	E	■	I	D	O	T	O	O	■	A	G	N	A	T	E
C	O	N	A	N	T	H	E	B	A	R	I	A	N	■	M	A	S	S	O	N
K	N	A	R	■	E	N	D	S	■	O	L	D	■	S	A	N	■	B	I	T
S	E	S	T	I	N	A	S	■	■	E	N	T	E	C	O	R	D	I	A	L	E
■	■	■	P	O	R	■	■	A	R	I	■	R	A	N	R	A	G	G	E	D
C	H	I	H	U	A	M	E	X	I	C	O	■	J	O	A	N	N	■	■	■
D	O	D	O	■	W	E	L	L	S	■	B	A	U	M	■	O	T	O	E	■
S	T	E	N	O	■	D	E	E	■	C	I	N	N	A	T	I	R	E	D	S
■	N	E	A	T	E	N	■	D	O	W	D	■	■	I	B	E	R	I	A	■
S	A	T	■	T	R	A	I	N	E	D	A	S	S	I	N	S	■	R	E	I
C	R	I	M	E	A	■	O	X	E	N	■	C	H	E	E	T	A	■	■	■
A	L	F	A	S	P	R	O	U	T	S	■	P	A	O	■	N	O	R	M	A
B	O	Y	D	■	■	U	T	N	E	■	O	O	M	P	H	■	U	I	E	S
■	■	M	A	U	N	A	■	R	E	P	O	S	S	E	D	C	A	R	S	■
A	T	L	E	I	S	U	R	E	■	R	E	F	■	■	L	A	H	■	■	■
C	H	E	N	R	E	P	U	B	L	I	C	■	H	A	M	S	A	L	A	D
E	R	A	■	G	D	S	■	B	I	C	■	L	I	D	S	■	N	O	L	I
T	I	N	C	U	P	■	M	I	S	S	I	P	P	I	M	U	D	P	I	E
E	L	N	I	N	O	■	I	N	S	O	N	G	■	T	A	N	G	E	N	T
N	L	E	A	S	T	■	A	G	E	N	D	A	■	S	N	O	O	Z	E	S

```
MASCOTS ■ TIMIDITY ■ OGRE
ATTACHE ■ UNCLOTHE ■ PEON
THEWHIRLEDSERIES ■ ETON
TONS ■ STASI ■ SASES ■ NOTE
EMO ■ RWANDAN ■ IDI ■ SULA
LESSEE ■ DANES ■ GRAFTED
■ THEROYALWHEE ■ COOTS
PAPRIKA ■ LEON ■ WORF ■
ERROR ■ NECK ■ LOSER ■ MSN
EMILE ■ CLEARLY ■ TINTYPE
KENL ■ WHICHDOCTOR ■ AWLS
ARCSINE ■ INAWORD ■ IMHIT
TSE ■ MERYL ■ SWAG ■ NIECE
■ OCAT ■ AILS ■ ESSAYED
BYFAR ■ WHACKSMUSEUM ■
LOWRISE ■ DINAR ■ ALISTS
ITHE ■ HID ■ SUNBELT ■ ERA
NEAL ■ OGEES ■ GUARE ■ IRAN
KALE ■ WHININGANDDINING
AMES ■ MISSPELL ■ OUTRACE
TOSS ■ ENMESHES ■ SPOILER
```

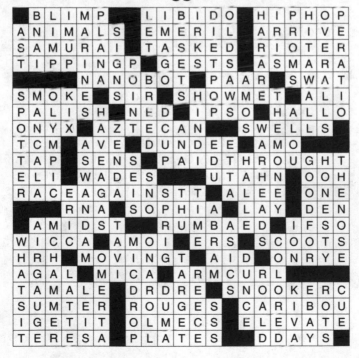

```
■ BLIMP ■ LIBIDO ■ HIPHOP
ANIMALS ■ EMERIL ■ ARRIVE
SAMURAI ■ TASKED ■ RIOTER
TIPPINGP ■ GESTS ■ ASMARA
■ NANOBOT ■ PAAR ■ SWAT
SMOKE ■ SIR ■ SHOWMET ■ ALI
PALISH ■ NED ■ IPSO ■ HALLO
ONYX ■ AZTECAN ■ SWELLS
TCM ■ AVE ■ DUNDEE ■ AMO
TAP ■ SENS ■ PAIDTHROUGHT
ELI ■ WADES ■ UTAHN ■ OOH
RACEAGAINSTT ■ ALEE ■ ONE
■ RNA ■ SOPHIA ■ LAY ■ DEN
■ AMIDST ■ RUMBAED ■ IFSO
WICCA ■ AMOI ■ ERS ■ SCOOTS
HRH ■ MOVINGT ■ AID ■ ONRYE
AGAL ■ MICA ■ ARMCURL ■
TAMALE ■ DRDRE ■ SNOOKERC
SUMTER ■ ROUGES ■ CARIBOU
IGETIT ■ OLMECS ■ ELEVATE
TERESA ■ PLATES ■ DDAYS
```

87

Puzzle 87 grid:

O	V	E	R		C	O	C	A	S		S	H	O	E	S		H	E	A	D
J	O	V	I		H	O	A	G	Y		M	I	X	U	P		O	S	L	O
A	L	E	C		E	X	P	E	N	S	E	T	Y	P	E		S	P	E	W
I	T	S	E	L	F		E	M	C	E	E	S		H	E	S	S	I	A	N
	B	A	A		L	E	A	S	E		C	O	D	A		E	S	E
O	V	A	R	Y		E	S	T		I	G	O	R		N	A	S	T	Y
B	E	Y	O	N	D	T	H	E	T	I	M	E	L	I	M	I	T	
I	R	O	N	E	R	S		S	A	R	A	N		A	U	T	O	B	O	T
E	T	U	I		A	D	S		W	A	G	O	N		D	I	N	E	R	O
	S	C	R	U	B		S	E	M	I	S		Z	E	N	E	R
W	E	N	T	T	O	O	F	A	R		R	E	C	K	L	E	S	S	L	Y
A	L	C	O	A		P	I	S	A	N		S	H	E	A	R	
R	I	A	L	T	O		S	E	D	A	N		E	L	S		A	P	E	D
S	E	A	D	U	C	K		D	I	R	A	C		E	S	O	B	E	S	O
	Y	E	A	R	B	O	O	K	P	H	O	T	O	G	R	A	P	H
S	T	O	A	T		I	O	N	S		I	P	O		D	A	R	N	S
P	O	I		T	A	S	K		B	A	L	E	R		E	S	L	
I	L	L	K	E	P	T		V	I	O	L	I	N		S	N	I	F	F	S
N	E	M	O		N	O	T	A	G	O	O	D	B	E	T		V	I	A	L
A	D	E	N		E	F	I	L	E		H	O	A	R	Y		E	S	S	O
L	O	N	G		A	F	T	E	R		A	G	R	E	E		S	H	O	T

88

Puzzle 88 grid:

R	A	M		C	O	M	A		T	R	I	P	S		S	P	H	E	R	E
I	D	O		V	E	E	R		O	H	A	R	E		H	E	A	P	E	D
F	I	N		J	U	S	T	O	N	E	M	O	W	E	R	T	H	I	N	G
F	E	A	R	O	F	H	Y	A	T	T	S		S	V	E	N		C	O	Y
S	U	S	H	I		T	O	T		A	D	A	G	E	
	T	E	N	S	I	L	E		U	P	O	N		M	O	N	D	O
C	R	E	A	T	I	V	E	R	I	O	T	E	R	S		E	L	T	O	N
H	E	R		P	I	A		S	P	E	A	K	T	O		D	E	L	L
O	T	I	S		P	E	S	T	L	E	S		O	R	D	E	R	L	Y
P	R	E	T	T	Y	S	H	O	E	R		G	E	N	O	A	N	
S	Y	S	C	O		E	M	T		R	O	T		N	E	C	C	O
	H	O	A	R	S	E		N	I	G	H	T	M	A	Y	O	R	S
D	E	P	A	L	M	A		T	O	S	H	I	B	A		E	M	U	S
I	V	O	R		I	M	P	L	O	R	E		C	A	T		P	S	I
G	I	L	L	S		P	R	I	A	M	R	E	A	L	E	S	T	A	T	E
S	L	E	E	T		A	U	L	D		A	L	L	Y	E	A	R	
	V	S	I	G	N		P	B	S		E	X	T	R	A
E	R	A		L	U	C	K		B	A	Y	E	R	M	I	N	I	M	U	M
D	O	U	B	L	E	Y	E	L	L	O	W	L	I	O	N	S		E	M	O
A	L	L	I	E	S		M	O	O	L	A		G	A	G	A		N	B	C
M	O	T	O	R	S		P	O	B	O	Y		S	T	A	Y		T	A	O

```
A M P L E ■ L A P D O G ■ ■ A D A G I O S
C A R O L ■ O N H I R E ■ E L E G A N C E
C H I C A G O T R A I N ■ N E A T I D E A
R E M A I L ■ ■ A L G E B R A ■ S T I L T
A R R ■ N A R C S ■ ■ R O O S T ■ ■ F L A
■ ■ O N E D I R E C T I O N T R A F F I C
C A S E ■ E D Y ■ Y U C K ■ ■ O G E E ■
O L E I N ■ O A S T ■ U T T E R R O T
Y E S N O D O U B T ■ L E A H ■ ■ R E L O
■ ■ ■ D E L T A ■ E A G L E S W I N G S
A M I S T A D ■ S E L I G ■ S I E S T A S
B O S T O N C R E A M ■ S C E N E ■ ■ ■
C L A Y ■ A U S T ■ P O I S O N F R E E
S T A L W A R T ■ ■ B O N N ■ ° Y I E L D
■ ■ C U P S ■ Z O O M ■ E A U ■ N A S A
F U N S M A S H I N G P U M P K I N S ■
A S E ■ ■ P E E T A ■ T A P A S ■ O H O
L O W E S ■ E R I T R E A ■ ■ S I G N A L
A P T I T U D E ■ R U S H T H E D O O R S
N E O N A T E S ■ I T S A G O ■ R O U T E
A N N E X E D ■ ■ P H O N I C ■ O F T E N
```

```
T O A S T ■ A W A R E ■ A P P S ■ S T A N
O A S I S ■ M A J O R ■ R I O T ■ A H S O
T H I N K D I F F E R E N T L Y ■ L E A H
O U S T ■ A S T O ■ ■ W I C K ■ S U N N I
■ ■ E A R T H ■ Y E S W E H A V E T H A T
A L E X E I ■ S T A G ■ ■ ■ A X E L S ■
P E I ■ T V M A ■ S T A R J O N E S ■
E A T F R E S H L Y ■ L I E G E S ■ J L O
■ ■ J O S T L E ■ S A B E R S ■ T E A T
B A C O N ■ ■ V A T S ■ R E S O R T T O
E V E R Y B O D Y L I K E S S A R A L E E
B O L D M O V E ■ P L A Y ■ ■ I V I N S
O W L S ■ W I E N I E ■ E N C A G E ■
P S I ■ P E N M E N ■ A D A B W I L L D O
■ ■ B O D E S W E L L ■ M C A N ■ I O U
■ D O U B T ■ ■ A I D E ■ S A T F O R
L E T G O O F M Y E G G O ■ C H L O E ■
E L E G Y ■ L E E D ■ ■ O H H I ■ A L A S
G U L L ■ D O Y O U H A V E A N Y M I L K
A X L E ■ D R E W ■ E L E C T ■ A A N D E
L E O S ■ T A R S ■ M A R K S ■ K N E A D
```

```
A R C S ■ ■ T I E R ■ C A K E ■ C H A M P
N O A H ■ B A L T O ■ A D A R ■ P E T A L
T H R E E F R E E T H R O W S ■ A R T I E
■ E P S I L O N ■ C U T R A T E ■ L I S A
■ ■ ■ E R A S E D ■ L E E S ■ V O I C E S
S T R E E T ■ R E A L R A R E W H A L E ■
C U E S ■ S C R A M S ■ ■ K E N N Y ■ ■
A N A C T ■ H E W S ■ D A I S E S ■ H O P
B A D H A B I T S ■ S U B ■ R U F O U S
■ ■ E J E C T ■ O W L I S H ■ P I N T S
S A F E ■ S H O E S E C T I O N ■ V E S T
P L U S H ■ I N S I D E ■ M A U V E ■ ■
E S T E E M ■ T E E ■ H E R M I T A G E
C O Z ■ L O O T E R ■ T A O S ■ C I V I L
■ ■ S P R E E ■ B A R N E S ■ M O N A
U N I Q U E N E W Y O R K ■ M C E W A N
P I N U P S ■ T I E S ■ S I T A R S ■ ■
D A D A ■ O V E R A C T ■ C A R A F E S ■
A C E R S ■ I R I S H W R I S T W A T C H
T I B E T ■ S E N T ■ A B E T S ■ S T A R
E N T R Y ■ E D G Y ■ S I R E ■ ■ T A M S
```

```
M A D E ■ S O D A ■ P A R M ■ J A R S
I B E T ■ C H R I S T E N D O M ■ A M A T
A L W A Y S H A S F O L I A G E ■ P I M A
T A I P E I ■ P O M E S ■ U L Y A N O V
A Z T E C ■ E V E R [GREEN] ■ A L L I N O N E
S E T ■ C I V I L ■ V A N ■ O P E R A S
■ ■ O H M A N ■ A P I N G ■ W E S ■
M O C K [BLUE] H E N S T A T E [YELLOW] S E A
E N O L A ■ S O W S ■ E L M ■ V S O P
T R U A N T S ■ L E D A ■ I A M ■ I T L L
H I G H S C H O O L ■ S E C R E T C O D E
O C H O ■ M O I ■ L A C E ■ E R I T R E A
D E E M ■ O L E ■ C O L S ■ M O I S T
■ D A N [BROWN] P R E T T Y I N [PINK] R A T S
■ S O B ■ U M A S S ■ N O I S Y ■
A R M O U R ■ M A T ■ R E L E T ■ W K S
C H O O S E U P ■ [ORANGE] B O W L ■ A G A I N
C O R N E A S ■ T I M O N ■ I N E S S E
E D G E ■ D E L A W A R E N I C K N A M E
S E A R ■ S T A Y I N A L I V E ■ U B E R
S S N S ■ O P E N ■ T Y P E ■ S I T S
```

95

CHEWBACCA CLUB LIDS
DEVIATION RIFE CELIE
SMALLTOWNSALON WHILST
LSU SOLD SEPIA ULT
PASSANT YULE RPI MOL
IMP MEWL REINDEERRIDE
GEAR DOIT DART SONG
SCREW PLUMB GAOL LAIR
THEFARMTEAM AGRI ETNA
YESSIR SWINGINGSIGN
SANGTO VOYAGE
ISNOTTOOINTO ONIONS
NAAN ETRE PROTESTPOET
KITS DODO SYRIA SOLAR
LIES FIFA GASP DATA
FOOTNOTEFONT SERT LEN
URN AVE LEAD LEEWARD
MMA RENEW STAY CRO
BOLGER WHATARETHEODDS
LOTUS EASE LOSESLEEP
ENVY SPUD AWKWAFINA

96

PECANS MISDEAL SCALAR
IROBOT ITSONME COSINE
SALOME LEANSIN RISING
HOOVERJAM JUSTBUNNIES
FRESNO LUIS UNAS
ASEA CAAN USCG PXS
ETAL ROLLINGINTHEJEEP
MILLS EON SPAY ETNA
AMI TATAS CLUE STEAM
JOCKOFTHEBAY GMAIL
REALTY TERRA ONEACT
RIALS GRAVEJIGGERS
ALOAD HESS ALONE LAP
COAT CLOY TIO SWEDE
MAKETHEJEANSLIST IBEX
EMS RAVI LIPS POLS
AIRE GAPS ARLENE
GARBAGEJUMP JUNEBUGGY
ICEAGE ONEIDAS REPAGE
BANTER SIDEONE OATIER
BREEDS STARTED SNOODS

```
C O E X I S T   T A C O N I C     G R U B
P H A R A O H   S H A P E L Y   C L A R A
L O S A N G E L E S T I M E S   A I D A N
S K Y Y   G R E   O B O E   T A T T I N G
    C A Y M A N   R I S K   D E T A I L
E D G A R   S A M E D I F F E R E N C E
S E A M O S S   C E E   S C A L E R
S E V E N T H G R A D E   D E R A L T E
O P E R   A M I E   C L U E   T O R Y
    I A M T O O   Z O O S   H E I N I E
A P T   R O O T O F A L L E V I L   E O S
L E A D E R   T R I P   R A F A E L
I N G E   B O B S   S I R I   N I K I
S H O P P E R   C A S H D I V I D E N D
    R O S I T A   T H O   G E N E S E E
T H R E E P O I N T S H O T   F A T W A
Y E A S T Y   S T A T   P A V L O V
R A M S E S I   I P O S   D I E   O A T H
E L M O S   P O W E R O F A T T O R N E Y
S E E R S   A M A T E U R   R I P E N E D
E R R S   D E R O S S I   O N A D I M E
```

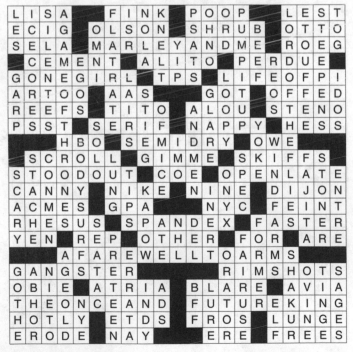

```
L I S A   F I N K   P O O P   L E S T
E C I G   O L S O N   S H R U B   O T T O
S E L A   M A R L E Y A N D M E   R O E G
  C E M E N T   A L I T O   P E R D U E
G O N E G I R L   T P S   L I F E O F P I
A R T O O   A A S   G O T   O F F E D
R E E F S   T I T O   A L O U   S T E N O
P S S T   S E R I F   N A P P Y   H E S S
    H B O   S E M I D R Y   O W E
  S C R O L L   G I M M E   S K I F F S
S T O O D O U T   C O E   O P E N L A T E
C A N N Y   N I K E   N I N E   D I J O N
A C M E S   G P A   N Y C   F E I N T
R H E S U S   S P A N D E X   F A S T E R
Y E N   R E P   O T H E R   F O R   A R E
  A F A R E W E L L T O A R M S
G A N G S T E R   R I M S H O T S
O B I E   A T R I A   B L A R E   A V I A
T H E O N C E A N D   F U T U R E K I N G
H O T L Y   E T D S   F R O S   L U N G E
E R O D E   N A Y   E R E   F R E E S
```

B	E	A	R	P	I	T			S	T	A	S	H	E	S		S	P	U	D
A	L	S	O	R	A	N		D	O	O	R	P	O	S	T		H	O	P	E
B	O	S	T	O	N	T	A	N	G	O	P	A	R	T	Y		E	A	T	S
E	P	E	E	S			S	A	G	E		N	A	E			N	A	C	R	E

(grid 99)

(grid 100)

The New York Times

SMART PUZZLES

Presented with Style

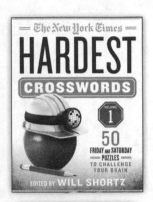

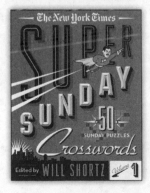

Available at your local bookstore or online at
us.macmillan.com/author/thenewyorktimes

 ST. MARTIN'S GRIFFIN